)ERS' GUIDES TO ESSENTIAL CRITICISM

JLTANT EDITOR: NICOLAS TREDELL

Readers' Guides to Essential Criticism
Series Standing Order
ISBN 1–4039–0108–2
(outside North America only)

You can receive future titles in this series as they are published by placing a standing order. Please contact your bookseller or, in the case of difficulty, write to us at the address below with your name and address, the title of the series and the ISBN quoted above.

Customer Services Department, Macmillan Distribution Ltd
Houndmills, Basingstoke, Hampshire RG21 6XS, England

Jacobean Drama

PASCALE AEBISCHER

Consultant editor: Nicolas Tredell

palgrave
macmillan

First published 2010 by
PALGRAVE MACMILLAN

Palgrave Macmillan in the UK is an imprint of Macmillan Publishers Limited,
registered in England, company number 785998, of Houndmills, Basingstoke,
Hampshire RG21 6XS.

Palgrave Macmillan in the US is a division of St Martin's Press LLC,
175 Fifth Avenue, New York, NY 10010.

Palgrave Macmillan is the global academic imprint of the above
companies and has companies and representatives throughout the world.

Palgrave® and Macmillan® are registered trademarks in the United States,
the United Kingdom, Europe and other countries

ISBN 978–0–230–00815–1   hardback
ISBN 978–0–230–00816–8   paperback

This book is printed on paper suitable for recycling and made from fully
managed and sustained forest sources. Logging, pulping and manufacturing
processes are expected to conform to the environmental regulations of the
country of origin.

A catalogue record for this book is available from the British Library.

A catalog record for this book is available from the Library of Congress.

10   9   8   7   6   5   4   3   2   1
19 18 17 16 15 14 13 12 11 10

Printed in China

CONTENTS

Sketches the difficulties in defining the term 'Jacobean', discusses the drama's association with decadence, explains the approach taken to the guide and summarises the chapters to follow.

The Critical Trail – Early Views to the Twentieth Century

Traces the development of criticism of Jacobean drama from the Restoration through to the early 1990s. The chapter considers, in particular, the Romantic criticism of Charles Lamb, S.T. Coleridge and William Hazlitt and the *fin-de-siècle* approaches of William Archer, A.C. Swinburne and John Addington Symonds. It then moves to the advances in theatre history brought forward by E.K. Chambers and G.E. Bentley and sets these alongside the theatrical and literary criticism of Muriel C. Bradbrook, A.C. Bradley, T.S. Eliot, Una Ellis-Fermor and L.C. Knights. Next, it considers the moralist criticism of the 1960s, as represented by Robert Ornstein, F.P. Wilson and T.B. Tomlinson. It concludes with an assessment of David Scott Kastan and Peter Stallybrass's *Staging the Renaissance*, which brought together essays by key figures in the 'New Historicism'.

Theatre History

Is concerned with the developments in theatre history that have resulted from the work of E.K. Chambers and G.E. Bentley. The chapter considers the work of Andrew Gurr in depth and compares his approach to that of some of his peers, including Keith Sturgess, Alan C. Dessen and Martin White. In Gurr's work, it traces the gradual shift from the use of Shakespeare-centred master narratives towards a more fractured view of theatre history. This shift is representative of a general trend in theatre history, as is evident in the work of the critics included in John D. Cox and David Scott Kastan's *New History of Early English Drama* and representative books by Tiffany Stern and Lucy Munro. The same fracturing, but with a firmer underpinning by critical theory, is also evident in the most recent work in the field brought together in the *Oxford Handbook of Early Modern Theatre*.

Textual Transmission

Describes the critical movement known as the 'New Bibliography' through a discussion of texts by W.W. Greg and Fredson Bowers. The chapter then outlines the 'New Textualist' reaction to this movement and illustrates the argument with examples from the work of Michael Warren, Gary Taylor, Stanley Wells and Jerome J. McGann. The New Textualism itself has since been critiqued and elaborated on, as is evident from a discussion of the arguments of John Lavagnino, Sonia Massai, Jeffrey Masten, Joseph Loewenstein and Zachary Lesser as well as from an analysis of recent and current editorial projects. Particular attention is paid to the Cambridge edition of the works of Jonson and the Oxford edition of the works of Middleton. MacDonald P. Jackson's, John Jowett's and Suzanne Gossett's work for the Oxford Middleton is considered as a way of shedding light on specific problems that arise when editing collaboratively authored plays.

Historical Contexts

Briefly discusses the criticism of E.M.W. Tillyard, which provoked a strong reaction by historically minded scholars in the late 1970s and early 1980s. In Britain, books by Jonathan Dollimore and Catherine Belsey respectively exemplify the 'cultural materialist' and politically engaged poststructuralist response to Tillyard's approach, while in North America, the work of Stephen Orgel, Jonathan Goldberg and Stephen Greenblatt is representative of the 'New Historicist' reaction against Tillyard and the older modes of historical inquiry. More recently, critics such as Stephen Mullaney, Douglas Bruster and Jean E. Howard have pushed historicist work in diverse directions, building a body of work which is represented in David Scott Kastan and Peter Stallybrass's *Staging the Renaissance* and in John D. Cox and David Scott Kastan's *A New History of Early English Drama*. The materialist and empiricist approach taken in the second anthology is representative of recent work in this field, as can also be seen in the criticism of Peter Lake and Michael Questier.

CHAPTER FIVE   73

The Genres of Jacobean Drama

Opens with a general discussion of the importance of genre as a critical category, drawing on the views of Rosalie Colie, Alistair Fowler and Heather Dubrow. The chapter then considers Jacobean dramatic genres and their criticism in turn: tragedy (the criticism of Muriel Bradbrook, Robert Ornstein, Dympna Callaghan and Michael Neill), revenge tragedy (the criticism of Fredson Bowers, Charles and Elaine Hallett and Eileen Allman), comedy (the criticism of C.L. Barber, Northrop Frye and Muriel Bradbrook), city comedy (the criticism of Brian Gibbons and Alexander Leggatt), tragicomedy (the criticism of Eugene Waith, Marvin Herrick, the authors brought together in Nancy Klein Maguire's collection of essays, as well as the work of Jeffrey Masten, Zachary Lesser and Lucy Munro), court masques (the criticism of Stephen Orgel, Roy Strong, the authors – especially Martin Butler – brought together in Peter Holbrook and David Bevington's collection of essays and the work of Clare McManus), the history play (the criticism of Irving Ribner, Judith Doolin Spikes, Martha S. Robinson, Teresa Grant, Mark Hutchings and Barbara Ravelhofer), and closet drama (the criticism of Albert H. Tricomi, Marta Straznicky, the authors brought together in S.P. Cerasano and Marion Wynne-Davies' collection of essays, and of Karen Raber).

CHAPTER SIX   100

Body and Race Scholarship

Begins with a consideration of the body scholarship or 'historical phenomenology', focussing on Mikhail Bakhtin's theorisation of festivity and the carnivalesque, Thomas Laqueur's investigation of the Galenic 'one-sex' body, Jonathan Sawday's inquiry into anatomical practices and tropes and Gail Kern Paster's analysis of the humoural body as represented in medical discourses and on stage. It then goes on to consider studies concerned with race, ethnicity and Islam, beginning with G.K. Hunter's essay on Othello before moving on to a discussion of books by Anthony Gerard Barthelemy, Ania Loomba and Kim Hall in the 1980s and 1990s. It concludes with a survey of more recent approaches, which have focused on 'geohumouralism' (Mary Floyd-Wilson), encounters with cultural others in the Mediterranean

(Daniel Vitkus), non-systematic xenophobias and shades of difference (Sujata Iyengar), and the performance of blackness on early English stages (Virginia Mason Vaughan).

Gender and Sexuality

Surveys three key analyses that have focussed on the issue of cross-dressing in Shakespeare's romantic comedies and Jacobean city comedy, contrasting the approaches of Lisa Jardine, Jean E. Howard and Stephen Orgel. It then proceeds to a wider investigation of gender and sexuality in feminist re-visions of Jacobean drama, concentrating on the criticism of Mary Beth Rose, Karen Newman and Wendy Wall, all of whom are influenced by the historicist work of the 1980s. The final part of the chapter is concerned with queer studies of Jacobean drama. It starts with a discussion of the work of Alan Bray, a historian, before moving on to the literary analyses of Jonathan Goldberg, Mario DiGangi, who discusses homoerotic friendship and Mary Bly, who combines queer studies and theatre history. It concludes with the criticism of Valerie Traub, whose focus on lesbian desire brings a much-needed corrective to the male focus of the other queer studies surveyed here.

Performance Studies

Opens with a survey of Shakespearean performance criticism, tracing its development from early studies, like J.L. Styan's, which sought to find evidence of early modern staging practices in modern performances, to Shakespearean performance studies, an approach which no longer seeks for authenticity and faithfulness to the Shakespearean texts but focuses on how modern performances create meanings that are relevant for today's audiences. Representatives of this latter school are Barbara Hodgdon, W.B. Worthen, Carol Rutter and the authors brought together in Diana E. Henderson's collection of essays concerned with Shakespeare on screen. The chapter moves on to discuss the development of 'Jacobean performance studies', a new critical field to which Susan Bennett, Martin White and Roberta Barker have contributed in various ways. Finally, it considers critical approaches to Jacobean drama on film, focusing on the one hand on a handful of French films of *Volpone* and, on the other hand, on the recent 'Jacobean' films by Marcus Thompson, Mike Figgis and Alex Cox.

Conclusion 158

Draws on each approach surveyed in the guide to point to avenues for future research and suggests ways in which the guide may be used in conjunction with other surveys in future years.

ACKNOWLEDGEMENTS

As William C. Carroll pointed out in his review of the year's scholarship in Tudor and Stuart drama in 2001, 'the range of work is beyond anyone's ability to consider with authority. So *caveat lector*'.[1] When considering the output not of a year but of more than a quarter century, this *caveat* must be multiplied by twenty-five. I am therefore the more grateful for the generous assistance I have received from friends, colleagues and students in the selection process and the writing and evaluation. Roberta Barker, Rob Conkie, Lukas Erne, Alison Findlay, Hannah Fish, Briony Frost, Sonia Massai, Clare McManus, Lucy Munro, Jyotsna Singh, Victoria Sparey, Tiffany Stern, Ann Thompson, Peter Thomson and Virginia Vaughan drew my attention to important texts in their respective areas of expertise. Apologies to them for being selective about their suggestions: in the end, I had to take some decisions for which I remain responsible. James Alsop, Jennifer Barnes, Jeremy Bloomfield, Philip Denning, Briony Frost, James King, Philip Schwyzer, Victoria Sparey, Daniel Williams and Zhiyan Zhang gave detailed and incisive feedback on individual chapters – thanks to all of them and to Phil Robinson. Karen Edwards' belief in the importance of teaching and textbooks has been an inspiration: I am so grateful for that (and for so much more). Laura Berndt spent a summer with me as a sharp-eyed and patient research assistant: many, many thanks to her for putting so much of her own enthusiasm and energy into getting the book ready for publication. Thanks, too, to Ashley Tauchert, Ges Macdonald and Andrew McRae at the University of Exeter for making this happen. Nicolas Tredell, a marvellously attentive reader, and Sonya Barker at Palgrave Macmillan have been a pleasure to work with: thanks to them for allowing me some flexibility; I hope the book is the better for it. It certainly *is* the better for the detailed and informed feedback of its peer reviewers, to whom I am very grateful. I thank the team at Macmillan Publishing Solutions for their hard work. Rhiannon and Glyn were the reason for writing this book and David's support and early rising habits made it possible for me to finish it.

I would like to dedicate this book to the students who helped to shape it.

Introduction: Defining 'Jacobean Drama'

'Jacobean Drama' is a term which, in the past, has often been used synonymously with the term 'Jacobean Tragedy' to describe, in John E. Cunningham's terms, 'plays of a certain atmosphere or flavour' that are 'very closely concerned with death and dying, with the air of the graveyard and the thoughts of men as they reached their end'.[1] In this, the plays of the Jacobean age are implicitly – and often explicitly – contrasted with 'Elizabethan Drama', the plays produced during the golden age of the English theatre closely identified with the leading figure of 'gentle' Shakespeare. In such uses of the period descriptors 'Elizabethan' and 'Jacobean',[2] the latter becomes everything that the former is not: decadent, violent, satirical, derivative, and it is this sense of decadence which constitutes the drama's appeal to many modern readers, who seek in the violence and transgression of the past a correspondence to the present.

The terminological muddle is complicated by the fact that, up to the 1960s, critics were prone to refer to *all* drama produced between the opening of the first public playhouse in 1576 and the formal closing of the theatres in 1642 as 'Elizabethan'. This is the usage we find not only in *The Elizabethan Stage* (1923), the massive history of the theatre by E. K. Chambers (1866–1954) that still looms large on our shelves and in our minds, but also in some of the most important critical appraisals of Jacobean drama of the mid-twentieth century, right up to Ralph J. Kaufmann's *Elizabethan Drama: Modern Essays in Criticism* (1961), which includes essays not only on Kyd and Marlowe, as one would expect from the title, but also on Jonson, Webster and even Ford, a Caroline playwright. The problem with such a usage of 'Elizabethan' as a portmanteau term is obvious: not only does the term stop being meaningful, but it also obscures the important developments that took place after 1603 which produced the distinctive flavour of Jacobean drama. When subsumed under the term 'Elizabethan', the drama of the Jacobean period is implicitly seen as derivative, as the product of an age to which it no longer belongs and therefore a misfit, whose bleak and cynical mood does not accord with the imagined gloriousness of the Shakespearean age of Elizabeth. The decision to focus this book on Jacobean drama as the corpus of plays that is defined historically as the plays written, mainly for the public and private stages in London, during the reign of James I, is a deliberate counter to the way in which the plays of this period have in the past been overshadowed by the term 'Elizabethan'. Putting the spotlight on the Jacobean period brings out the distinctiveness of its theatrical world, a world of which Shakespeare is still a significant part, though his Jacobean plays can, in this light, more readily be seen as part of a wider theatrical context by which he was influenced as much as he contributed to it. After more than thirty years of scholarly activity that has sought to understand early modern drama in its historical, political and cultural contexts, it seems timely to bring together in one book the critical milestones that have worked to disentangle 'Jacobean Drama' from the 'Elizabethan'.

The beginning of the 'Jacobean' period can be difficult to pinpoint. Glynne Wickham, for example, uses the year 1597 as his starting point because that year saw the Elizabethan Privy Council's order that all the London Playhouses be suppressed, bringing with it the professionalisation of acting.[3] 1599–1600, the years which saw the construction of the Globe and Fortune theatres as well as the establishment of two rival companies of boy actors, could also be considered a convenient starting-point. The date which I will, on the whole, opt for in this Guide, is nevertheless 1603: it sees not only the accession of James I and a corresponding change in the political and cultural environment, but, crucially, the conferring of royal patronage upon all the London playing companies. While this did not bring about an instant change in the nature of the relationship between the players and their audiences, it does mark the beginning of a shift towards a tighter allegiance to the court as opposed to the city. In terms of developments in theatre architecture, the accession of James, and Queen Anna of Denmark's enjoyment of court masques, led to the introduction of Inigo Jones's proscenium-arched stages in 1604–5 which, while at first quite insignificant in their influence on the public playhouses, were eventually to revolutionise the English stage.[4]

By contrast, defining the end of the 'Jacobean' period for the purposes of this book is quite straightforward: not only did John Fletcher, the leading playwright of the King's Men, die that year, but the restrictions on playing during Lent in 1625 were followed by a prohibition on playing following the death of the King, which was followed by an outbreak of the plague that saw all theatres closed for eight months. As a result, the Admiral's or Palsgrave's/Elector Palatine's Men, the company that had been the principal rival of the King's Men throughout James's reign, ceased their existence as an independent company and the Lady Elizabeth's company, which had evolved out of various groupings of former boy companies and which premiered plays as important as Middleton's *Chaste Maid* and Jonson's *Bartholomew Fair*, was also broken up.[5] There is thus a clear distinction to be made between theatres of the Jacobean reign and the Caroline, which, once the theatres reopened, largely saw a consolidation of playing arrangements with a stable number of playing companies.

This book will thus make an argument in favour of recognising the drama produced during the reign of King James I as marked by a shift from the public playhouses to an increasing use of smaller indoor venues (also known as 'private' playhouses) and the growing importance of drama at court. At the same time, it will also use the adjective 'Jacobean' in a looser way that returns us to John Cunningham's perception of the drama's distinctive 'flavour' in the period. This involves a more flexible periodisation, in which we accept that 'the characteristic preoccupations and tones of early seventeenth-century tragedy had already been anticipated in the work of Kyd and Marlowe [arguably the two most influential Elizabethan authors of tragedies] and were definitively established by five plays first performed between 1599 and 1604', namely Shakespeare's *Hamlet* and *Othello*, Marston's *Antonio's Revenge*, Jonson's *Sejanus* and Chapman's *Bussy d'Ambois*.[6] These tragedies bring to the fore the key ingredients of the popular perception of 'the Jacobean', namely a heady mixture of revenge, cynicism, self-awareness, complex plotting, corrupt courts, sexual excesses and perversions, secret murders, with spies and flatterers surrounding the charismatic but flawed hero. In comedy, too, what we now recognise as the distinctive flavour of Jacobean city comedy was anticipated in the satirical plays performed by boys' companies in the private playhouses at the turn of the century. 'Jacobean', then, while referring to a strictly delimited period, is a useful term that allows me to include in the book studies that analyse the plays that anticipate the drama performed during James' reign. It also allows me to touch on, for example, Peter Greenaway's *The Cook, The Thief, His Wife and Her Lover* (1989) as a 'Jacobean' film, since it aims to reproduce a 'Jacobean' mood of sexual excesses, spectacular violence, cynicism and stylish plotting.

The purpose of this book is to discuss the criticism of Jacobean drama as defined above rather than to analyse any specific plays of the period or, indeed, the criticism of specific plays. If some plays gain particular prominence in specific chapters – for example, *As You Like It*, *Epicoene* and *The Roaring Girl* in the section on cross-dressing – this is motivated by their importance to the issues under discussion and the wish to provide a stable point of comparison between critical approaches rather than a wish to privilege them for their own sake (or a desire to claim *As You Like It* as a Jacobean play, for that matter). While Shakespeare is manifestly part of the theatrical culture of Jacobean England and the period saw the production of some of his most important plays, this Guide will, as much as this is ever possible, treat him as but one among all the playwrights active in Jacobean London and will privilege criticism that is concerned with Shakespeare's contemporaries over criticism that takes Shakespeare as its exclusive subject. The focus of the book will further-more be on the critical present and future rather than the more distant past. Readers will be guided to a selection of the 'giants' of twentieth-century criticism in Chapter 1 and, where relevant, in later chapters, but my aim is principally to point my readers towards the works that enable an understanding of current debates and a selection of the most innova-tive critical departures since the 1980s. It is with this focus in mind that I am only including the dates of birth and death of critics whose work pre-dates the 1960s: criticism written after that time points towards the present and constitutes an early part of current debates.

To understand these debates, however, requires that we first turn to the critical trails that led up to them. Accordingly, my next chap-ter will consider, in necessarily broad brushstrokes, the rediscovery of Shakespeare's contemporaries by Charles Lamb at the beginning of the nineteenth century and the influence his work had on Romantic critics. Later in the century, the Romantics' endorsement of the contemporaries gave way to a more divided view of the plays, with moralists decrying the self-same decadence that was valued by *fin-de-siècle* aesthetes. In the twentieth century, the theatrical revivals and attempts at authentic stag-ing by the Elizabethan Stage Society combined with the efforts of textual critics and theatre historians to give a 'scientific' grounding to the study of the drama. Meanwhile, influential critics followed T. S. Eliot's lead in focusing on the language of the plays, often adding a moral commentary to their analysis of the drama. In the later twentieth century, the influ-ence of critical theory and the emergence of newer methods of historical investigation led to the comprehensive reassessment of Jacobean drama to which the remainder of the book is dedicated.

This comprehensive reassessment would not have been possible without the joint developments in theatre history and the study of textual transmission, to which Chapters 2 and 3 are dedicated. In both fields, early twentieth-century attempts at bringing a more 'scientific' methodology to bear on the textual and documentary evidence came under attack in the second half of the century, as more material evidence came to light and poststructuralist theory invited scholars to acknowl-edge and embrace multiple viewpoints and instability. In theatre history, I trace the movement towards, first, a rejection of theory and a search for empirical evidence around the turn of the millennium, and second, a tentative return to an acknowledgement of the intrinsically theoretical nature of attempts to re-imagine the early modern theatrical world in more recent work. In textual studies, theory has always been central to the field, whether in the work of the 'New Bibliographers' who shaped the texts as we still often encounter them today on our shelves, or in the 'New Textualists', whose revisionist attack on the 'New Bibliography' relied very markedly on the poststructuralist thinking of Roland Barthes and Michel Foucault. I close the chapter on textual transmission with an overview of the most significant editorial developments that have a direct impact on the nature of the texts we rely on to study Jacobean drama.

Chapter 4 is concerned with the two critical schools which arguably have had the greatest influence on the ways in which Jacobean drama is approached today: the 'New Historicism', which is closely identified with a group of North American critics and its British counterpart, the 'cultural materialism' influenced by the work of Raymond Williams. I use the chapter to outline the different approaches of these critics and the ways in which they aim to use historical methodologies to expose the ideological structure and tensions apparent in Jacobean drama. I then turn to more recent approaches that take issue with some of the tenets of New Historicism and outline some of the avenues that have opened up for present-day scholars.

Historical contexts are not the only context in which plays are read, however. For centuries, one of the primary ways in which audiences and readers have approached the drama has been to set each play into an intertextual dialogue with other plays of the same genre. Understanding the rules governing generic distinctions and the ways in which individual plays violate or respect those rules has always been a crucial ingredient of literary analysis. It is therefore not surprising that the study of generic forms is still flourishing even as it is often looked at as rather old-fashioned. Chapter 5, accordingly, is concerned with the genres of Jacobean drama and pays particular attention to the smaller genres and sub-genres – the masque, city comedy, revenge tragedy, tragicomedy and closet drama – that are the most characteristic of the Jacobean period. It is symptomatic of the vigour of the field as a whole, I would suggest, that it is in the analysis of these quintessentially Jacobean genres that we find some of the freshest approaches to the drama.

The following two chapters, on the body and race and on gender and sexuality, follow specific sets of avenues that have been opened up by the work of the historicist and materialist critics and by the new attention to the politics of private life that has resulted from the race and gender activism of the 1960s and 1970s. Much of the most vibrant work on Jacobean drama is intimately concerned with the human body, its physical make-up, its conceptualisation in medical discourses and conduct manuals of the early modern period, its racial characteristics and its gender in a theatre whose performers were all white males. I start with a consideration of the work of the four critics (Mikhail Bakhtin, Thomas Laqueur, Jonathan Sawday and Gail Kern Paster) who have had the greatest influence on our conceptualisation of the early modern body and its relationship to its culture. I then move on to the work of race critics who have taken issue with the drama's presentation not only of blackness but also of whiteness, leading to investigations that have changed the way we view the relationships between England and its trade partners and colonies. In the chapter on gender and sexuality, I move on to consider more closely issues surrounding the staging of femininity on an all-male stage and the ways in which the female characters of Jacobean drama may be read as ideological constructs. New historicist and cultural materialist criticism have had a marked impact on the study of gender and sexuality, as is also evident in the queer studies of Jacobean drama with which the chapter ends.

The book concludes with a consideration of the work-in-progress that is the development of performance studies of Jacobean drama. Based, to a large extent, on the work of Shakespearean performance studies, the analysis of Jacobean drama on stages and screens is the newest of the approaches treated in this book and is therefore also one of the most challenging. The theoretical underpinning of the field is still rudimentary and I discuss the many questions that have been raised so far by the pioneers of Jacobean performance studies. I end with a discussion of the few critical appraisals of the available corpus of films of non-Shakespearean Jacobean drama. As the corpus expands and more criticism becomes available in print, this promises to be a vigorous and wide-ranging critical field that engages with the work of theatre historians, textual critics, historicists, and genre critics as much as it already does with the analyses of the body, race, gender and sexuality, as we begin to recognise the power of performance to encompass and engage with a multiplicity of concerns and approaches.

CHAPTER ONE

The Critical Trail – Early Views to the Twentieth Century

Jacobean drama and the romantics: the creation of a literary and critical corpus

It is something of a commonplace to assert that the period 1603–25 produced some of the most extraordinary drama in English literature. This view is reflected in the currently widespread pedagogical and critical practice of studying Shakespeare within the context of the plays of his contemporaries. Such an attitude towards Jacobean drama, however, would have been almost unthinkable before 1808, the year which saw the hugely influential publication of *Specimens of English Dramatic Poets Who Lived about the Time of Shakespeare* by Charles Lamb (1775–1834). Before the appearance of Lamb's annotated anthology, the plays of Chapman, Marston, Dekker, Heywood, Middleton, Rowley, Webster, Tourneur, Field, Massinger and Ford had disappeared almost entirely from stage, print and cultural awareness. Of the Jacobean dramatists other than Shakespeare, only Ben Jonson, Beaumont and Fletcher and, to a much lesser extent, Middleton, seem to have substantially survived the upheaval of the Civil War and found a new life on the Restoration stages, where the first play to have been performed after the return of Charles II was Jonson's *Epicoene*.[1] But even there, their survival often came at the cost of being rewritten to fit contemporary demands for decorum in style, for reserve in the portrayal of violent emotions and actions, and for sensitivity to altered political circumstances. While in the eighteenth century the plays of Shakespeare continued to be valued and to appear both in theatres and important critical editions, by mid-century even Jonson and the previously highly popular Beaumont and Fletcher canon were falling out of favour in the theatre,[2] with Theophilus Cibber (1703–58) commenting that 'Beaumont and Fletcher's plays are not acted above once a season, while one of Shakespear's [*sic*] is represented almost every third night'.[3] By the end of the century, in spite of the calls of lonely voices like that of George Coleman (1732–94), in his 'Critical Reflections on the Old English Dramatic Writers',[4] for the restoration of the work of a larger number of Jacobean dramatists to the stage, Shakespeare had almost entirely eclipsed all his fellow play-wrights.

Enter Charles Lamb, and with him the rediscovery of much of the Jacobean dramatic corpus. Some of Lamb's 'specimens' are selected from collections and editions (of Jonson, Beaumont and Fletcher, and Massinger) that were still generally available, but more than a third of the texts he included could only be found 'in the British Museum and in some scarce private libraries'.[5] The texts he thus makes accessible are highly selective and quite brutally edited: Lamb has no trouble admit-ting that he has 'expunged, without ceremony, all that which the writ-ers had better never have written' and has got rid of some 'superfluous' characters, to boot.[5] His inclination is towards the passionate and tragic, reflecting the predilections of his Romantic readers. He bewails the 'insipid levelling morality to which the modern stage is tied down' and extols the 'vigorous passions, and virtues clad in flesh and blood, with which the old dramatists present us'.[6] As a result, much of the criti-cal commentary of the nineteenth century, based as it was on Lamb's selections, followed his bias and focussed more on scenes of high emo-tion than on comedy, masques or Arcadian pastorals. The shortness of Lamb's selected passages, moreover, in conjunction with the, at most, scanty contextualisation of the dramatic action, reveals Lamb's convic-tion that these texts are to be read as poetry rather than drama.[7] This is also confirmed by the notes that are interspersed between some of the extracts.

From the notes one can also glean the patriotism that animates Lamb's enterprise: for example Heywood, of whom he writes as of an old friend, has the virtue of being animated by a 'true hearty Angli-cism of feelings' that shapes his 'Christianism'.[8] Above all, Lamb is someone who, through both selection and commentary, judges the plays and playwrights with regard to their morality (Marston, for instance, is a 'worn-out Sinner'[9]), their poetic value, and their merit relative to Shakespeare, who, though excluded from the anthology, is the ultimate point of reference. His comments on Heywood are representative:

■ Heywood is a sort of *prose* Shakspeare [sic]. His scenes are to the full as natural and affecting. But we miss *the Poet*, that which in Shakspeare [sic] always appears out and above the surface of *the nature*. Heywood's characters, his Country Gentlemen, &c. are exactly what we see (but of the best kind of what we see) in life. Shakspeare [sic] makes us believe, while we are among his lovely creations, that they are nothing but what we are familiar with, as in dreams new things seem old: but we awake, and sigh for the difference.[10] □

In line with many predecessors, contemporaries and successors, Lamb sees in Shakespeare the perfect combination of 'Nature' and poetry or 'Art' to which all other Jacobean playwrights could, at best, aspire, but never surpass.

The many reprints of Lamb's *Specimens* throughout the nineteenth century not only assured the wider circulation of Jacobean plays but also prompted the composition of a number of pieces of criticism by figures as weighty as S. T. Coleridge (1772–1834), Alexander Dyce (1798–1869), William Hazlitt (1778–1830) and Leslie Stephen (1832–1904). The longevity of Lamb's influence can be perceived from the fact that A. C. Swinburne (1837–1909) dedicated his *Age of Shakespeare* (1908) to him and declared Lamb to be 'the strongest as well as the finest critic that ever was found worthy to comment on the most masculine or leonine school of poets in all the range of English literature'.[11]

Coleridge influentially shared Lamb's distrust of spectacle and his focus on playtexts as poetry and also followed him in using Shakespeare as the ultimate point of reference. Of Shakespeare's contemporaries, Ben Jonson is the only playwright Coleridge considers to be 'original': 'he is, indeed, the only one of the great dramatists of that day who was not either directly produced, or very greatly modified, by Shakspeare [*sic*]'.[12] On the whole, however, Coleridge muses that '[t]he more we reflect and examine, examine and reflect, the more astonished are we at the immense Superiority of Shakspear [*sic*] over his contemporaries – & yet what contemporaries!', he adds, in an exclamation that justifies the attention he then goes on to lavish not only on Jonson, whom he praises for his morality and profound philosophy, but also on Beaumont and Fletcher and Massinger.[13] While Shakespeare is superior to all his contemporaries in his wit, these playwrights equal him 'in all of the other and as I should deem higher excellencies of the Drama, Character, Pathos, Depth of Thought, &c.'[14] Coleridge is greatly taken by the verse of Beaumont and Fletcher, who he wishes had written poetry rather than tragedy. Coleridge is most clearly showing the influence of Lamb's *Specimens* on his own perception of Jacobean drama: like Lamb, Coleridge resists reading the plays as plays rather than poetry. While he praises the poetry of Beaumont and Fletcher, he deplores the use to which they put their poetic talents: whereas 'Shakespeare always makes vice odious and virtue admirable', 'Beaumont and Fletcher do the very reverse – they ridicule virtue and encourage vice: they pander to the lowest and basest passions of our nature'. Where 'our sweet Shakspeare [*sic*]' managed to portray noble passions, in the plays of 'Massinger, and Beaumont and Fletcher, it really is on both sides little better than sheer animal desire'.[15]

Lamb also had a tangible impact on William Hazlitt's influential *Lectures on the Literature of the Age of Elizabeth, Chiefly Dramatic* (1820) which cover

most of the playwrights anthologised in *Specimens*. Hazlitt's lectures share
and develop many features of Lamb's anthology. Even more than Lamb,
Hazlitt endorses Romantic and patriotic values, extolling 'the natural genius
of the country' that fostered Jacobean drama, rendering it, like the best of
'Our literature', '[g]othic and grotesque; unequal and irregular; not cast
in a previous mould, nor of one uniform texture, but of great weight in the
whole, and of incomparable value in the best parts'.[16] Jacobean drama, in
brief, is 'nature's handiwork', and that handiwork is predicated on 'the
genius of Great Britain'.[17] Hazlitt, too, shares Lamb's antitheatrical bias –
he finds that 'some of his more obscure contemporaries have the advantage over Shakspeare [*sic*] himself, inasmuch as we have never seen their
works represented on the stage; and there is no stage-trick to remind us
of it'.[18] Accordingly, he, too, treats the texts as poetry rather than drama
and focuses on passages of particular poetic beauty, praising Beaumont
and Fletcher for being 'lyrical and descriptive poets of the first order' while
deploring the fact that '[t]hey are not safe teachers of morality.'[19] Literary
criticism is thus intermingled with moral judgement that can, at times,
affect Hazlitt's perception of a playwright's style: thus, he implies, there
is a link between Massinger's 'repulsiveness of manner' and 'harsh and
crabbed' style on the one hand and his 'perversity of will' on the other.[20]

Hazlitt is also especially interested in characterisation. He treats characters
as real people and as old friends, who, together with a select group of play-
wrights, help him 'get through the summer or the winter months': 'Ben
Jonson, learned Chapman, Master Webster, and Master Heywood, are there
[…] Bellafront soothes Matheo, Vittoria triumphs over her judges, and old
Chapman repeats one of the hymns of Homer, in his own fine translation!'[21]
Shakespeare is also part of this fantasised group of friends and keeps resur-
facing throughout the lectures as the absolute measure of perfection. In fact,
Hazlitt is quite open about the fact that his lectures are ultimately designed
to lead to a greater appreciation of Shakespeare:

> ■ He was not something sacred and aloof from the vulgar herd of men, but
> shook hands with Nature and the circumstances of the time, and is distin-
> guished from his immediate contemporaries, not in kind, but in degree and
> greater variety of excellence. He did not form a class or species by himself,
> but belonged to a class or species. His age was necessary to him; nor could
> he have been wrenched from his place, in the edifice of which he was so con-
> spicuous a part, without equal injury to himself and it. [...] [Shakespeare's
> contemporaries] are indeed the scale by which we can best ascend to the
> true knowledge and love of him. Our admiration of them does not lessen our
> relish for him; but, on the contrary, increases and confirms it.[22] □

While the idea of Shakespeare's absolute superiority is nothing new,
what is novel and important here is the determination to set him

in his dramatic context. Shakespeare is no more timeless than his fellow dramatists, and if he is Hazlitt's friend and contemporary, then so are they.

Not only the Romantics, but also the *fin de siècle* 'decadents', headed by Oscar Wilde (1854–1900), saw the Jacobeans as fellow-spirits. In this, they were in stark opposition to someone like William Archer (1856–1924). A playwright and translator of Ibsen, Archer found it necessary to castigate the plays of John Webster, and with them, the legacy of Lamb, in order to pave the way for the new drama he was representing: 'it is high time', he asserted in 1893, 'that the whole Lamb tradition should be subjected to careful scrutiny'.[23] Archer mocks the lack of realism in Webster's portrayal of the Duchess's grief and accuses Webster of providing insufficient motivation for his characters, of a 'fatal lack of clearness', of 'unskilfully mov[ing]' his 'frigid, mechanical, brutal' horrors and of not constructing his plays properly.[24] Lamb and Swinburne, Archer argues, may 'have mistaken a low form of drama for a high, and even the highest, because they found it robed in regal purple of pure poetry'. In truth, the drama of Shakespeare's contemporaries 'pandered [...] to the mob' in 'gratifying the popular taste for gruesomeness and gore, because their own imagination was haunted in a strange uncanny fashion by the legendary crimes of the Italian Renaissance'.[25]

On the other hand, for someone like the sexologist Havelock Ellis (1859–1939), who edited the first 'Mermaid Series' volume of *Thomas Middleton: The Best Plays of the Old Dramatists* (1887, with an introduction by Swinburne) or John Addington Symonds (1840–93), a poet, cultural historian of the early modern period and writer on homosexuality, Jacobean dramatists and their audiences could not be quite so easily distanced and condemned.[26] For Symonds, writing on Webster and Tourneur, the Jacobean dramatists may well be flawed and owe a debt to Shakespeare and Kyd, but they fully deserve our attention in their own right: 'The outlines sketched by Kyd were filled in with touches of diseased perversity and crippled nobleness by Tourneur in his Vendice, and were converted into full-length portraits of impressive sombreness by Webster in his Flamineo and Bosola'.[27] While the language of disease and perversity looks as if it were taken from Archer's condemnation of the drama, Symonds does not find this a negative feature – after all, the sombreness of Webster is 'impressive' and Symonds does not dispute Webster's claim to 'the right to view human fates and fortunes with despair, to paint a broad black background for his figures, to detach them sharply in sinister or pathetic relief, and to leave us at the last without a prospect over hopeful things'. Webster, quite simply, is 'Shakespeare's greatest pupil in the art of tragedy'.[28] No wonder, then, that in Oscar Wilde's *The Picture of Dorian Gray* (1890), Sibyl Vane's death is compared to 'a strange lurid fragment from some Jacobean tragedy, [...] a wonderful scene from Webster, or Ford, or Cyril Tourneur'.[29] For *fin-de-siècle* play-wrights and poets, who read Jacobean tragedies for their aesthetic quali-ties, it is the very luridness of these plays that is 'wonderful'.

The twentieth century: establishing a critical tradition

The advent of a more 'scientific' approach to Shakespeare in the latter half of the nineteenth century that led to such a major editorial enter-prise as the publication of the Cambridge *Shakespeare* between 1863 and 1866 eventually also led to a division between those who believe in autonomous dramatic texts, texts that have to be looked at in their own right as literary texts, and the contextualisers, who insist that texts can only be considered within relevant contexts, whether these be textual or historical. Criticism of the former kind is informed by individual taste and focussed on style, characterisation and morality, thus linking it to nineteenth-century critical traditions, whereas the latter is shaped by the conscious application of some methodology and aims at detachment from its subject and absence of judgement. The his-tory of the criticism of Jacobean drama in the twentieth century sees, at first, the division between these two types of approaches, followed by a gradual absorption of the more purely 'literary' criticism by the 'contextualisers'.

A radical break with Romantic and *fin-de-siècle* aesthetic criticism is immediately perceptible upon opening any of the four volumes that make up *The Elizabethan Stage* (1923) by E. K. Chambers (1866–1956), the foundation stone of much of twentieth-century criticism of Jacobean drama. Influenced by the Elizabethan revival in the theatre led by William Poel (1852–1934), whose Elizabethan Stage Society sought to stage the drama of Shakespeare and his contemporaries in 'Elizabethan' style, Chambers sought to bring together all the availa-ble knowledge about early modern staging conditions. Almost entirely absent from the work are open judgements as to the literary or moral value of any of the plays or playwrights. Gone, also, is the notion that the plays are to be read as poetry. Instead, Chambers focuses on all the aspects of the plays that mark them as drama written to be per-formed in specific venues by specific people. He applies what he calls the 'historic method' which is more nuanced, he suggests, than much of the work of his contemporaries, whose judgements rest upon conclu-sions about staging and theatre architecture that are not founded upon the thorough analysis of all the available evidence.[30] Rigour and depth of scholarship, combined with an impressive width of scope, are, then, the key features of these volumes in which Chambers redefines the 'context' of Jacobean drama. No longer does contextualisation, as in Hazlitt, mean the appreciation of Shakespeare's contemporaries as a means towards a better understanding of Shakespeare himself. It is true that Shakespeare remains a privileged figure in that he is, on the whole, excluded from *The Elizabethan Stage* in order to have the two-volume *William Shakespeare: A Study of Facts and Problems* (1930) dedicated to him alone.[31] But the purpose of Chambers' book is the provision of as complete a historical backdrop to *all* dramatic production in early modern England as could be compiled out of the evidence available at the time of publication.

The result is a resource which, though in some ways dated, remains invaluable both for its main texts and for its voluminous footnotes and fourth volume consisting of appendices in which crucial documents are reprinted. Chambers colourfully depicts the courts of Elizabeth I and James I, and explains the workings of the Royal Households and the role of entertainments such as masques, pageantry and court plays within those households. He tackles the question of which factions vied for control of the stage in the sixteenth and early seventeenth centuries and, in the process, goes as far as to give a detailed account of the rise of antitheatrical sentiment among Puritans in Calvinist Geneva during the sixteenth century. This leads him to a no less detailed contemplation of the circumstances that led to the rise of the profession of acting 'as a regular profession, in which money might with reasonable safety be invested, to which a man might look for the career of a lifetime'. This, he points out, is an essential development if we are to understand the workings and status of Jacobean theatre:

> ■ The player of the seventeenth century is in fact as necessary a member of the polity as the minstrel of the twelfth or the fourteenth; with this distinction that, in London at least, he is a householder and not a vagrant, and is therefore able to perform his function on a larger scale and with a fuller use of the methods and advantages of co-operation.[32] □

Chambers thus paves the way for the type of modern criticism – to be discussed at greater length in this Guide in the chapters on theatre history and textual transmission – which ceases to see the playwright as the sole creative force behind the surviving plays and instead acknowledges the influence of a variety of interrelated historical factors and the agency of a large number of figures involved in the production of plays.

One of these factors, which is meticulously investigated by Chambers and is also currently receiving increased scholarly attention, is the role played by the companies of players as economic and artistic groupings. While Chambers is ready to admit that his 'detailed chronicles [...] of all the companies traceable in London during any year between 1558 and

1616' 'too often [...] [lapse] into arid annals of performances at Court or in the provinces',[33] this is more than made up for by the usefulness of the information provided for any scholar wishing to investigate, for example, the companies' repertories. Less useful, because more comprehensively superseded by current scholarship, is Chambers' account of the history and structure of the public and private playhouses. The same can be said of his section on 'The Printing of Plays', which he openly acknowledges is indebted to his 'friend Mr. A. W. Pollard'[34] (1859–1944) – a giant of textual criticism – and in which he, for instance, repeatedly asserts Shakespeare's lack of involvement in the publication of his plays, a claim which has now been convincingly refuted.[35] On the other hand, Chambers' description of early modern staging at Court and in the theatres is still well worth reading, even if it, too, has been supplemented and modified by more recent scholarship. Even if superseded in parts, what makes Chambers' volumes endure as possibly the most 'essential' work of criticism on Elizabethan and Jacobean drama altogether is the way they bring together previously disparate pieces of evidence that are interpreted with characteristic differentiation and discernment.

Chambers' work is carried on, with equal care if not quite equal flair, by G. E. Bentley (1901–94) – and, as we learn from his acknowledgements, his wife – in *The Jacobean and Caroline Stage* (1941–68). Bentley's purpose is clearly stated as 'to carry on the admirable survey made by Sir Edmund Chambers in *The Elizabethan Stage* from 1616, his terminal date, to the closing of the theatres in 1642'.[36] To this purpose, he dedicates seven volumes which are, he says, 'intended for references purposes and not – grisly thought – for consecutive reading',[37] though large parts of Volume One, which deals with dramatic companies and players, are well worth reading consecutively. Because the intended reader is the scholarly researcher hunting for a specific piece of information, the methodically organised volumes are accompanied by footnotes and appendices that are, if anything, still more exhaustive than Chambers'. Throughout, Bentley follows Chambers in his conscious avoidance of 'the popular error of considering the plays as non-dramatic literary documents', endeavouring to 'keep them in their proper theatrical context' instead.[38] That said, the fact that Bentley provides discussions of individual plays at all – however 'historical' these are in the instance – combined with his inclusion of a selective bibliography for each play, reveals Bentley's awareness of how his work is implicitly at the service of the type of critic whom he accuses of reading the plays as non-dramatic literary documents. By mid-century, the purism of Chambers' 'historical method' is beginning to be somewhat diluted and to acknowledge more readily that it is at the service of literary interpretation.

How such literary interpretation could profit from the work of the likes of Chambers and Bentley is possibly best exemplified by the work of Muriel C. Bradbrook (1909–93), whose *Themes and Conventions of Elizabethan Tragedy* (1935) and *The Growth and Structure of Elizabethan Comedy* (1955) remain important texts in genre study and will be discussed as such in Chapter 5 of this Guide. For the current narrative, what is important is the way Bradbrook's use of Chambers in *Themes and Conventions* is openly seen by her as a way of reacting against the school of criticism of 'Coleridge, Hazlitt and Lamb' who, she says, 'were interested almost exclusively in characterisation' because 'they were influenced by the current dramatic theory, which was Realism; and the dominant literary form, which was the novel'.[39] The nineteenth-century critics' expectations about consistent characters, Bradbrook argues, could not help but be frustrated by 'Elizabethan' methods of characterisation which followed conventions that were appropriate for the non-realistic public playhouse stages and repertory companies. Her discussion of conventions of acting and presentation, type-casting, different types of plot construction and of the audience's training in listening and rhetoric are all designed to highlight the distance between the early modern and the modern periods and to enable her reader to understand 'how an Elizabethan would approach a tragedy by Marlowe, Tourneur, Webster or Middleton'.[40] As a result, her analysis of the plays in the second part of her book treats them firmly as 'drama' rather than 'literature' or 'poetry'.

Bradbrook is especially attuned to the features that distinguish early modern from Realist drama, commenting on the stylisation of the plays, their use of Humorous, non-naturalistic characters, their patterns of imagery and standard plot structures. If at times her statements about conventions are rather too categorical, considering that they are sometimes based on pure speculation, they at least tend to err on the side of emphasising the alien rather than the familiar. There is no evidence I know of, for example, to support her imaginative supposition that 'a painted board before an open trap seems the likeliest method of represent[ing]' the action of 'characters [...] leap[ing] into the river'.[41] It is Bradbrook's awareness of the larger picture of early modern dramatic production, which is closely allied to her sense of the alienness of that culture, that leads to her most illuminating comments, as when she explains of *The Changeling* that '[t]he subplot is connected with the main plot chiefly by implication. It acts as a kind of parallel or reflection in a different mode: their relationship is precisely that of masque and antimasque, say the two halves of Jonson's *Masque of Queens*'.[42] This is the sort of observation that can only come out of literary criticism that has been informed by a historically aware study of the Jacobean dramatic context.

Despite Poel's 'Elizabethan revival' and the trend towards more 'scientific' criticism which can be observed in editorial practice and stage-centred studies such as Chambers' and Bradbrook's, some critics persisted in regarding the plays as purely literary or even poetic texts.

The approach to the drama and elegant style of writing of the nineteenth-century gentleman scholar continued to flourish well into the twentieth century, where, within Shakespeare studies, A. C. Bradley (1851–1935) became its most prominent representative. His tendency towards 'character criticism' in *Shakespearean Tragedy* (1904) has been too famously debunked by L. C. Knights's 'How Many Children Had Lady Macbeth?' (1933) to need any further explanation here.[43] But it is worth noting that his application of an Aristotelian framework to early modern tragedy – blaming some 'fatal flaw' for the downfall of the hero/heroine and seeking to identify some uplifting factor and moral in the protagonist's final moments of self-awareness and the resulting 'catharsis' – had an enduring impact well beyond the limits of Shakespeare studies, affecting the criticism of other Jacobean writers, as well. It is also worth pausing on the profound suspicion of the stage that informs many of Bradley's comments. The imposition of Aristotelian and Hegelian frameworks and Bradley's antitheatricality are particularly clear in his comments on *King Lear*, which he declares to be 'too huge for the stage'.[44] The play frustrates him in many ways. On the one hand, Gloucester's blinding, he feels, 'is a blot upon *King Lear* as a stage-play' because 'the mere physical horror of such a spectacle would in the theatre be a sensation so violent as to overpower the purely tragic emotions, and therefore the spectacle would seem revolting or shocking'.[45] On the other hand, the ending of the play also offends Bradley's 'dramatic sense', since it does not finish with Lear and Cordelia's rescue and the death of their enemies. Cordelia's and Lear's deaths, he finds, are unnecessary since 'the tragic emotions have been sufficiently stirred already'.[46] It never seems to occur to Bradley that the brutality and bleakness of this play could be dramatically effective in ways not dreamed of in his Aristotelian philosophy. Nor does Bradley seem to consider the historical or dramatic context of the play particularly relevant for his interpretation of it: Shakespeare is not Bradley's friend and contemporary as he was for Hazlitt, but he is timeless and 'universal' in a way unthinkable for someone like Bradbrook.

Less shackled by preconceptions about tragedy than Bradley, though equally indebted to the nineteenth-century heritage, are the vastly influential essays on various Jacobean dramatists in the 1920s and 1930s by T. S. Eliot (1888–1965), which are brought together in his *Selected Essays 1917–1932* (1932). It is worth noting, here, that Eliot's approach to Jacobean drama is not disinterested: it is related to his quest for an innovative poetic practice which could engage with the world of the early twentieth-century – hence his allusions to Jacobean drama in *The Waste Land* (1922). The long essay misleadingly entitled 'Seneca in Elizabethan Translation' (1927), which discusses the Roman playwright's influence on a large range of Elizabethan and Jacobean plays, is a good starting-point. Where Bradley attacked Shakespeare's representation of the 'revolting and shocking' blinding, Eliot quite simply accepts that 'the Elizabethan tragedies are remarkable for the extent to which they employ the horrible and revolting'. This does not, however, lead him to a condemnation of *King Lear*. Instead, he simply goes on: 'It is true that but for this taste and practice we should never have had *King Lear* or *The Duchess of Malfy* [*sic*]; so impossible is it to isolate the vices from the virtues, the failures from the masterpieces of Elizabethan tragedy'.[47] Bradley's attempt to bring late nineteenth-century notions of decorum in staging to bear on Shakespearean tragedy makes way, in Eliot, for some equally dubious 'daring generalizations concerning the temper of the epoch' that explain the 'sanguinary character' of the plays as the result of 'some fundamental release of restraint'.[48] (At least, Eliot's generalisations have the virtue of acknowledging the historical distance between the Jacobean period and the twentieth century). Like Lamb and Hazlitt, Eliot's assessment of the drama's brilliance is coloured by patriotic chauvinism: 'the genius of no other race', he claims, 'could have manipulated the tragedy of horror into the magnificent farce of Marlowe, or the magnificent nightmare of Webster'.[49] Also like his predecessors, Eliot reserves a special place for Shakespeare in this as in all his Jacobean essays. If Eliot is unafraid to condemn *Titus Andronicus* in the harshest terms, this does not prevent him from seeing Shakespeare as having had a greater impact on the work of his contemporaries and successors than he probably deserves credit for:

■ The direct influence [of Seneca] is restricted to the group of Marlowe and to Marston; Jonson and Chapman are, each in his own way, more sophisticated and independent; the later or Jacobean dramatists, Middleton, Webster, Tourneur, Ford, Beaumont and Fletcher, found their language upon their own predecessors, and chiefly upon Shakespeare.[50] □

The focus on language in this passage is representative of the essay as a whole: the 'horrors' of the drama are mainly a linguistic feature for him, a matter of how the verse is handled.

The handling of verse is also Eliot's principal concern in his essays on individual authors. He concludes, for example, that 'Heywood's versification is never on a very high poetic level, but at its best is often on a high dramatic level',[51] or that Tourneur 'was a master of versification and choice of language'.[52] While this sort of judgement of a playwright's poetic ability often appears a little off-hand and rests on Eliot's personal taste, some of the conclusions he reaches upon analysing the language of the plays are more rewarding. In 'Ben Jonson' (1919), a particularly well-considered essay, Eliot declares that Jonson's poetry is 'of the surface' in that 'his emotional tone is not in the single verse, but in the design of the whole'.[53] This leads him to consider that design and to conclude that Jonson has more affinities with Marlowe than with Shakespeare and 'the Shakespearians, Webster, and Tourneur'.[54] Whereas Shakespeare's characters appear to have a life beyond the play in which they appear, in Marlowe's and Jonson's plays, 'the life of the character is inseparable from the life of the drama'. And that 'life of the drama' is one which exists, Eliot finds, 'without a plot', something which requires 'immense dramatic constructive skill' to achieve.[55] The study of language, in Eliot's criticism of Jonson, thus leads to a study of characterisation and Jonson's method of simplification and, eventually, to an analysis of the dramatic technique and plot construction in which he comes to some pithy and startling conclusions. Eliot's fame ensured that his interpretations of the plays and judgements on the dramatists remained influential for many years, so that the notion that Middleton, for example, has no distinct 'personality' and 'has no point of view' or 'message' is one that has had to wait several decades to be revised.[56]

One of the reasons why Eliot's essays on the Jacobean dramatists had such an immediate impact upon other critics is that he made a convincing case for their plays' affinities with modern-day tastes. Jonson, in particular, is an author the 'present age' would find sympathetic because in his plays: 'There is a brutality, a lack of sentiment, a polished surface, a handling of large bold designs in brilliant colours, which ought to attract about three thousand people in London and elsewhere'.[57] If this was Eliot's sentiment in 1919, by 1937, when Una Ellis-Fermor (1894–1958) published *The Jacobean Drama: An Interpretation* in the run-up to World War II, the feeling that there might be something in common between the Jacobean period and the present had only deepened. Ellis-Fermor finds the drama characterised by a 'sense of defeat', a 'preoccupation with death' and a 'spiritual uncertainty' that go with both periods' 'fear of the impending destruction of a great civilization'.[58] The two main influences Ellis-Fermor identifies as contributing to the 'sinking of the clear exaltation of Elizabethan dramatic poetry into the sophisticated, satirical, conflicting mood, deeply divided, of the Jacobean drama' are Machiavelli, responsible for the calculating hero who is deprived of a spiritual dimension, and Seneca, who 'opened to [the playwrights] the language of undefeated despair'.[59]

The value of Ellis-Fermor's study, however, does not lie in her fairly conventional tracing of Machiavellian ideas and moments of stoic endurance and Senecan verse in the plays. Like Eliot, who is a tangible influence on her thinking, Ellis-Fermor instead sets out to identify the essential quality of each of the playwrights she discusses, identifying the features that single him out from his contemporaries. If some of her comments, especially on dramatic technique, are rather impressionistic and vague, as when she discusses the 'implied musical notation' of Act Five of

The Duchess of Malfi, many of her observations capture important aspects of the drama.[60] Long before the advent of feminist criticism, Ellis-Fermor gently directs the reader's attention towards the sorts of issues that will animate that form of criticism, pausing on Webster's heroines and suggesting that Middleton 'is one of the few writers of Jacobean comedy who is not so obsessed by the differences between the sexes as to be unable to see the likenesses'.[61] Ellis-Fermor also seems somewhat ahead of her time in her assessment of Beaumont and Fletcher. On the one hand, she condemns their tragicomedies, in terms that are possibly even harsher than Hazlitt's and Eliot's, for their irresponsibility, their 'weakness of motivation' and 'fundamental unsoundness which from time to time builds beauty of sentiment and conduct on insecure foundations'.[62] On the other hand, Ellis-Fermor also points out that in these plays 'there is a marked increase in explicit statement and in discussion [...] of topics of still living and immediate concern; the nature of kingship, of friendship, of honour (particularly of woman's honour), of the conduct proper to a gentleman'.[63] These are rich veins that have been mined since to great effect by a spate of more recent scholars, with Jeffrey Masten, for example, linking the discourses of friendship and gentlemanly conduct to the issue of homosexuality and the collaborative playwrighting of Beaumont and Fletcher (see Chapter 3 of this Guide).

If Ellis-Fermor was probably unaware of the ways in which her study would resonate with future forms of criticism, *Drama and Society in the Age of Jonson* by L. C. Knights (1906–97), which was also published in 1937, is a self-consciously pioneering attempt to use some of the ideas provided by Marxist analysis of economic conditions for an analysis of Jacobean drama. Knights' stated aim is to determine the relations between dramatic literature and 'the prevailing mode of economic production and exchange' in the Jacobean period. To Knights, Jacobean drama represents a test case for the validity of applying Marxist thinking to literature since 'the drama, more obviously than any other form of art, is a social product; in the plays produced in the early seventeenth century, if anywhere [...] we should be able to trace the connexion with the economic bases of society'.[64] Crucially, Knights sees the period as one in which two modes of life and economic organisation came into conflict, broadly seen as the 'medieval' structuring of trade and industry through guilds and of country life through agriculture and the manor versus the 'modern' large-scale development of capitalist enterprise. It is the coexistence and friction of these two contradictory modes of social organisation which, he suggests, led to the extraordinarily socially aware drama of the period.

Knights' section on 'The Background', in which he describes the inherited economic order, the development of capitalist enterprise, new elements in the national life such as enclosures, trade depressions, the dislocation of social classes, the importance of money and the 'social

theory' of the period, is still informative and valuable for its frank probing of Marxist ideology. He cautions against the facile assumption that
the structuring of Elizabethan society into a 'gradation of estates' was
'merely a way of "keeping the poor in their place"' and stresses the
social responsibility that was inherent in that system.[65] The dramatists
he discusses – Jonson, Dekker, Heywood, Middleton and Massinger – all
share, he suggests, in an 'enlightened conservatism' that made them
respond critically to the social and economic upheavals that punctuated
the reign of James I, with the 'continued abuses of the patent system'
forming the background to the Midland riots of 1607 and the 'disorgani-
zation of the staple woollen industry in 1616'.[66] This is where Knights'
attempt at Marxist criticism begins to wear thin and to reveal its true
colours: 'the reactions of a genuine poet to his environment', he asserts,
'form a criticism of society at least as important as the keenest analysis
in purely economic terms', and that criticism, it seems, must of necessity be nostalgic for 'the good life' associated with medieval structures,
however much these, too, were oppressive to the poor.[67]

   In the second part of Knights' book, the author's relief at the fact that
he may now leave history and Marxist theory behind to some extent
and concern himself with literature and poetry instead is so obvious as
to be funny:

■ A study such as this lies largely outside the field of strict literary criticism; but without a background of criticism to refer to it is impossible to
say anything at all, and I propose to begin [...] by selecting one play and
merely trying to explain why I find it admirable.[68] □

What follows is a largely 'literary' analysis in the vein of Eliot, to whom
he repeatedly refers. Thematically, this analysis is organised around the
'anti-acquisitive attitude' Knights sees in Jonson and his contemporaries and which he traces back to Christian and medieval values. As the
book moves from Jonson to Dekker and Heywood, it becomes increasingly clear that Knights' chosen topic keeps forcing him to stray far from
his instinctive home ground of literary analysis and to discuss material
that he would normally go out of his way to avoid. Not only does his
subject matter make him consider comedies rather than tragedies, but
the quality of the plays he includes in his study is much more variable
than he would wish. Of Dekker, he says:

■ With a few exceptions Dekker's plays are uniformly dull, and the effort
of attention they require – the sheer effort to keep one's eyes on the
page – is out of all proportion to the reward. They were, however, 'best
sellers' [...] and as an index of contemporary taste and opinion they
provide some information that is relevant to this study.[69] □

To present-day students and critics who have been brought up with the cultural materialist/New Historicist criticism of the last quarter of the twentieth century, this squeamishness about 'bad' writing in this 'old historicist' text seems extraordinary. It is, however, an excellent reminder of the fundamental shift in attitude towards the criticism of Jacobean drama that we now take for granted. Knights' book, like no other, reveals the painful wrench the transition from aesthetic and purely 'literary' to historically informed and political criticism represented for many practitioners. It serves as a useful reminder of why that transition took such a long time to be effected.

Certainly, the transition heralded by Knights is not yet in evidence in the 1960s, which saw the publication of Robert Ornstein's *The Moral Vision of Jacobean Tragedy* (1960, see also pp. 75–6), Ralph J. Kaufmann's collection *Elizabethan Drama: Modern Essays in Criticism* (1961), which brings together essays by the most important scholars on Elizabethan and Jacobean drama of the previous three decades, and T. B. Tomlinson's *A Study of Elizabethan and Jacobean Tragedy* (1964). While Ornstein does engage with the historical context, painting a picture of the Jacobean period as one in which old ideals are replaced by new ways of life influenced by market forces, none of these books is, properly speaking, historical in its approach to the plays. The plays are very much read for their poetry and for the 'moral vision' that they propagate – or fail to propagate. If there is a keynote to these three books, in fact, it is that struck by the opening chapter on 'Elizabethan and Jacobean Drama' in Kaufmann's anthology, in which F. P. Wilson notes 'a change in the temper of comedy' around 1603, which was accompanied by a corresponding difference in the genres of romantic drama and tragedy, which in the Jacobean period became full of 'surprises of plot' and 'surprises of feeling, surprises which are encouraged by the tragicomedy which [Jacobean] writers affected. How the thermometer of passion goes up and down in a single scene of Beaumont and Fletcher!', exclaims Wilson, who goes on to comment on the 'superficiality and [...] the impoverishment of their ideas and their language'.[70]

While Wilson shies away from using the term 'decadence' in his chapter, no such restraint is exercised by Ornstein and Tomlinson. The latter even dedicates the final part of his book to the topic of 'The Decadence', which he finds to be 'not merely a threat but a commanding principle' for Webster, Tourneur and Middleton and a simple truth about the tragicomedies of Beaumont and Fletcher.[71] Earlier in his book, Tomlinson singles out *The Revenger's Tragedy* as a rare play to portray corruption without being entirely contaminated by the 'social and moral decadence' of its subject matter. The play's 'poetic richness' which is felt – often all too uncritically – to be characteristically 'Jacobean' is, for Tomlinson, specific to Tourneur (to whom he decisively attributes the play) and not a more widespread feature of Jacobean drama.[72] *The Revenger's Tragedy*, says Tomlinson, 'was a very great achievement, but it was obviously the high point of an old tradition, not the beginning of a new'.[73] The new Jacobean drama, as exemplified by the work of Middleton and especially Webster, is seen very much in terms of chaos, decay and the movement towards death. For Tomlinson,

> ■ *The Duchess of Malfi* is [...] the only Webster tragedy which clearly escapes the charges of decadence so often levelled against the Jacobeans generally. 'Decadence' proper is the result of dramatists thinking of themselves merely as lesser copies of a Shakespeare or a Marlowe, content therefore to play upon worn-out Elizabethan themes and attitudes. [...] In *The Duchess* Webster has something to say, and it is still – as it is not, for instance, in Ford – something of value.[74] □

With *The Revenger's Tragedy* and *The Duchess of Malfi* thus separated from the rest of Jacobean drama and seen as rare examples of 'something of value' to study (*The Changeling* is another play that is described as having a 'depth of focus unique in Jacobean [...] drama'),[75] one may wonder why Tomlinson chose to write a book on the subject at all, and it also becomes clearer why his and Ornstein's books are such rare examples of full-length studies of Jacobean drama in the mid-twentieth century: described as being of little literary and moral value, it was simply not worth reading in the age of formal analysis, stylistic appraisal and moral criticism. It was to take a new generation of critics in the late 1970s and 1980s, whose work will be discussed in detail throughout this Guide and who had a much stronger interest in understanding not the poetry and morals as much as the historical relevance and political force of Jacobean play-texts, for the drama to become the subject of sustained criticism and vibrant debate.

Staging the Renaissance: critical practice opens up

By 1991, which saw the publication of *Staging the Renaissance: Reinterpretations of Elizabethan and Jacobean Drama*, Jacobean drama could no longer comfortably be read as 'poetry', nor could it be considered unproblematically without taking its historical material and cultural contexts into account. Aesthetics was displaced by theory and politics as formalist approaches and the New Criticism, which had gone particularly stale in Shakespeare studies, were losing their footing in a rapidly changing critical environment. In the manifesto-like introduction to their ground-breaking collection of new work published between 1979 and 1989 by the most important critics of that decade and beyond, David Scott Kastan and Peter Stallybrass remark on the 'significant shift in the very ways in which the drama is conceived and approached':

■ Returning in some sense to the historical interests of an even earlier scholarly age, recent criticism of the drama increasingly has insisted upon it not primarily as a 'poetic' and individual art, but as a theatrical and collaborative activity, demanding a focus both on its discursive complexities and on the institutional conditions in which it was produced. [...] Feminism, Marxism, poststructuralism, and psychoanalysis have productively transformed the ways in which we now conceive of texts and representation, while at the same time a renewed attention to historical specificity, necessitated precisely by the largely metaphoric if not metaphysical appeals to 'History' of many of these theoretical initiatives, has emphasized the importance of the particular, and often contradictory, material determinants of the Renaissance stage.[76] □

Key words in this passage are 'historical specificity', 'contradictory' and 'material determinants'. The political and/or critical theories of Feminism, Marxism, post-structuralism and psychoanalysis, as applied to Jacobean plays in the anthologised essays, are systematically grounded in the material culture of the period (hence the denominator 'cultural materialism'), with the authors keen to embed the texts in various very specific historical contexts (hence the denominator 'New Historicism') and to bring out the tensions and contradictions inherent in any text that originates in as hotly contested a public sphere as were the Jacobean theatres.[77] Gone is the emphasis on the 'genius' of individual playwrights and the beauty of their verse: the focus here is on 'the multiple and complex collaborations that the theater demanded between patrons and players, playwrights and printers, playhouses and playgoers', and the judgements we find in the volume concern the politics rather than the versification of the drama. The object of study is destabilised and fractured at the same time as the critics themselves are more aware of their own historically contingent points of view and the ways their attempts at reconstructing history are 'necessarily mediated, provisional, and incomplete'.[78]

The combination in this watershed publication of an intense awareness of tradition with a destabilising break with it is evident in the very form the volume takes. Like many of the works of criticism I have discussed in this introduction (Hazlitt, Bradbrook, Ellis-Fermor, Knights), the volume is divided into a first part concerned with the 'background' (here entitled 'The Conditions of Playing') and a second part concerned with literary interpretation (here entitled 'The Plays'). But instead of the single voice and single critical approach, the collection presents us with a whole choir of voices, each singing in a slightly different key and yet achieving a surprisingly musical if sometimes intriguingly dissonant sound. It is this choir, to extend the metaphor yet further, that composed the score which today's critics of Jacobean drama are still using as the basis for their variations and riffs.

What the volume includes as relevant 'background' to the drama strays beyond the boundaries set by Chambers in 1923. In the opening essay, for example, Steven Mullaney directly challenges the emphasis laid on theatre architecture by traditional giants of theatre history such as Chambers, Bentley and Wickham. More important than their design, he insists, was the location of the theatres in the 'transitional zone' of the London liberties.[79] Later in the volume, Jean E. Howard proposes another adjustment of point of view about the same issue: to her, the location of the theatres is less important than the fact that there were theatres at all, that what had once been an activity that took place within 'the controlled space of the nobleman's house' was now something public and accessible to women, who thus became 'both spectacles and spectators, desired and desiring' in ways that troubled antitheatrical writers like Stephen Gosson.[80] A related focus on femininity as spectacle governs Lisa Jardine's chapter on 'Boy Actors, Female Roles, and Elizabethan Eroticism', which challenges the notion, implicit in the work of Chambers, Bentley and even Bradbrook, that theatrical cross-dressing was a simple convention that did not cause 'moral uneasiness' or provoke 'misdirected' desire.[81] Such 'misdirected' eroticism is a component of the theatre that Chambers would never have dreamed of seeing as remotely mentionable let alone important. Here, however, it is turned into a highly significant 'background' to the drama by Jonathan Goldberg's assertion that 'Marlowe's theatrical milieu, as hospitable to homosexuality as any institution in the period can be said to have been [...] is the place [...] where the counter-voices of the culture were acted out'.[82] Finally, textual criticism, which had been included by Chambers but confined to a small, derivative, chapter, takes on a much more central role in this volume thanks to the inclusion of essays by Stephen Orgel and 'Random Cloud' (Randall McLeod writing under the pseudonym he uses for his most provocative work). Influenced by poststructuralist theory and the 'New Textualism' (see Chapter 3) Orgel's insistence on 'the basic instability of the text' and Cloud's marvellous rant about editors' smoothing-out of the 'fragmentation' and 'multiplicity' of dramatic characters present a challenge not only to editors, but also to readers who are enjoined to be much more textually aware when approaching Jacobean drama through modern editions.[83]

Not just the 'background' to the drama has changed. As the selection of plays in the second part of the volume reveals, what is worthy of more detailed analysis has also been redefined to reflect shifts in the wider culture. Thus, for example, the feminist movement of the 1970s, which brought with it the centrality of gender as a critical category, is also responsible for the 'resurrection' of long-forgotten texts written by women – hence the volume's inclusion of Margaret W. Ferguson's essay on Elizabeth Cary's *Tragedy of Mariam*. Additionally, a play like *Epicoene*, which does not even feature among the eighteen Jonsonian plays and masques discussed in Bradbrook's *The Growth and Structure of Elizabethan Comedy* (1955), now upstages *Volpone* and *The Alchemist* and receives a chapter of its own in which Karen Newman productively revisits Marx's equation of women and commodities to elucidate the play's representation of talkative women as 'a threat to order and male sovereignty, to masculine control of commodity exchange, to a desired hegemonic male sexuality'.[84] Postcolonialist criticism's concern with race and identity, on the other hand, means that plays such as *The White Devil*, which have always been central to the Jacobean canon, are subjected to renewed scrutiny to reveal, as in Ann Rosalind Jones's New Historicist juxtaposition of the play with Thomas Coryat's travel narrative *Crudities* (1611), the bizarre way in which the reprehensible Italian courtesan is 'associated with the undercivilized behavior of the Irish'.[85] The canon, even where it remains unaltered, is thus redefined by 'issues' and theories: a Marxist concern with economic relations and class structures governs Kastan's selection of *The Shoemaker's Holiday* just as Stallybrass' use of psychoanalysis and of Mikhail Bakhtin's theory of the grotesque body (see pp. 100–1) determines his focus on *The Revenger's Tragedy*.

The purpose of the present book is to look again at the work of many of the authors anthologised in *Staging the Renaissance* and to explore their, their peers' and their successors' contributions to the criticism of Jacobean drama. In what follows, I will consider only the most indispensable criticism that predates the 1980s and concentrate instead on the research that has been carried out since then. *Jacobean Drama: A Reader's Guide to Essential Criticism* is concerned with guiding its readers through the various strands of this research and pointing them towards the latest developments in the various fields. It is clearly impossible to be comprehensive in the coverage of 'essential' criticism and this book will provide only a fragmented, unstable picture, in which the concentration on specific works and issues will live side-by-side with broader narratives of critical history. In its very inconsistency, however, this book might be a fair reflection of the field itself, marked as it currently is by self-conscious destabilisation of prior certainties and a trend towards building a picture of Jacobean drama out of fragments of detailed historical, theoretical and literary investigation. This picture, to be accurate, must start with the two basic foundations on which the drama itself rests: the theatres in which the plays were first performed and the books in which they were first printed.

CHAPTER TWO

Theatre History

Traditional 'master narratives': from Chambers and Bentley to Gurr and Dessen

E. K. Chambers's *The Elizabethan Stage* (1923) and G. E. Bentley's *The Jacobean and Caroline Stage* (1941–68) remain the two most essential and influential reference works on the shelves of any historian of the Jacobean theatre, even if some of Chambers's conclusions are increasingly coming under attack as 'very much a product of his time'.[1] Andrew Gurr, whose long and distinguished career has been entirely dedicated to writing about the theatre of the period, tellingly admits in his Preface to *The Shakespearean Playing Companies* (1996) that his history is essentially a revision of Chambers and Bentley. The main difference between their work and his book is that 'besides supplying a longer historical perspective, some corrections of fact, and a large input of new material' which has become available in the intervening years, Gurr intends to '[shift] the focus back to the plays and to their highly mobile social and political contexts'.[2] The work of the theatre historian in the late twentieth century, it appears from this, was essentially a matter of updating the research of Chambers and Bentley both in terms of the new data that has been discovered and with respect to the new directions criticism of Jacobean drama in general has taken since the 1980s.

Clearly, that is not all that theatre historians have been doing since Bentley set down his pen in 1968: theatre history is a field in which a lot of very exciting new work, which can hardly be described as a mere topping-up or refocusing of Chambers and Bentley, is currently being carried out. But before one can move on to the more iconoclastic research I will turn to at the end of this chapter, it is essential that one should feel entirely at ease with the theatre of the period. To this end, the best place to start is Gurr's informative account of different aspects of early modern theatre in London (while bearing in mind that his interpretation of the facts is informed, as his titles reveal, by a Shakespearean bias).

Gurr's first foray into the field, *The Shakespearean Stage, 1574–1642* (1970) very quickly established itself as an authoritative, comprehensive survey of the theatre of the period that integrated, especially in its revised editions of 1980 and 1992, the findings of many important mid to late-twentieth-century theatre historians. As a result, his description of the public playhouses, for example, brings together all the available evidence concerning the shapes of the Theatre, the Fortune, the Globe, the Swan and the Red Bull playhouses and modifies the assumed spaces of these buildings in small but important respects that have had a bearing on the physical shape of the reconstructed Globe Theatre in London. Reassessing the extant evidence about these buildings, as some of Gurr's hypothetical formulations in this section reveal, is not a straightforward business. In the absence of the archaeological evidence he is campaigning to obtain, Gurr is aware that many of his conclusions are inevitably precarious (though there is some hope that new excavations on the Rose Theatre site will reveal more solid evidence in due course).[3]

Gurr's chapters on 'The Players' and 'The Staging' in *The Shakespearean Stage* also remain useful introductions to the subject of early modern performance techniques. Gurr succinctly introduces his readers to some of the key performers of the period (Alleyn, Burbage and Field, among others) and discusses the kind of training players underwent. This leads him to speculate about the large amount of type-casting that must have taken place. While the assumption that 'consistent type-casting of the major roles is the easiest way to cope with the demands of any reper-tory system' has been challenged in some quarters,[4] it has also recently received renewed support, as we shall see, in the work of Tiffany Stern. Type-casting must have been widespread, and it must have led to a cer-tain amount of acting according to types. To establish how such typed acting might have looked, Gurr consults a wide variety of sources includ-ing Bulwer's wonderful illustrations of sign language conventions for the purpose of instructing seventeenth-century would-be orators. While Gurr concedes that these 'illustrations belong more properly with dumb-show than acting with words', he does also hypothesise that such 'conventions were the shorthand of stage presentation, and in a packed repertory, with plays performed at high speed, there can have been little chance for deeply studied portrayals of emotions at work'.[5] However much, in the early seventeenth century, actors were developing the art of 'person-ation', 'a relatively new art of individual characterisation', Gurr's praise of the 'naturalism' characteristic, in particular, of the King's Men remains inflected by his acknowledgement of how strongly that 'naturalism' must have been attenuated by conventions of both acting and stagecraft which would strike a modern viewer as highly stylised.[6]

Gurr's *Playgoing in Shakespeare's London* (1987) shifts the focus from the players and theatres to the audience and seeks to arbitrate, to some extent, between Alfred Harbage's assumption of an 'artisan' audience for the early modern theatres and Ann Jennalie Cook's research, which suggests that playgoers were of 'privileged' social status.[7] Working with Cook's figures, Gurr concludes that 'Cook's is a more plausible stereotype than Harbage's, but it is still a thorough oversimplification'.[8] Gurr proceeds to reproduce the available and largely familiar evidence, examining it from a variety of angles. He starts on relatively safe ground with a consideration of what the physical conditions of playhouses can tell us about the audience. Even here much of his argument is, perforce, speculative and leads him into tight corners from which there is no elegant escape: when discussing 'the need for toilets', for the existence of which, he notes, 'there is regrettably little evidence', he is led to 'suspect that the Globe offered no privy for the defecation of solids closer than the river, and that buckets served for the passing of urine. Privacy there was none, and how women managed we can only guess'.[9] This little excursion into the toilet habits of playgoers may not be conducive to resolving the question of their social class, but it does offer a lively glimpse of what theatregoing may have involved and is characteristic of the combination of attention to detail and imaginative extrapolation in the work of theatre historians.

How little is actually known about the physical make-up not only of the outdoor public playhouses but also of the indoor spaces is obvious not only in Gurr's admissions about the need to 'guess', but also from a juxtaposition of *Playgoing* with Keith Sturgess's *Jacobean Private Theatre*, which was published in the same year. Sturgess's book discusses the buildings, audiences, playwrights and repertories of the Blackfriars, Cockpit/Phoenix and Salisbury Court theatres in great detail, concluding with a few fascinating imaginary reconstructions of performances of key Jacobean texts in each of these venues. Gurr tells us that 'none of the indoor playhouses would accommodate more than about a quarter of the amphitheatre capacity',[10] while Sturgess asserts, just as confidently, that the 'audience capacity of the private playhouses was probably no more than a third of that of their public counterparts'.[11] Sturgess's caveat that 'we must bear in mind that the results, however precise they look, rest on no more than informed guesses' is an important one: it is vital to remember not to take any such statements at face value and see such contradictions as opportunities for further research.[12] The last word on the issue was not spoken in 1987: for more up-to-date views it is well worth consulting the chapters on 'The Theatres' by John Orrell in *A New History of Early English Drama* (1997), the fuller account (with illustrations) by Martin White in *The Cambridge History of British Theatre* (2004), as well as the six detailed and illustrated chapters in the 'London Playhouses' section of Richard Dutton's *The Oxford Handbook of Early Modern Theatre* (2009, see pp. 38–9). A more interactive and vividly visual view of Jacobean indoor theatres is afforded by Martin White's DVD and website *The Chamber of Demonstrations*, which includes scholarly articles, interviews with scholars and theatre practitioners, as well as original practice stagings in an indoor playhouse (the Wickham Theatre at the University of Bristol) based on the Inigo Jones/John Webb designs for a Jacobean private theatre.[13]

If the physical evidence about spaces for the audience is uncertain, evidence about the 'mental composition' of the early modern audience is even more difficult to read. Based on a range of documents, including all the known references to playgoing listed in a valuable appendix, Gurr finds 'rather more evidence for divisions between audiences in their social and cultural character than in their learning or intellect'.[14] The key notion here is that of several audiences, attending different playhouse venues, which displaces the earlier assumption of a singular audience, however socially varied, attending a generic early modern playhouse. Gurr is developing a differentiated conception of the early modern theatrical culture in London as varied and constantly evolving: different playhouses, public and private, catering to specific social groupings whose interests and predilections change in accordance with changes in the political and cultural climate.

This investigation of the ways in which various theatrical companies catered to distinct tastes and social groupings is carried further in Gurr's next two books, *The Shakespearian Playing Companies* (1996) and *The Shakespeare Company, 1594–1642* (2004). Since the latter is an elaboration of the former with a firmer focus on Shakespeare as an organising figure, I will concentrate here on the earlier book.

In the first part of *The Shakespearian Playing Companies* Gurr aims, in eight chapters covering topics from travelling to patronage and the changes specific to the year 1603, to provide 'A History of the London Companies from the 1560s to 1642'. Scott McMillin aptly summarises this history as

■ [turning] on several pivots: the formation of the Queen's men in 1583 as a monopoly company and as the largest troupe yet in the professional theater; the 'deal' struck by the patrons of the Chamberlain's men and the Admiral's men in 1594, by which their companies became a 'duopoly' and were able to settle into the Theatre and the Rose without fear of competition; [...] the decision of the same company to rebuild the Globe after the disastrous fire of 1613, a choice which Gurr attributes to their attachment to the popular theater despite their success at the elite Blackfriars; and finally, the reorganization of companies behind the King's men after the plague closure of 1625.[15] □

Gurr's attempt at generalisation and coherence breaks apart in the second half of the book, however, where the same material is re-presented in the guise of detailed histories of individual companies, each of which is dealing with roughly the same time period from a different angle and offers an alternative narrative to that provided in the first part of the book. The tension between the book's first and second parts is suggestive of the increased fracturing of the field. This sense of fracturing and multiplicity is increased once we realise that even in the second part of the book, the organisation of the material under headings such as 'Worcester's/Queen Anne's/Revels Company, 1562–1625' is unable to mask the fact that we are speaking of a company here which had at least two different patrons and whose composition and identity varied widely in the 63 years of its existence.

When it comes to the subject of Gurr's next book, the company he increasingly takes to calling 'the Shakespeare Company' in an attempt to give it a greater sense of coherence and identity while cashing in on the kudos of Shakespeare, Gurr's unifying project is undermined by his division of the company's history into two distinct chapters. Gurr breaks his account of this company in 1608, the year King James consolidated the company's pre-eminence by compensating them for the closure of the theatres because of the plague and the players decided to start using the Blackfriars private playhouse for their winter seasons while continuing to perform in the Globe in summer. While we may be talking about the same grouping of *people*, the chapter break indicates that we are talking about different types of *enterprise*: the King's Men before 1608 are a different kind of business from the King's Men after 1608. This begs the question of what, exactly a 'company' is: is it a grouping of players, an allegiance to a noble patron, a business structure, or a collection of plays and properties?

While such questions are raised by Gurr's research, Gurr himself does not attempt to answer them. His concern is rather with the outline of a large-scale map of companies and their repertories across the period, and he succeeds in highlighting broad patterns and in putting some flesh (information about the kinds of plays performed by specific companies) on the bones (information about the make-up and finances of each company) provided by Chambers and Bentley. Gurr makes a strong case for a recognition of how theatrical corpuses may be organised not so much in terms of authorial figures – whether single or collaborative – as in terms of the companies who commissioned and owned the play-texts and who were subject to the vagaries of impresarios, patrons, players' shifting allegiances, financial constraints and political crises and manoeuvres. This is arguably the most influential insight provided by *The Shakespearian Playing Companies*, which has since led to new and provocative work (see, for example, my discussion of Bly in Chapter 7 of this Guide).

Gurr, obviously, is not the only important figure in traditional theatre history – he is, above all, the most prolific and widely read representative of the kind of narrative theatre history centred on Shakespeare which is gradually being replaced by newer kinds of approaches. It is actually worth remarking here how the broad trajectory of Gurr's career is symptomatic of the field of theatre history in the past three decades: he moves from generalising statements about the whole period to increasingly focussed attention on the material specificities of particular moments, companies, and texts, thus paralleling trends within the broader critical community. Before I move on to those, however, another traditional scholar who at the very least deserves a mention here is Alan C. Dessen. For three decades, his work has been dedicated to reimagining the ways plays were staged by looking closely at the stage directions of all surviving play-texts. One result of this research is the rich resource provided by the *Dictionary of Stage Directions in English Drama, 1580–1642* (1999), a reference work (co-edited with Leslie Thomson and regularly updated on a website) based on a data-base of around 22,000 stage directions.[16] The interpretative use to which such directions can be put is illustrated by Dessen's *Elizabethan Drama and the Viewer's Eye* (1977), *Elizabethan Stage Conventions and Modern Interpreters* (1984) and *Recovering Shakespeare's Theatrical Vocabulary* (1995).

One of these, *Elizabethan Stage Conventions* will have to serve as my illustration of Dessen's major contribution to theatre history. Crucially, Dessen starts 'with the assumption that there is much we will never know (e.g., what the stage at the Globe actually looked like to a spectator)'.[17] This leads him to a consideration of what we *can* know about early modern staging: the stage directions that have come down to us in print. These, he points out, are not easy to interpret since they use a specialised 'language' which theatrical practitioners and critics no longer speak. The aim of his book, accordingly, is to 'reconstruct or recover some Elizabethan playhouse conventions', with a particular emphasis on 'techniques or procedures that appear to us odd, illogical, or intrusive'.[18] Dessen explicates such techniques – for instance, the shooting of an arrow, or Gloucester's 'fall' from the Dover cliff – with a refreshing respect for the authors of the stage directions as theatrical professionals 'who not only knew [their] craft well but also knew [their] theatre from the inside, both its potential and its limits'.[19] He resolutely opposes any interpretation of stage directions influenced by post-nineteenth-century notions of theatrical realism and urges his readers to reconsider the drama within a non-illusionist mode: even more than Gurr, he insists on the stylised nature of early modern acting techniques. He also helpfully questions the authority of the evidence he uses, differentiating different types of play-text (and hence, stage direction) according to their probable provenance and following Richard Hosley in distinguishing between 'theatrical' and 'fictional' stage directions.[20] Like Gurr, Dessen takes interpretative risks and comes up with stimulating, if sometimes dubious, answers to difficult questions. Thus, for instance, his suggestion that, because 'several moral plays from Queen Elizabeth's reign [...] provide evidence for an allegorical or symbolic logic behind stage violence', such a logic may well have governed the staging of violent acts in Jacobean plays such as *The Atheist's Tragedy* or *A Woman Killed With Kindness* has the potential to alter quite radically our conception not only of the stagecraft of these plays but also of their emblematic and moral significance.[21] One may wish to quarrel with many of Dessen's interpretations, but they do provide a powerful and impressively well-researched corrective to the lazy assumptions that are, as he repeatedly reminds us, encouraged by modern editorial and staging practices.

Fracturing the narrative: new ways of writing history

In its almost doggedly empirical attention to the stage direction as an individual piece of evidence and its awareness of contradictory interpretative possibilities, Dessen's work, to some extent, anticipates the positivist nature of much recent work in theatre history. The impossibility of Gurr's unifying attempt to provide a master narrative accounting for all aspects of theatrical production in London in the period has now been widely recognised. John D. Cox's and David Scott Kastan's wide-ranging anthology of commissioned essays *A New History of Early English Drama* (1997), and the collection of essays commissioned, from some of the same authors, by Jane Milling and Peter Thomson for *The Cambridge History of British Theatre* (2004), are representative of the work carried out in theatre history around the turn of the millennium. The Cox-Kastan anthology can be seen as the pendant, within theatre history, to Kastan's earlier 'literary' co-edited anthology *Staging the Renaissance: Reinterpretations of Elizabethan and Jacobean Drama* (1991), which I discussed in the Introduction. Just as *Staging the Renaissance* assembled the materialist literary criticism of some of the most influential researchers of the 1970s and 1980s, the *New History* brings together some of the most important figures of theatre history. The anthology amounts to a sharply focussed snapshot of the field at the end of the twentieth century.

What distinguishes the *New History* not only from *Staging the Renaissance* but also from earlier theatre history is its deliberate avoidance of playwrights and plays as organising principles and a return to 'history'. In some ways, the anthology heralds a turn away from literary criticism and back to a more empirical study of factual evidence – what Diana Henderson, in the context of Shakespeare studies, describes as 'an archive fever that followed from the critique of historical master-narratives and was later abetted by a backlash against the less accessible (and sometimes more philosophically challenging) forms of theory'.[22] Accordingly, this anthology will re-appear as an essential text within my chapter on historical contexts (Chapter 4). The anthology is also striking in its deliberate fusing of theatre history and textual criticism: since much of the evidence about one field informs research in the other, they are treated together in the third part of the anthology, which is dedicated to 'Early English Drama and Conditions of Performance and Publication'. Therefore, several of the arguments I am tracing here will also resurface in the chapter on textual transmission (Chapter 3).

The agenda for the anthology is clearly set by Stephen Greenblatt's 'Foreword' and the editors' 'Introduction: Demanding History'. Countering the 'master narrative' school of criticism with a Shakespearean bias, Greenblatt insists that the *New History*

■ does not tell a simple story. It does not invite the reader to imagine that the theatrical activities of several centuries were an elaborate preparation or rehearsal for the career of William Shakespeare, nor does it offer a straightforward, unitary definition of the objects – the textual and material traces of the past – that it analyzes. It forgoes the satisfaction of linear narrative and literary triumphalism in order to present a more capacious, confusing, and complex picture of early drama.[23] □

As *Staging the Renaissance* did in its grounding of literary criticism of Jacobean drama in material culture, *New History* insists on the *materiality* of theatre history and privileges the object – the printed text, the archival or even archaeological evidence – over the historical narrative, the author or the poetry and plot of a play. In fact, the content of the drama is clearly displaced here in favour of the material conditions of its creation: playing spaces, social spaces, costumes, censors, patrons, audiences, printers are treated with the same seriousness as originators of the drama as playwrights. Where Gurr had deprecatingly contrasted the output of 'the Beaumont-and-Fletcher factory' with the single authorship of Shakespeare as the pinnacle of dramatic writing,[24] the *New History* has no prejudices against 'factories' and treats playwrights principally as collaborators and revisers of each other's plays: drama is a 'collective activity that ties the play to history' and demands that we relinquish the traditional 'singular focus on texts'.[25]

Where *New History* most significantly departs from the agenda of *Staging the Renaissance* is in its attitude towards theory. The former volume had embraced theory as a way of reconceptualising the plays and included essays informed by psychoanalysis, feminism, queer studies and cultural materialism. In *New History*, only the materialism of 'cultural materialism' properly remains as the editors explain that 'theory has now brought us to the place where we must respond to its challenges by producing not more theory but more facts, however value-laden they may be, that will illuminate the historical conditions in which early drama was written, performed, read, published, and interpreted'.[26]

Flying in the face of the continuing framing of much critical investigation of Jacobean drama by theoretical concerns, theatre history is here
programmatically declared to be a field that has, for the time being,
exhausted the possibilities opened up by theory and that is returning to
empiricism – albeit a self-consciously post-theoretical empiricism – as its
main mode of inquiry.

Determining what is 'essential' reading in this 565-page tome in which
every essay contains a gem is an impossible task. Nevertheless,
I will hazard to single out three essays, starting with Peter H. Greenfield's
chapter on 'Touring'. Using the *Records of Early English Drama* (*REED*) that
have been painstakingly collected by a cohort of theatre historians over
many years, Greenfield argues for a view of touring that is radically different from the 'antiprovincial' narrative proposed by earlier scholars.[27]
Touring, he argues, was an integral part of what Jacobean companies
did, not an act of desperation, and earlier accounts emphasising how towns
paid players off to prevent them from performing hide the fact that '95
percent of the records indicate that entertainers were allowed to play,
were rewarded, or were otherwise successful'.[28] This is a powerful corrective to the privileging of London that characterises much of theatre
history, including many contributions to the Cox-Kastan anthology.

The next essay, '"Cloathes worth all the rest": Costumes and Properties'
by Jean MacIntyre and Garrett P. J. Epp, draws attention to the material
value of these objects. Costumes are important not only because they indicate a character's social class and occupation, but also, surprisingly, because
they may have determined what sort of play a company commissioned.
The authors note that 'Between 1617 and 1621, the King's Men produced
at least three plays set in the Netherlands, which had to be costumed in the
distinctive and well-known Dutch fashion, and between 1620 and 1625
they put on no fewer than eight plays calling for Spanish dress'. This, they
explain, may well be a result of the company 'having costumes proper
to those countries' and trying to recoup their investment.[29] Topicality, it
seems, is not just a matter of what is happening in the political arena,
but also of what is available in the company's costume store. This sort of
insight has a crucial impact on what is perceived as a relevant 'context' for
materialist criticism.[30] One important consequence of this type of work is
that when objects take on centre-stage positions, the plays in which they
appear and the playwrights who imagine their presence are pushed yet
further to the sidelines of theatre history.

The third essay in the Cox-Kastan collection which I want to highlight is Peter Thomson's 'Rogues and Rhetoricians: Acting Styles in Early
English Drama', which interrogates what a 'character' is. What makes
Thomson's contribution especially valuable is his framing of it in terms of
modern stage practice and his acknowledgement of the influence of the
thinking of the Russian director Konstantin Stanislavsky (1863–1938),

who is at the origin of naturalistic 'method' acting, on contemporary actors' and audiences' conceptions of 'character as subjectivity'.[31] Thomson's return to the practicalities of the early modern theatre and his reminder that actors were not given the full text of the play, but only their own 'parts' with short cues attached, is a forceful reminder of how important a respect for the nitty-gritty of theatre history is to counter the excesses of character-based literary and psychoanalytical criticism.

Rehearsal practices and actors' parts are also central to Tiffany Stern's *Rehearsal from Shakespeare to Sheridan*, which has had a considerable impact on the field since its publication in 2000. Like Dessen and Thomson, Stern sees the early modern theatre as fundamentally different from our own and emphasises the need to understand the physical circumstances surrounding performance – specifically, the material form of plays and the rehearsal practices of the players – in order to avoid misreading the plays. In Stern's defiantly untheoretical study the postmodern fragmentation of theatre history as a field slyly insinuates itself into her project as she dismantles the play-texts into actors' parts, displaces the primacy of the author as an originating figure and challenges the existence of 'character' in the vein of Thomson. Stern's book draws on a wider variety of sources than is usual, taking in not only references to rehearsals in the play-texts themselves but also material found in prologues and epilogues, pamphlets, biographies and account books. She discusses 'rehearsal' (a word which she insists 'did not necessarily signify a re-hearing or recurrent event')[32] in a number of theatrical contexts: country plays, academic performances (including the disingenuously 'educational' and 'private' performance of boy actors), and the professional theatre of the public playhouses.

The aspect of Stern's research which poses the most fundamental challenge to how the actor's craft is commonly viewed in our Stanislavsky-influenced rehearsal-intensive theatrical culture is her insistence that actors not only learned their roles from 'parts' or 'parcells' but that the principal mode of rehearsal was individual 'study', sometimes in the presence of an '"instructor" who was either author, prompter, manager, or friend to the actor'.[33] Faced with the need to put on a great number of plays in quick succession, she finds, players relied heavily on typecasting and often dispensed with group rehearsal altogether. This, she argues, often led to situations where the first performance of a play was also the first time the actors got a sense of the play as a whole and were dependent on the prompter who, she explains 'was something like a conductor, bringing into harmony actors who were largely familiar only with what they had to do individually; he prompted words, timing and basic blocking'.[34] The first performance, in Stern's account, appears to have been a particularly exciting occasion not only because that is when audiences had the power to accept or reject the play, but also because that is when the company's reliance on 'parts' could pay dividends because of the way such parts included subtle authorial directions:

■ [P]laywrights [...] seem to have enwrapped their 'direction' into the form in which they wrote their plays in the first place: they produced texts that, divided in parts, would bring about the action required in performance – without the actor necessarily needing to understand what is going on. One instance of this is the 'premature' or 'false' cue – the part that apparently gives the actor who is to speak his cue too early. □

This she illustrates with a speech in *The Merchant of Venice* in which Shylock gives the hapless actor playing Solanio his cue ('have my bond') four times before Solanio is finally allowed to speak his line. Each time Shylock gives a premature cue, he immediately tells Solanio to be quiet, so that

■ [w]eighed down with the irritation and embarrassment of repeated false cues, the actor playing Solanio will have been wrought to a pitch of uncompromising anger by the time he was actually permitted to speak. The interruption and the shouting down are provided for by the part, and the anger required, rather than being 'directed' in advance, is created in performance.[35] □

The very absence of a rehearsal in the modern sense of the word thus seems to have led to a particularly lively – and life-like – performance. This insight requires that we rethink the ways plays were scripted and performed in quite fundamental ways.

In her attacks on 'Revision studies', which Stern accuses of 'rely[ing] on assumptions about the role of the author in the preparation of a play that simply will not stand up against the facts',[36] she furthermore productively engages in a dialogue with some of the most radical twentieth-century thinking in textual criticism. As I will explain further in my next chapter, revision studies, exemplified prominently by the collection of essays *The Division of the Kingdoms* (1983) and the subsequent edition, by Stanley Wells and Gary Taylor, of the Oxford *William Shakespeare: The Complete Works* (1986), is 'founded on the assumption that there were several collaborative group rehearsals before performance which were "directed" by Shakespeare'.[37] Stern's contestation of the notion that there were several such company rehearsals also puts an end to this theory. Instead of rehearsal, it is 'performance itself that emerges as a major forum for revision'.[38] Actors, she argues, not only changed their lines both accidentally and deliberately (clowns especially 'seem to have been expected to embellish and even partially write their texts'),[39] but they were also responsible for cuts in the dialogue which, crucially, left their cues intact. Theatre history, in *Rehearsal*, as in *Shakespeare in Parts*

(2007), Stern's co-authored book (with Simon Palfrey) which further explores the implications of her work on actors' cues, thus repeatedly overlaps with textual studies in ways that make it difficult to disentangle the two fields.[40]

This is also true of Lucy Munro's *Children of the Queen's Revels: A Jacobean Theatre Repertory* (2005). Influenced by Gurr's *Shakespearian Playing Companies*, Munro's book also takes on board the developments showcased in the Cox-Kastan anthology and especially in Roslyn Knutson's work on theatrical repertories. Munro's work is refreshing, in the context of the sometimes dry materialist historicism and the rejection of theory that dominates turn-of-the-millennium theatre history, in that it is informed by poststructuralist theory, queer studies and textual criticism and brings back a reader-friendly narrative conceptualisation of her subject without ironing out contradictions or losing the close attention to detail and context characteristic of materialist criticism (for example, in her discussion of the importance and value of costumes and a haberdasher financier for a company of 'constantly growing' actors).[41] Her history of the 'avant-garde' boy company which challenged the adult companies with its metatheatrical plays between 1603 and 1613 is, if anything, almost overwhelmed by the amount of information she provides in both the text and the five appendices detailing the company's repertory, record of court performances, lists of actors and referenced biographical summaries.

Munro begins with a company 'biography' consisting of 'a series of smaller, overlapping narratives' that allow her to consider all the different agents involved in the making of a play, from playwright, actors and shareholders (who take on an unexpectedly and possibly undeservedly central role in her account) to playhouse functionaries, patrons, audiences and publishers.[42] Particularly suggestive, in her opening section, is Munro's analysis of the potential effects of the boy actors' transvestism not only in terms of gender but also, crucially, in terms of age and social class. Her focus on the company's repertory pays rich dividends in her discussion of plays written for the Whitefriars playhouse (especially *May Day*, *Epicoene* and *Amends for Ladies*), which all 'experiment with the figure of a young man who is disguised as a woman' and in which 'the potential slippage between "male" and "female" possible in the juvenile troupe, with its mixture of actors in their teens and early twenties, is used to create disturbing and comic effects'.[43]

The core of Munro's book is dedicated to an inquiry into how a repertory or company approach can enrich our understanding both of the interactions between audience and play(ers) and of the development and functioning of dramatic genres. While in her chapter on tragicomedy, as we will see (pp. 88–9), Munro goes as far as to argue for the theatre company's decisive role in shaping this new genre, in her chapter on comedy, Munro insists on the 'combative' relationship between audiences and the Queen's

Revels comedies. The comedies 'actively interrogate the social identities associated with the spectators': rank, she argues, is exposed by these plays as essentially performative.[44] Importantly, Munro does not assume a uniform audience for these plays but rather insists on the 'multivocality of theatre' and the corresponding diversity of the spectators, especially in their reactions to jokes about social class.[45] The comedies of the Children of the Queen's Revels invite different readings and responses from different members of the audience, and the resulting laughter, she argues, 'disrupts the reconciliatory conclusion towards which comedy is orientated'.[46] As a whole, Munro's book presents a powerful argument against the traditional playwright-centred approach to the drama: using a company as an organising principle allows her to approach the plays in a way that sheds new light on the evolutions of generic categories and the role of the audience in shaping the plays.

Munro's return to theory is representative of the most recent trends in theatre history, as represented in the hefty *The Oxford Handbook of Early Modern Theatre* (2009). This collection of cutting-edge essays, which accepts Munro's emphasis on the playing company rather than the playwright as an organising principle, brings together both familiar names (including Gurr, Dessen, Stern and Munro) and the research of younger scholars working on what Richard Dutton, the volume's editor, calls 'the research frontiers' of theatre history (see, for example, the splendid essay on 'Adult Playing Companies, 1613–1625' by James J. Marino, which critically orders old information in a new way and Eva Griffith's essay on 'Christopher Beeston: His Property and Properties', which uses a manager rather than a specific company or playwright as an organising principle).[47] Significantly, the entire volume is introduced by an essay by William Ingram which explicitly engages with the way in which theatre historians in recent years have shied away from theory and avoided discussing their methodology, while producing narratives and emplotments that make historiography look remarkably similar to fictional writing. He thus attacks the seemingly theory-free nature of 'our preferred practice', which he characterises as 'positivist or essentialist', and calls for an approach to theatre history that is more aware of its theoretical underpinnings – to claim that the theory is implicit in the practice and not engage with it is 'imprecise, evasive, and in some cases perhaps not entirely honest'.[48] Ingram also calls for a practice that acknowledges the lack of documentary evidence, the contingent nature of that evidence and the multiplicity of interpretations and narratives that may be constructed from surviving sources.

The ensuing volume does, to a large extent, deliver just such a practice: the thirty-five essays, which cover playing companies, formal and informal playing spaces, and social and theatrical practices, repeatedly draw attention to various theories and the scarcity or circumstantial nature of their evidence. The conception of theatre history and the early modern theatre in this volume is far less positivist and distinctly more relativist and post-modern in its embracing of multiplicity than the picture conveyed in the Cox/Kastan anthology a decade earlier. Theatre history is here slowly evolving into a more self-conscious practice, and as more evidence about the period emerges in sources such as *REED*, it is also gradually building up a picture of Jacobean theatre which is ever less about Shakespeare, the King's Men and London and ever more concerned with a much broader spectrum of playwrights, companies and playing spaces. Such a widening of the focus is also taking place in the closely related field of textual criticism, the subject of my next chapter.

CHAPTER THREE

Textual Transmission

The study of the textual make-up of Jacobean drama is the most foundational of the approaches outlined in this Guide, in that every time we read a play by a Jacobean dramatist that play has been transmitted to us in a way that has inevitably altered its nature. It is therefore crucial that we understand at least in a rudimentary fashion the ways in which editorial work in the past century has shaped Jacobean drama for the present-day reader. It is also important that we understand some of the debates that have arisen since the 1980s from an investigation of early modern print culture.

Once more, the figure of Shakespeare looms large in the field. In the introduction to his 100-page Appendix to *Shakespeare in Print*, in which he attempts to provide 'as full a reckoning of the early editions [of Shakespeare's plays] ever possible', followed by 'a sampling of Shakespeare publishing in more recent centuries', Andrew Murphy admits that '[c]ompiling an exhaustive listing of all the editions of Shakespeare ever published would be an impossible task'.[1] Doing something similar for any of Shakespeare's contemporaries would be much more manageable and would reveal the vastness of the gap between Shakespeare's popularity in print and that of his rivals. If texts such as Edward Sharphams's *The Fleer* have not been reprinted between the early seventeenth century and 2006, when it was freshly edited by Lucy Munro, that says a lot about the recent nature of the resurgence of interest in editing and printing such long-forgotten plays.

That renewed interest, perhaps perversely, is linked to the crucial developments that have taken place in the editing of Shakespeare's plays, as it is the attempts to produce scholarly editions of his works that have generated the debates that animate the wider field of textual studies.[2] Working in very large brushstrokes, the movement in textual studies in the twentieth century can be said to have started with a school of thought now know as the 'New Bibliography', which dominated the early part of the century up to the advent of poststructuralist thinking (marked, in critical theory pertinent to this field, by Roland Barthes' 'The Death of the Author' (1967)).[3] In the latter part of the century, the dominant mode of textual thought became the 'New Textualism',[4] which reacted against and destabilised the New Bibliography, leading to a drive towards *Unediting the Renaissance*, as the title of Leah Marcus' book of 1996 put it.[5] Today, editors and textual scholars are still trying to find a way to negotiate between these two extremes, with widely respected editors and textual theorists, such as N. W. Bawcutt in 2001 and Lukas Erne in 2008, passionately arguing once again for the importance of the role of the editor as a mediator between the early modern texts and the present-day reader.[6] The very fact that Erne's latest book is designed to 'demonstrate how important it is to train ourselves to become better readers not just of Shakespeare but also of modern editions' and to see present-day editors as the early modern author's 'collaborators' shows how much the textual make-up of plays, precisely because it has been so comprehensively problematised by scholarship in the last thirty-odd years, has become part of the object of study when we read Jacobean plays.[7]

New Bibliography

The 'New Bibliography' is a movement spearheaded by three friends, W. W. Greg (1875–1959), R. B. McKerrow (1872–1940) and A. W. Pollard (1859–1944), who were reacting against the lack of scientific rigour they found in the important editions of the nineteenth century. Their friendship and collaboration resulted in an unusually coherent body of work which was influential far beyond Shakespeare studies. I will throw a spotlight on two texts that can be said to, in various ways, encapsulate the thinking of these scholars: firstly, Greg's influential 'The Rationale of Copy-Text' (1950–1), a lecture that 'became something of a sacred text in the editorial community',[8] and secondly *On Editing Shakespeare and the Elizabethan Dramatists* (1955) by Fredson Bowers, a North American disciple who adopted and refined New Bibliographical methods, some would say to absurdity.

In 'The Rationale of Copy-Text', Greg takes issue with the previously accepted supposedly scientific 'mechanical method' of selecting 'whatever extant text may be supposed to represent most nearly what the author wrote and to follow it with the least possible alteration', making of this text the 'copy-text' for one's edition that would be followed slavishly wherever there was not an obvious mistake for the editor to correct.[9] Greg criticises this approach for the way it blindly accepts readings which, while logically possible, may well be wrong in that they might not represent what the author actually *intended* to write (for example, the reading in question could be a scribe's or compositor's plausible guess about the meaning of an illegible handwritten word). Greg therefore suggests that we distinguish between 'substantive' readings of the text 'that affect the author's meaning or the essence of his expression, and others, such in general as spelling, punctuation, word-division, and the like, affecting mainly its formal presentation, which may be regarded as the accidents, or as I shall call them "accidentals", of the text'.[10] While Greg is quite happy for an editor to follow his copy-text in its accidentals, he argues that 'whenever there is more than one substantive text of comparable authority', the editor has a responsibility to choose the reading which in his necessarily fallible judgement 'is likely to bring us closer to what the author wrote than the enforcement of an arbitrary rule'. What he is fighting, then, by insisting on the editor's 'duty and necessity of exercising his own judgement' is what he refers to as 'the tyranny of the copy-text', which has led past editors to accept all substantive readings found in their copy-text even where they were of doubtful provenance and were therefore unlikely to represent the authorial text.[11]

It is this desire to recover as closely as possible the author's writing, and the implicit distinction between the extant imperfect documents and the idealised authorial text that drives New Bibliographical thinking. Since, in almost all cases, knowing what the author wrote is impossible because hardly any authorial manuscripts of early modern plays survive, understanding exactly which types of manuscript the earliest extant printed play-texts were based on becomes crucial for the editor when assessing which substantive variant is more likely to represent the author's intended wording. This is the motivating force behind Fredson Bowers' dense little book *On Editing Shakespeare and the Elizabethan Dramatists*. Bowers writes with the supreme authority of someone who will, as he famously states in the book, 'strip the veil of print from a text' and provide editors with the methods necessary to find the holy grail of 'what the author wrote', to return to Greg's equally famous formulation.[12]

Evidently ill-at-ease with Greg's notion that this goal can be reached through an application of judgement unsupported by more 'scientific' methods, Bowers proceeds to distinguish between thirteen different types of text which the first printed edition of a play may have been based on. These range from an author's 'foul papers' ('the author's last complete draft in a shape satisfactory to him') all the way to the almost comically hypothesised '"foul papers," fair copy, prompt book, or transcript of a prompt book of a memorial reconstruction of the text without direct transcriptional link with any manuscript derived from author's autograph'[13]– a type of text which A. B. Pollard had, early in the century, demonised as at the basis of a 'bad quarto'.[14] The task of the editor of a modern critical edition is firstly to identify the type of text an early print edition was based on and then, on the basis of that identification, to proceed to decide which of the available early editions of a play is closest to the authorial foul papers. This is the text that is to be used as the copy-text and which is to be further examined for traces of the work carried out by 'the compositor or compositors who type-set the book' so as to enable a distinction between 'variant readings of a revised edition as either authoritative or compositorial'.[15] It is on the basis of such evidence that Bowers imagines the edifice of Shakespearean editing to be built, piling one 'sure fact' thus inferred on another, till 'the final capstone' may be 'placed on Shakespearian scholarship and a text achieved that in the most minute detail is as close as mortal man can come to the original truth'.[16]

New Textualism

Bowers' concluding image of the 'original truth' to be editorially reconstructed has a quasi-religious fervour about it which, one suspects, seeks to obfuscate the shakiness of some of the foundations on which this permanent edifice is built. For one, the 'foul papers' that represent authorial thinking may never have existed – in one of a series of articles attacking New Bibliographical principles, Paul Werstine has pointed out that this category of text, while widely postulated in the writing of McKerrow and Greg, has not been empirically found to exist.[17] The issue, however, is larger than the mismatch between postulated constructs and material evidence of their existence. The New Bibliographers' focus on identifying the agents who interfered in the transmission of the text between the author and the printer drew attention to the fact that a text cannot be thought of as the product of the lone author. Texts, as Jerome J. McGann argued in the early 1980s, are 'socialised'. There is no such thing as 'an *Ur*-poem or meta-work whose existence is the Idea that can be abstracted out of all concrete and written texts which have ever existed or which ever will exist'. Instead,

■ the works of an artist are produced, at various times and places, and by many different sorts of people, in a variety of different textual constitutions (some better than others). Each of these texts is the locus of a process of artistic production and consumption involving the originary author, other people (his audience[s], his publisher, etc.), and certain social institutions.[18] □

Seen from this angle, there is nothing intrinsically 'wrong' with choosing as one's copy-text not the printed version of the play closest to hypothetical authorial foul papers, but, say, the version that is most likely to be derived from a promptbook. The 'authority' for the substantive readings in such a text, therefore, stems not from proximity to 'what the author wrote' but from its emergence from the creative community of the early modern playhouse.

This insight came to fruition in two related publications that represented a significant shift in textual scholarship known as the 'New
Textualism'. The first is Gary Taylor and Michael Warren's collection
of essays in *The Division of the Kingdoms: Shakespeare's Two Versions of
King Lear* (1983). Countering Greg's declaration, based on New Bibliographical principles, that 'an editor has no choice but to take the folio
as copy-text' when editing *King Lear*,[19] the group of young textual critics
who contributed to *The Division* re-examined the Quarto and Folio texts
of *King Lear* and concluded that the two texts represent two separate
versions of the play that carry equal authority, with the Folio text quite
likely to be an authorial revision for the opening of the Blackfriars theatre in 1610–11. By paying close attention to the original documents
of Shakespeare's plays, they showed that many of the features that
were once taken as signs of textual corruption could as easily constitute
evidence of authorial revision.

The second milestone in 'New Textual' scholarship is Stanley Wells
and Gary Taylor's edition of *William Shakespeare: The Complete Works* for
Oxford (1986), which was complemented by the vast *William Shakespeare: A Textual Companion* (1987). Rather than insist on their ability or
even desire to recover the 'original truth' of Shakespeare's text, Taylor's
introduction explicitly states that '[n]o edition of Shakespeare can or
should be definitive'.[20] This awareness creates freedom for the editor:
the freedom to make unconventional choices, to privilege one type of
text over another and thus shed new light on well-known texts. What
made this edition revolutionary was the fact that the editors took full
advantage of this freedom. Their stated aim was, among other things,
'to explore in detail the textual consequences of the theatrical origins
and intentions of the great bulk of Shakespeare's work' and 'to investigate the possibility of authorial revision'.[21] Their understanding of the
promptbook as – invoking McGann's terminology – 'a socialized text, one
which has been communally prepared for communication to a wider
public', and of Shakespeare himself as someone who 'devoted his life
to the theatre' leads them consistently to choose as their copy-text 'the
text closer to the prompt-book of Shakespeare's company', privileging
the theatre over authorial intention.[22] For *King Lear*, Taylor's involvement in *The Division of the Kingdoms* seems to have had a particularly visible impact on the edition, for it becomes the cornerstone of the editors'
argument for understanding Shakespeare as a reviser of his own work,
which is characterised by 'textual instability'.[23] Accordingly, the edition
is the first *Complete Works* to print two texts of *King Lear*: *The History of King
Lear* based on the 1608 Quarto, and *The Tragedy of King Lear*, based on the
Folio text. Along different but related lines, the editors also take the radical step of reconsidering the Shakespearean canon and, in an influential
move, ascribe the authorship of *Timon of Athens* to both Shakespeare and

Middleton and argue that Middleton was the reviser not only of *Measure for Measure*, but also of *Macbeth*.

The Oxford *Shakespeare* shook the world of textual criticism; it was attacked, defended, and has generated much new textual thinking and editorial work. Firstly, its insistence on textual instability, coinciding as it did with the development of electronic media, led to an exploration of new ways of presenting variant texts. Two essays in Lukas Erne and Margaret Jane Kidnie's *Textual Performances: The Reconstruction of Shakespeare's Drama* (2004), a collection that sees itself as the successor of *The Division of the Kingdoms* twenty years on, engage with this issue. John Lavagnino's 'Two Varieties of Digital Commentary' wistfully looks back to the initial optimism about the possibilities afforded by the new media, which had led some to believe that print would be replaced by electronic editions. In fact, Lavagnino contends, online commentaries prove to be of limited use and one should distinguish between 'commentary intended as a companion to reading and commentary intended as a scholarly reference'.[24] Lavagnino's wistful reflections are juxtaposed with Sonia Massai's excited account of her work on an internet edition of *Edward III*, which allows her to highlight textual instability by using animated type that alerts the reader to press-variants. Furthermore, she includes the full texts of all available editions of *Edward III* up to 1905, as well as extracts from all of the more recent editions. Her essay and edition thus represent one extreme of present-day editorial practice: that which, while providing critical guidance, ultimately shifts the responsibility for interpretation onto the reader, who is now conceptualised as a *'user*, or what can be described as a "Barthesian" reader'.[25]

Secondly, the scholarship on which the Oxford *Shakespeare* was built and its acknowledgement of Shakespeare's collaborations renewed scholarly interest in the playwrighting and collaborative practices not only of Shakespeare but also of his contemporaries. I want to single out just three of the provocative book-length studies that share this focus, beginning with Jeffrey Masten's *Textual Intercourse: Collaboration, Authorship, and Sexualities in Renaissance Drama* (1997), which reacts against the deeply engrained cultural perception of Shakespeare as *the* individual Author and argues for 'the inappropriateness of an authorially based canon in this period'.[26] With reference to the Oxford edition's production of the two-text *King Lear*, Masten shrewdly points out how the editors, in spite of their intention to demolish the New Bibliographical insistence on a single text, authorise their two-text *Lear* with reference to the single author Shakespeare: what they argue for is *authorial* revision rather than collaborative revision. Collaboration, Masten insists, is a dispersal of authorship and authority, rather than a simple doubling of it, and he forces us to reflect on the different early modern meanings of the word 'author', which conjoins notions of writing, fatherhood and authority, producing a distinctly gendered perception of authorship which he then traces in a number of plays by Shakespeare, Beaumont, and Fletcher. His recognition that these playwrights 'wrote within a paradigm that insistently figured writing as mutual imitation, collaboration, and homoerotic exchange' enables a surprising but fruitful textual intercourse between textual studies and queer studies (see pp. 131–9).[27]

A different approach, which uses Jonson as a counter-example to the collaborative practices highlighted by Masten, is taken by Joseph Loewenstein in *Ben Jonson and Possessive Authorship* (2002), which shows that focus on the production of texts need not exclude studying a single author. Where Masten had followed Michel Foucault in arguing that there is an anachronism in our assignation of early modern play-texts to single authors,[28] Loewenstein's analysis of Jonson's 'possessive' authorship shows that a century before copyright became enshrined in law, play-printing practices in Jacobean London enabled new ways of thinking about authorship which, while contingent on specific circumstances, did, to some extent, anticipate modern notions of single authorship.

In his investigation of the trajectory of Jonson's career, Loewenstein notes that his 'marketing of authorial attention, the advertisement of books as newly revised by their authors' from the 1590s onwards is a feature that is not exclusive to Jonson. Focussing his analysis on the prefatory materials and the presentation of texts, Loewenstein finds that in his earlier quartos, Jonson sought to 'work out typographic devices that reinforce or replicate effects proper to the theater' in a way that showed his perception of print as an ideal form of theatre.[29] The publication of *Sejanus* in 1605, followed by significant editions of *Volpone* (1606), *Catiline* (1607) and *The Masque of Queenes* (1609), marks a turning-point and paves the way for the publication of the 1616 folio *Workes* because of the way it foregrounds Jonson's own authorial agency and diminishes the role he accords to the theatre. For Loewenstein, the milestone represented by the printing of Jonson's 1616 folio *Workes* must be understood as the result of a long gestation period in which Jonson's 'authorial identification with printed writing' matured in response to multiple circumstances and agents from the worlds of politics, the theatre and, not least, of printing.[30] The 1616 *Workes* are the result of a congruence of circumstances that are very particular to the Jacobean period, with printers and stationers wrangling over the rights to texts at the same time as playwrights wish to establish greater control over their plays. That control, of course, could only ever be temporary, as even Jonson has had to relinquish the publication of his works to present-day editors and printing presses in media whose existence he could never have anticipated.

Zachary Lesser's *Renaissance Drama and the Politics of Publication* (2004), on the other hand, fully accepts Masten's critique of our standard use of authorial canons and shifts the focus from authors to publishers (the person sponsoring the printing of the play, not necessarily the printer him/herself). The literary 'canon' in Lesser's innovative study becomes the group of works produced by a specific publisher for his specialist group of readers. The works belong together because their publisher thought them all to be appealing to his particular group of readers to whom he marketed these books as commodities. Plays, seen from this perspective, 'may carry radically different meanings and politics not only between [their] printed and [...] performed versions, but even between two otherwise-identical printed editions brought out by two different publishers'.[31] Lesser insists that '[s]tudies of the economic conditions under which *books* were exchanged can and should lead us to new under-standings of the *texts*, and the politics, of those books' and he reminds us that whereas plays in the theatre had to appeal to as wide an audience as possible,[32] in print they had to be appropriate for specific niche markets and might well have been selected and even revised accordingly.

The key question Lesser asks of every book he analyses is this: what makes this particular text appropriate for publication by this publisher at this particular time? The results can be astonishing, as becomes clear, for example, in his analysis of Webster's *The White Devil*, in which he suggests that the play was seen as participating in a larger debate about the role of women in society. Its publisher, Thomas Archer, produced books that ideologically covered both sides of the debate – what Lesser calls '*dialogic publishing*'.[33] If we want to understand the play the way it was understood by its first readers, Lesser argues, we therefore have to read it alongside these other works, in particular Joseph Swetnam's *Araignment of Lewde, idle, forward and unconstant women* (1615) and Rachel Speght's counter-attack in *A Mouzell for Melastromus* (1617). Looking at *The White Devil* and the other plays published by Archer reveals how the individual texts incorporate the dialogic structure of their print publication, as they represent exam-ples of companionate marriage alongside images of 'safe danger', of more challenging examples of femininity and matrimony that are ultimately contained by the plot. A focus on the publication of texts thus results in a fascinating new reading of the plays, with literary interpretation inextri-cably linked to textual transmission in a way which also has a bearing on how plays ought to be presented to present-day readers.

Editing Jacobean drama today

The kind of research into the circumstances surrounding the production and printing of plays surveyed above, together with the model of the Oxford *Shakespeare*, has had a profound influence on present-day editing of Jacobean drama. Such research is at the heart of a major editorial project, under the general editorship of David Bevington, Martin Butler and Ian Donaldson, to produce the Cambridge Edition of *The Works of Ben Jonson*. Due to be published in 2010, the edition's rationale and methods can be accessed through the project website and through *Re-Presenting Ben Jonson: Text, History, Performance*, a thought-provoking collection of essays by several of the scholars involved in the project.[34] *Re-Presenting Ben Jonson* highlights the increased desire to dismantle the edifice of Jonson's *Workes*, in which he shaped his authorial persona through elisions and revisions, in order to give the reader more of a sense of the actual trajectory of Jonson's career. Printing the plays and poems in chronological order rather than in the arrangement Jonson put them into 'would open up the illusion of the works' inner, ahistorical coherence by rendering visible the inconsistent career moves, the points of uneven development, the collaboration and hack work, foregrounding the awkward contingencies and responses to circumstance that the Folio tends to gloss over'.[35] The influence of recent textual criticism is obvious here, as the editors consider deliberately ignoring Jonson's authorial intentions, as expressed in the Folio, to recover instead a more 'theatrical' and 'socialised' version of plays such as *Every Man Out of His Humour*, whose quarto of 1600 presents a substantially different text from the heavily revised 1616 folio text.[36] An awareness of textual instability and a desire for editorial transparency are also at the heart of the decision to complement the modern-spelling print edition with an electronic edition. The choice of modern spelling arises from a desire to put Jonson on an equal footing with Shakespeare: the project website comments that the critical practice of presenting old-spelling quotations from Jonson alongside modern-spelling quotations from Shakespeare 'perpetuates the popular notion of Jonson as a less accessible, more formidably learned writer than Shakespeare'.[37] The electronic edition will be 'accompanied with an archive of old-spelling texts derived from the folios, quartos and other early editions, digitized images of the manuscripts (where quality permits), and with other contextual, critical and historical data (including early biographies, legal documents, masque records and so forth)'.[38] The open-ended nature of the electronic medium will furthermore enable the updating of the plays' performance histories, returning Jonson firmly to the realm from which he emerged: the theatre, rather than the print shop.

Ben Jonson is not the only author who is receiving a high-profile textual make-over: he is beaten to the line by Thomas Middleton in the Oxford University Press team with Gary Taylor and John Lavagnino's *The Collected Works of Thomas Middleton*, a gargantuan enterprise on the model of the Oxford *Shakespeare*, which was published in 2007.[39] Involving sixty-odd scholars, the edition follows the layout of the Oxford

Shakespeare, replicating, in the book's presentation of one volume of primary texts complemented by a companion volume, the editorial claim to equal status for Middleton and Shakespeare. Taylor insists that 'Rather than simply applying to Middleton modes of editorial practice and critical theory developed to represent another author [i.e. the Oxford *Shakespeare*], we have sought to present Middleton's works in the manner most appropriate to their production and (re)production in early modern culture'.[40] There is nevertheless a lot about this edition – beyond the involvement of Taylor and John Jowett – that is immediately recognisable from the Oxford *Shakespeare*. Not only is it clear that the work for the Shakespeare edition is the starting-point for the inclusion of *Timon of Athens*, *Macbeth* and *Measure for Measure* in the Oxford *Middleton*, but it shares that edition's defiantly modest assertion that '[t]his edition does not claim to be definitive'.[41] That may be so, but it is hard to imagine that in our lifetime it will be superseded by another complete collection of Middleton's dramatic and non-dramatic works, though beyond doubt the edition is already sparking a renewed interest in the author, with various 'companion' volumes already in preparation (Cambridge's *Middleton in Context*, edited by Suzanne Gossett, is due to be published in 2010).

One aspect of Middleton's work and the culture he operated in that is consistently highlighted in this edition is the casualness and frequency of collaborative writing practices in the theatre. In this respect, a particularly important chapter in the companion volume, *Thomas Middleton and Early Modern Textual Culture: A Companion to the Collected Works*, is MacDonald P. Jackson's 'Early Modern Authorship: Canons and Chronologies'. Jackson strongly states the 'party line' of the edition when asserting the importance of 'the sense we receive of "one significant, consistent, and developing personality"' (citing T. S. Eliot on Shakespeare) 'behind the diverse works associated with a major [...] author's name' and hence the importance of decisions about what works to include in the Middleton canon.[42] His contribution to the volume is 'an overview of the issues raised' by attribution scholarship 'and of the different categories of evidence deployed, in any attempt to establish the canon of an early modern author'.[43] He contrasts the secure knowledge we have of Middleton's authorship of *A Game at Chess* with a play like *The Revenger's Tragedy*, for which attribution scholars have had to rely on the 'stylistic and sub-stylistic features of the texts themselves' to arrive at an authorial attribution.[44] Many of the plays included in the edition are the result of Middleton's retouching of old plays by other writers or of his collaboration with them on a new play – as Jackson notes, '[i]n the frequency with which he collaborated, Middleton is more representative of his age than Marlowe, Jonson, or Shakespeare'.[45]

Measure for Measure and *The Spanish Gypsy* in the Oxford *Middleton* will serve as examples of the various problems involved in editing such plays. The former is edited by John Jowett, who had been involved in the Oxford *Shakespeare* that had popularised the attribution of the play's revision to Middleton. Presenting that same text in the Oxford *Middleton*, however, is problematic: as Jowett explains, since we only have the version of the text which was adapted in 1621 and printed in the 1623 Shakespeare Folio, '[a] Middleton edition that conventionally edited the 1621 text would [...] do little other than reprint *Measure* from the Oxford Shakespeare'. Rather than see this as a limitation on the options available to the editor for the *Middleton* volume, however, Jowett sees an opportunity here 'to affirm the adaptation itself as the prime object in view'.[46] Using a variety of type-faces, Jowett distinguishes between cancellations and additions, making visible to the reader the process of rewriting which has been obscured by conventional editions that integrate the play in the Shakespeare canon.

Different problems were faced by Suzanne Gossett, the author of the introduction to *The Spanish Gypsy* (edited by Gary Taylor) and the editor of Rowley and Middleton's *A Fair Quarrel*. In a recent article in which she reflects on 'Editing Collaborative Drama' more generally, Gossett provides an excellent overview of the key problems faced by the post-New Textual editor. She begins by reflecting on the increasing trend, in editions of 'collected works' by early modern authors, including Shakespeare, towards possibly excessive inclusiveness of works in which they had, if not a hand, then at least a little finger.[47] *The Spanish Gypsy* is included in the Oxford *Collected Middleton* simply on the strength of its title-page attribution to Middleton and Rowley, even if recent scholarship has established the play as a collaboration between Ford and Dekker. The danger with this sort of editorial policy, she argues, is that the name on the cover of the collection will inevitably skew the editor's approach to the play and encourage an attempt to make the play 'fit' the rest of the author's oeuvre. It also leads to an implicit, if not explicit, hierarchy, in which one author is declared to be more important than his collaborator(s). This is complicated by the fact that the editor is expected to stress the collaborative aspect of the play while simultaneously arguing for its success as a work of art, a claim which is often based on finding in it an artistic 'unity'. In her introduction to *The Spanish Gypsy*, it is therefore not surprising to find that Gossett, while admitting the relatively small contribution Middleton made to the actual writing, stresses the one contribution he made that gives the work its unity and links that unity to Middleton: Middleton, she states, 'is the most likely candidate for composing the "plot" or scenario for the play, linking its four narratives into a polyphonic whole, and then assigning scenes and subscenes to the playwright best suited to each'.[48]

Another problem with all the editions of 'collected works' that are in preparation or have recently been published is the fact that nearly all general editors have opted for modern-spelling renderings of the works of Shakespeare's contemporaries. For plays written collaboratively, this tends to 'eliminate some or all of the traces of collaboration that the editor believes she recognizes' – idiosyncrasies of spelling and punctuation are flattened out by editorial intervention even where the editor would wish to highlight the multi-authored nature of the text.[49] When the collaboration is not synchronic (two authors working on a play together and at the same time) but diachronic (one author revising the work of another some time after its first completion, as in *Measure for Measure*), the questions of authorship and what to do with the parts of the play that were altered by the second hand become even trickier. Whatever the nature of the collaboration and the scholarly consensus about who wrote what part of a play, 'the presence of a second writer in any section complicates a one-to-one connection between "life" and "text", between individual intention and dramatic result, throughout'. Accordingly, the discussion in introductions to such plays tends to shift from individual psychology to 'accounts of interpersonal relations and theatrical developments', giving such introductory and contextual discussions a focus that distinguishes them from single-author editions.[50] Again, Gossett's own introduction to *The Spanish Gypsy* is an excellent example: it is explicitly signposted as an 'attempt to examine what *Gypsy* meant to its authors and audiences in 1623' – a statement that directs attention away from the individual to the collective.[51] The Oxford *Middleton*, then, is not only a major scholarly achievement, but it is also a telling example of the difficulties faced by editors of Jacobean drama today.

In her reflections, Gossett draws not only on her experience of the Oxford *Middleton* but also on the work she is currently doing as one of the three General Editors of Arden Early Modern Drama, alongside John Jowett and Gordon McMullan. Arden Early Modern Drama is an open-ended series of single-text scholarly editions of dramatic texts by dramatists writing between the late fifteenth and seventeenth centuries, which was launched with Gossett's own edition of *Philaster* and editions of Webster. The series applies and adapts the editorial rationale behind Arden 3 to a substantial number of Jacobean plays. As such, it promises to be a worthy challenger to three other editorial projects concerned with bringing non-Shakespearean drama to a wider scholarly and theatrical community.[52] The long-established Revels series is the brain-child of Clifford Leech in the 1950s and provides excellent scholarly editions, based mainly on New Bibliographical principles but with more recent editions showing the impact of New Textualist thinking. For example, Lee Bliss's 2004 edition of Beaumont and Fletcher's *A King and No King* provides an eclectic text in which the first quarto, which 'is at least two removes from the authors' final draft',[53] is the copy text, but which takes on board New Textualist arguments about the 'socialised' text when it integrates staging-related readings taken from the second quarto, whose authority is derived from its playhouse provenance. Revels editions provide a substantial editorial apparatus and are also in part available in a simplified and updated form as Revels Student Editions, which slim down the textual information but provide a reader-friendly commentary and introduction. A second, even more long-established rival is the New Mermaid series, which has a less extensive scholarly apparatus than the Revels and which caters principally to the theatre, school, college and undergraduate markets with affordable, reliable texts and introductions. Finally, a more recent phenomenon is the Globe Quartos series which consists of slim little modern-spelling editions of barely known plays either revived at Shakespeare's Globe or produced by the theatre's Education Department as part of their 'Read Not Dead' initiative. The editions are produced relatively quickly, with hardly any introduction and editorial apparatus, to provide playgoers and readers with a copy of otherwise unavailable play-texts. Editing Jacobean drama today thus takes a variety of different shapes: from single-author collected *Works*, to e-texts that highlight textual instability and editorial traditions for a specialist reader, to various series that target either academic or general readers (or both). For the serious student of Jacobean drama, the text itself is possibly the most important of the 'historical contexts' I will explore in the next chapter.

CHAPTER FOUR

Historical Contexts

The study of the extratheatrical historical contexts that had an impact on the creation and reception of Jacobean drama is not only one of the most well established of the critical approaches to the plays, but also one that has seen some of the fiercest debates in the past century. In the 1980s, the traditional way of reading literary texts as responding and alluding to specific historical events (for instance in the work of John Dover Wilson or Theodore Spencer) was attacked by the mainly North American 'New Historicist' movement and the 'cultural materialist' school of thought in Britain. They also took issue with the type of historical contextualisation offered by E. M. W. Tillyard's influential *The Elizabethan World Picture* (1943), which saw literary texts as illustrative of state ideology (the world picture of Tillyard's title, which he imagined as strictly hierarchical and ordered), with little scope allowed for the expression of alternative views. Tellingly, Tillyard proclaimed that 'all the violence of Elizabethan drama [in which he includes Jacobean plays] has nothing to do with a dissolution of moral standards: on the contrary, it can afford to indulge itself just because those standards were so powerful'.[1] Far from challenging the norms and the 'universal order' of 'the chain of being' that extended from God down to inanimate objects, literary texts were seen to reinforce that order, so that in *King Lear*, for example, Edmund's scepticism about his father's superstitions simply confirms that he is 'one of those superlatively vicious men whom the stars and their own wills have joined to produce'.[2]

New Historicist and cultural materialist work in the 1980s and 1990s, by contrast, revolutionised the field, amid fierce controversy, by seeking to emphasise the many-voiced nature of culture and the relativity of history. Instead of relating a literary text to a specific political event, thus restricting its range of meanings, literary texts now began to be read as part of a larger network of cultural texts (including art, architecture and non-literary texts, such as pamphlets, conduct manuals, sermons, medical texts, etc.) and to emphasise the contradictions inherent in the various discourses available in early modern England. For this, critics have drawn on the one hand on the poststructuralist thinking of Michel Foucault (on power) and, on the other hand, on the Marxist thinking of Louis Althusser (on ideology) and Raymond Williams's reflections on culture. In the new millennium, the newer historicist methodologies have become conventional to an extent that signals their decline: as Douglas Bruster notes, there is a tendency now for 'approaches [to be] reshuffled rather than rethought, leaving the field busy but without the direction it once had'.[3]

Rethinking historicism in the 1980s: 'cultural materialism' and 'new historicism'

Reading Jonathan Dollimore's *Radical Tragedy* (1984) today allows us to get a sense of the 'direction', the radical energy characteristic of the rethinking of historicism in the 1980s. Dollimore's book has been hailed as the founding text of cultural materialism, a critical practice that combines historical investigation with a Marxist agenda. In his 'Introduction to the Second Edition' of 1989, Dollimore takes a step back to re-assess his work and situate it at the intersection of cultural materialism and gender critique. *Radical Tragedy*, Dollimore admits, is

■ an arrogant book, one which not only reads Jacobean tragedy differently, but presumes to challenge a politically conservative way of doing criticism; a book which claims to be interdisciplinary, oppositional, intellectually challenging rather than academically stifling, politically engaged rather than spuriously impartial.[4] □

For Dollimore, the inspiration for such oppositional and politically engaged criticism comes not only from poststructuralist thinking and from the work of twentieth-century avant-garde playwrights and theatre practitioners but also from the Jacobean tragedies themselves. Especially important, for Dollimore, are the unconventional tragedies of 'John Webster, who has been acutely problematic for a critical tradition which has wanted to keep alive all the conservative imperatives associated with "order", "tradition", the "human condition" and "character"'.[5] Dollimore sees the Jacobean period as one of crisis, in which the 'Elizabethan world picture' posited by Tillyard was struggling to maintain its ideological grip on a theatre that represented emergent oppositional views, with the drama addressing the 'crisis of confidence in those holding power'.[6] Jacobean tragedies, he insists, are obsessed with chaos rather than order and they

■ attack, in particular, the idea of a particular, retributive, providence by (for example) undermining the dramatic conventions which embody it.

They also challenge the basic premise of providentialism as it grows out of, and draws upon, natural law: the idea of a teleologically encoded law governing the nature, identity and inter-relationships of all things and, ultimately, the very *telos* [i.e., the aim] of the universe itself.[7] □

Against the divinely ordered universe of Tillyard, Dollimore thus sets a conception of Jacobean tragedy (as exemplified by Webster's tragedies as well as *Sejanus, King Lear, Revenger's Tragedy* and *Antony and Cleopatra*) as embodying the emerging forces of disorder, decay, stultification and social dislocation.

As his treatment of Tillyard's 'Elizabethan world picture' indicates, a distinction which is central to Dollimore's analysis and that originates in Raymond Williams's thought is that between residual, dominant and emergent ideologies. Culture 'is not a unitary phenomenon' and Jacobean tragedies, as Dollimore insists again and again, reveal the tensions between various competing ideologies, 'interrogat[ing] ideology from within, seizing on and exposing its contradictions and inconsistencies and offering alternative ways of understanding social and political process'.[8] In this, early modern writers like Michel de Montaigne (1533–92) anticipate the thinking of modern philosophers such as Louis Althusser, bringing to their understanding of ideological structures a scepticism that 'is central to Jacobean tragedy'.[9]

Not only do Jacobean tragedies challenge the established ideology, but the concept of 'man' itself is decentred, as instead of the subject owing his identity and purpose to a divinely appointed order, 'man' is revealed to be the construct of political and social forces and tensions. Dollimore thus takes a clear stance against what he calls the 'essentialist humanism' of his critical forebears, from Coleridge to Bradley and Eliot, who conceptualised their task as one 'of re-affirming the universal values associated with man's essential nature' and who sought to find a unity, coherence and closure in the drama which is simply not there in Jacobean tragedy.[10] There, Dollimore asserts, closure

▪ is usually a perfunctory rather than a profound reassertion of order (providential and political). We may feel that such closure was a kind of condition for subversive thought to be foregrounded at all. But we should recognise too that such a condition cannot control what it permits: closure could never retrospectively guarantee ideological erasure of what, for a while, existed prior to and so independently of it.[11] □

It is in this strong sense that the subversion that takes place in Jacobean tragedy is not effectively contained by its gesturing towards closure and order that is the most characteristic feature of Dollimore's cultural materialist practice.

This aspect of his work is picked up by Catherine Belsey, whose influential and 'mildly polemical' *The Subject of Tragedy: Identity and Difference in Renaissance Drama* (1985) combines the emphasis on subversion with a thorough analysis of contemporary discourses on gender and subjectivity.[12] Echoing Dollimore's attack on 'essentialist humanism', Belsey rebels against the understanding of the subject as transhistorical, universal – and male. Subjectivity, she asserts, 'is discursively produced and is constrained by the range of subject-positions defined by the discourses in which the concrete individual participates'. Any such discourse is 'always embattled, forever defending the limits of what is admissible, legitimate or intelligible'.[13] Belsey concentrates on early modern tragedy because of the way in which it 'can be seen as a focus of the contests for the meaning of subjectivity and gender' in the period and allows the voices of women to be heard.[14] While her 'project is to construct a history of the meanings which delimit at a specific moment what it is possible to say, to understand, and consequently to be', she remains aware that the past she is constructing is itself 'an interpretation which is in a sense an anachronism'.[15] The concerns of the present inevitably colour the construction of the past.

Tellingly, Belsey subdivides her book into two sections: 'Man' and 'Woman'. In the first, she traces the emergence of 'liberal humanism' in the second half of the seventeenth century, as the medieval conception of the human being as discontinuous (consisting of both body and soul) made way for a conception of the bourgeois subject as unified. She links this to the shift from the emblematic theatre of the moralities to the introduction, in the Jacobean masque, of perspective scenes and the proscenium arch. These innovations in theatre architecture began, in the manner of 'Classic realist theatre', to '[isolate] the world of the fiction from the world of the audience' and to present 'unified subjects' that reflected the spectators' 'own imaginary unity'.[16] For Belsey it is no coincidence that this development is contemporary with the rise of Stuart absolutist ideology.

The Jacobean period is therefore of especial interest to her, since 'the stage brought into conjunction and indeed into collision the emblematic mode and an emergent illusionism. The effect was a form of drama capable at any moment of disrupting the unity of the spectator'.[17] In such a theatre, self-assertion as we find it in the heroes of early modern tragedy is often 'ironic, pathetic rather than heroic, or alternatively monstrous, precisely *in*human', as in the protagonist of *Richard III*. The soliloquy, through which the modern free-standing individual presents himself, internalises the moral conflicts and the discontinuities of the allegorical tradition of the moralities. The humanist subject is therefore always haunted by the discontinuity and conflicts he seeks to exclude, is always precarious in his claim to unity, knowledge and autonomy.[18]

This view of the male subject is countered in the second part of the book by Belsey's focus on 'Woman'. Using Alice Arden's murder of her husband in 1551 and the various re-presentations of the crime, including the domestic tragedy *Arden of Faversham* (anonymous, ca. 1590), as her starting-point, Belsey examines the changing status of women within marriage. Marriage moved from 'the Anglican and absolutist position [...] that marriage was indissoluble' to the 'liberal position' of some Puritan groups who 'defined marriage as a civil covenant' which 'depended on consent'.[19] As a consequence, Alice Arden's crime can be read as 'a defiance of absolutism' that 'drew attention to the problem of [her] sexuality, and of the institution which had failed to hold it in place'.[20] What can be found in plays such as *Arden* is 'a series of contests for the place of women in the family and in society, which may in turn be understood as struggles to install women as subjects'.[21] With women not allowed to speak for themselves and forced to hold the contradictory subject position of someone who is equated with children *and* with adults, 'the speech attributed to women [...] tended to be radically discontinuous, inaudible or scandalous'.[22] This is obvious from Belsey's incisive analysis of *The White Devil, A Woman Killed with Kindness* and, most interestingly, Elizabeth Cary's *The Tragedy of Mariam*, in which the female playwright problematises her outspoken heroine's contradictory subject position.

While Cary's play 'seems to oscillate between endorsement and disapproval of Mariam's defiance', Belsey argues that in many plays women who speak out are demonised as 'personators of masculine virtue'.[23] In Jacobean tragedies like *The Changeling, Macbeth* and *Antony and Cleopatra*, the eloquent and heroic heroines are also portrayed as masculine and deadly. Cleopatra is especially interesting in this context, for through her suicide she 'becomes agent of her own destiny', an 'absolute subject' who, while a woman and mother, refuses femininity, becoming 'plural, contradictory, an emblem which can be read as justifying either patriarchy on the one hand or an emergent feminism on the other, or perhaps as an icon of the contest between the two'.[24] A play like *The Duchess of Malfi*, on the other hand, 'stands as a perfect fable of emergent liberalism' which 'valorizes women's equality'.[25] The love of the Duchess and Antonio is figured as the antithesis of the political in a way that represents the period's increasing linking of love and marriage in conduct manuals. Tellingly, this reading of *Malfi* leads up to a conclusion which Belsey subtitles 'changing the present': hers is a historical criticism whose ultimate aim is not the re-reading of history in itself, but rather the fostering of a more differentiated, politicised understanding of the past that enables us to grasp better the way the present is constructed and may therefore be changed. It is this sense of political engagement in historically oriented criticism which was to prove a powerful influence on feminist and queer studies and on the study of race, as can be seen in the work of most of the critics I discuss in Chapters 6 and 7 of this Guide.

While English cultural materialism is distinctive for its reliance on Raymond Williams, its overtly political interest in the subversion of the dominant order and the dislocation of 'essentialist' or 'liberal' humanism, in North America the 'New Historicism', while sharing in the interest in material culture and the discursively created subject, had a less overtly politicised agenda. New Historicists have tended to counter the cultural materialists' 'stress on unresolved conflict' and subversion with an emphasis on 'strategies of containment which, while admitting subversive tendencies, have also neutralised them'.[26] Much of this important work on the historical and political context of early modern drama in the late 1970s and early 1980s focused on the Jacobean masque and influenced both Dollimore and Belsey. Stephen Orgel's *The Illusion of Power: Political Theater in the English Renaissance* (1975) is one such work. Orgel reminds us that the masque's court setting and its use of aristocratic actors make it radically different from drama performed in public playhouses. Private theatres 'are the creation of their audiences, and are often designed not only for a particular group but for a particular production or occasion'.[27] The productions that took place in venues such as the Cockpit-in-Court or the Great Hall and the Banqueting House were 'celebrations of royal power and assertions of aristocratic community'.[28] Because of the expectation that court dramas would express 'the age's most profound assumptions about the monarchy' and include 'strong elements of ritual and communion, often explicitly religious', the plays of the King's Men, when they were asked to play at court, changed not only in their audience but also in the 'function of the performance'.[29] The play was now directed at the monarch, with the rest of the audience watching both the play and the monarch watching the play from the 'one perfect place in the hall from which the illusion achieves its fullest effect'. Seating arrangements at a performance therefore 'became a living emblem of the structure of the court. The closer one sat to the monarch the "better" one's place was, an index to one's status, and, more directly, to the degree of favor one enjoyed'.[30] The theatrical space itself was politicised.

Orgel argues that the scenic effects and 'surprises' for which Inigo Jones, the masque designer who presided over Jacobean courtly spectacles, was famous, 'bore very little relation to the action of the drama, taking place, for the most part, only in the intervals between the acts'.[31] In such 'interludes of wonder', Orgel suggests,

■ the theater itself became an entity; the stage was not the setting for a drama, but was itself the action. And its transformations were those of the human mind, the imagination expressing itself through perspective, mechanics, the imitation of nature, creating a model of the universe and bringing it under rational control. Such a theater [...] has little to do with plays; it is, indeed, in certain ways antidramatic. But it proved peculiarly appropriate to the special audience who commanded its creation.[32] □

Orgel thus reads the scenic spectacles of the masque as a philosophical and even a political statement that expresses the will not only of the masque's designers, but even more so of its royal audience, rendering visible profound truths about the King's power and liberality. The idealised fiction that formed the main masque was a celebration of the aristocratic community that was 'both Platonic and Machiavellian; Platonic because it presents images of the good to which the participants aspire and may ascend; Machiavellian because its idealizations are designed to justify the power they celebrate'.[33] Masques, then, are a surprisingly good way of accessing royal ideology, and subtle shifts, Orgel contends, mark important changes in the royal political ideology.

In his readings of three Jacobean masques, *The Masque of Queens*, *Oberon* and *Neptune's Triumph for the Return of Albion*, Orgel demonstrates how the roles aristocratic performers played in masques were thus 'not impersonations but ideals', expressions of the way the Jacobean court wished to be perceived.[34] In the last of these masques, designed to celebrate Prince Charles's return after the fiasco of the 'Spanish Match' (Charles's failed expedition to Spain to secure the hand of the Spanish Infanta in 1623–4), there is an alarming mismatch between the staged political myth of the sovereign royal will and the political reality of the increasingly wilful commonwealth and squabbling French and Spanish ambassadors, which led to the cancellation of the performance. A reading of the masque allows us to access James's disconnected view of political reality towards the end of his life, anticipating the even more autocratic reign and dangerous separation between court and commonwealth of the Caroline period.

To some extent, Orgel's 'historicism' in this book is still traditional, reading the spectacles against specific historical circumstances. His acknowledgement of the mismatch between royal myth and the political reality, however, shows the strong awareness of the coexistence of competing ideologies. Also crucial, in this book, is his recognition that literature – the text of the masque – is dependent for its meaning on other forms of texts (e.g. Inigo Jones's drawings and designs, or even the respective positions of monarch and courtiers in the audience), and that all these texts together and the social and power relationships they embody amount to a structural complex that expresses a political ideology. It is these features of Orgel's work that anticipate the work of Stephen Greenblatt and pave the way for the New Historicism.

Greenblatt's *Renaissance Self-Fashioning From More to Shakespeare* (1980) is generally credited with launching this movement. It is a less angry and aggressive book than Dollimore's even though it is in many ways its precursor (Dollimore acknowledges a debt to Greenblatt). Because it does not primarily deal with Jacobean drama, it is relevant for the present discussion chiefly in its 'Introduction', in which Greenblatt outlines his provocatively novel methodology. This involves juxtaposing seemingly unrelated 'texts' as a way of accessing the processes whereby early modern subjects fashioned themselves. His introduction makes it clear that his rationale for such an approach comes out of the work of Clifford Geertz, an influential anthropologist who argued that humans themselves should be understood as 'cultural artifacts'.[35] Literature, Greenblatt maintains, functions 'as a manifestation of the concrete behavior of its particular author, as itself the expression of the codes by which behavior is shaped, and as a reflection upon those codes'. It is thus deeply implicated in the culture and the ideologies that govern that culture, but must not be seen 'exclusively as the expression of social rules and instructions', as this would allow it to be 'absorbed entirely into an ideological superstructure' (which is what tends to happen in Tillyard's work). Nor must we 'drift back toward a conception of art as addressed to a timeless, cultureless, universal human essence' (thus joining Dollimore in his attack on 'essentialist humanism'), or 'as a self-regarding, autonomous, closed system' (a reference to Formalist approaches and New Criticism).[36] What Greenblatt attempts is 'a more cultural or anthropological criticism' that is concerned with

■ the interpretive constructions the members of a society apply to their experiences. A literary criticism that has affinities to this practice must be conscious of its own status as interpretation and intent upon understanding literature as a part of the system of signs that constitutes a given culture; its proper goal [...] is a *poetics of culture*.[37] □

What we now call the New Historicism, then, is an attempt to create such a 'poetics of culture', to understand how the self that expresses itself in a work of art and/or through language is a collective construction that is never free from interpretation. The New Historicist critic must investigate 'both the social presence to the world of the literary text and the social presence of the world in the literary text'. Always, the text is seen as deeply embedded both in the ideological matrix of the culture and in the material world from which it emerges – hence Greenblatt's constant 'returning to particular lives and particular situations, to the material necessities and social pressures that men and women daily confronted'.[38] The larger narrative Greenblatt proposes is clearly and deliberately selective, fitful and fragmented, with Greenblatt explicitly eschewing 'any comprehensive "explanation" of English Renaissance self-fashioning': it is a mode of criticism that values the individual case study and the story it tells above the grand overview and generalisations.[39]

That said, the six interlinked stories Greenblatt puts together in this book, drawing on Foucault's perception of the discontinuity of history and on Lacanian psychoanalysis, do together produce an overarching narrative centred on canonical authors. That narrative tells us about how individuals are shaped by the structures of power that govern their lives and how it is impossible – or near-impossible – to resist or subvert the ideological system. The only way in which this is possible is through what, in his chapter on *Othello*, Greenblatt describes as 'improvisation': 'the opportunistic grasp of that which seems fixed and established'.[40] But even Shakespeare's exceptional propensity for improvisation, the sense of empathy that allows him to enter into the consciousness of his characters, is subversive only to a limited extent: 'After all, the heart of a successful improvisation lies in concealment, not exposure; and besides, [...] even a hostile improvisation reproduces the relations of power that it hopes to displace and absorb.'[41] While it can be said that 'Shakespeare relentlessly *explores* the relations of power in a given culture', Greenblatt contends that it is much more difficult to argue that his plays evince a 'release from the complex narrative orders in which everyone is inscribed'.[42] Where Dollimore had stressed the inability of closure, in Jacobean tragedy, to erase the subversion that had preceded it, Greenblatt's stress is on how even Shakespeare cannot entirely shake off his ideological fetters, even if he does explore them more intensely than others.

Jonathan Goldberg's *James I and the Politics of Literature: Jonson Shakespeare, Donne and Their Contemporaries* (1983) takes its 'anthropological' approach from Greenblatt and applies it to the Jacobean period, building on the work of Stephen Orgel, to whom the book is dedicated. Goldberg considers not only the Jonsonian masque but also the public theatre, James I's own writings and Donne's poetry alongside a whole range of artefacts, from coins to architecture and portraiture, extending Orgel's argument about the influence of the King's political myth on the literature of the period. In Goldberg's analysis, that myth is omnipresent and is consciously fashioned by a King whose use of an imperial register deliberately contrasted with Elizabeth's carefully cultivated image of a monarch who entered into a relationship of mutual love with her subjects. Drawing on the style of classical Rome, 'James played at being apart, separate'. His adopted 'style of gods' allowed him to claim 'deity as the emperors had done before him' and to portray himself as the husband and father of his state.[43]

One crucial way in which James propagated the ideological construction of his absolute and free monarchical authority was by using 'writing as an instrument of royal power'.[44] Goldberg illustrates this argument by closely examining the *Masque of Queens*, where

■ Text and monarch stood in the same relationship to the performance onstage; at the masque, there was another silent text, the king himself. As much as Jonson's invention, he was the soul of the masque. Silent, uncostumed, offstage, no part of the visible design, yet there would be no design without him. All the words, all the spectacle aim at him. He embodies the mystery of the masque. His is the permanent form of the masque, its life beyond words, a living image, represented.[45] □

Here, Orgel's implication of royal authority in the creation of the masque is pushed further, as James himself becomes an embodiment of the masque; both king and masque are permanent textual expressions of royal power.

Absolutist claims are also embodied in the trope of *arcana imperii*, the mysteries and secrets of state that inform Jonson's conception of Sir Politic Would-Be in *Volpone*, and in the trope of the king as actor, which regularly surfaces in the drama of the period. In *Basilikon Doron* (1599), his treatise on kingship, James used this trope to point to the transparency of the king, the way his actions are always observed on the one hand, and on the other hand to indicate how public show is 'obfuscating and opaque' and how 'the king's outward behavior may be at variance with the inner man'.[46] The equivocation of royal language can be found again in the drama. It is the playwrights' ability to play on the contradictions inherent in the king's own discourse that lies at the bottom of the characteristic 'doubleness of the Jonsonian masque' which 'managed to delight the sovereign and yet did not shirk criticism'.[47] On the public stage, the Roman tragedies of *Julius Caesar, Sejanus, Coriolanus, Catiline* and *The Roman Actor* best reflect James's performance of absolute power following a Roman template. It is in these plays' representation of the ruler's body as both opaque and transparent, Goldberg suggests, that we see the 'inherent theatricalization' of political power and the rhetoric of power in the Jacobean period.[48] Throughout the book, the drama (and literature more generally) is thus shown to be inseparable from politics, the one inflecting and reproducing the other, with Jonson and James emerging as instrumental figures in the creation and representation of the contradictions inherent in Jacobean absolutist ideology.

'Mature' historicisms: the late 1980s and early 1990s

While Goldberg's book could be faulted for its exclusive and, ultimately, reductive concern with monarchical power and ideology, with its concentration on the royal court and the spectacles that stage it and are staged in it, Stephen Mullaney's view of the ways in which the drama can be said to be 'political' in the period is more flexible and centrifugal.

Mullaney's *The Place of the Stage: License, Play and Power in Renaissance England* (1988) is representative of the second wave of New Historicist work that integrated some of the cultural materialists' insights and applied the established methodologies to new areas. His focus shifts from the ideological centre of Jacobean royal displays to the margins of the city, the spaces beyond the city walls where the Elizabethan theatres were first located. It is his understanding of the heterogeneity of culture (in a contrast with Goldberg that is particularly striking when the two books are read one after the other) that informs his analysis of the impact the physical location of the theatre had on the drama, whose main intertext here is the city of London itself.

Based on John Stow's *Survay of London* of 1598, Mullaney reads the city as 'a symbolic text that was both inscribed by the passage of power and communal spectacle, and interpreted or made accessible through such ritual processes'.[49] The spaces beyond the city walls on which he concentrates were known as 'the Liberties' and were areas of paradoxical freedom, both under city jurisdiction and beyond manorial rule. In these heterogeneous spaces

■ [w]hatever could not be contained within the strict bounds of the community found its place [...], making the Liberties the preserve of the anomalous, the unclean, the polluted, and the sacred. [...] If within the city walls the ideals and aspirations of community were staged in an extensive repertory of civic rituals and cultural performances, then the margins of the city served as a more ambivalent staging ground: as a place where the contradictions of the community, its incontinent hopes and fears, were prominently and dramatically set on stage.[50] □

The plays Mullaney reads in the light of the marginal position of the theatres are liberated by that position; they are placed at 'a critical distance [...] that provided the stage with a culturally and ideologically removed vantage point from which it could reflect upon its own age with more freedom and license than had hitherto been possible'.[51] The players themselves were seen as analogous to the lepers who had preceded them in their movement from the city to its outskirts: like the lepers, they were 'figures of categorical ambivalence'.[52] They may have turned theatres into an institution, but theirs was an institution that was not recognised by city authorities in the way the corporate guilds they imitated were. Theatre, in Mullaney's view, was intrinsically scandalous and provocative, a product of the ideology of the time which also questioned that ideology.

Mullaney's argument about the movement of the drama from the marginal position of the Liberties in the Elizabethan period to the culturally and ideologically central position it achieved in Jacobean

London moves back and forth between the Elizabethan period and the Jacobean. To the latter he dedicates his detailed readings of three of Shakespeare's Jacobean plays, ending with *Pericles* because this is the play which, for him, points towards the more elite audience of the Blackfriars theatre and, ultimately, beyond the popular stage towards the birth of the novel. His interpretations are informed by a concern with the theatre's power to subvert the dominant ideology which finds its source in the cultural materialist work exemplified in *Political Shakespeare*, the collection of essays Dollimore co-edited with Alan Sinfield in 1985. The resulting readings reveal the theatre's ability to express and critique James's assumption of absolute and Machiavellian power.

I want to pick Mullaney's chapter on *Measure for Measure* as an illustration of how he uses his conceptual framework for literary interpretation. Following Goldberg, Mullaney reads *Measure for Measure* as a quintessentially Jacobean play. He also openly acknowledges Foucault's influence when he describes the play as 'a compressed history and genealogy of [exemplary] power and of the cultural pressures that would, in the course of the sixteenth century, necessitate its increasing theatricalization'.[53] Mullaney relates Duke Vincentio's disguise as a friar to the abolition of the ceremonial of confession after the Reformation and links his exercise of exemplary justice at the end of the play to James's own predilection for exemplary executions that were accompanied by unexpected royal pardons. Crucially, for Mullaney, the play includes the character of Barnardine, who 'represents the limits of even the Duke's power to control or contain, to induce and subvert the desires of his subjects'. In fact, 'as a figure of uncontained license Barnardine is also a figure for the social and cultural terrain occupied by Elizabethan and Jacobean drama'.[54] Mullaney thus uses the liminal location of the theatre as a point of entry into readings of the drama that probe it for moments of resistance, subversion and license.

As Douglas Brooks was to state merely eight years after the publication of *The Place of the Stage*, '[i]t would be difficult to overestimate the extent to which Mullaney's book broke new ground [...] for subsequent scholars of early modern drama and culture'.[55] Mullaney was faulted by his reviewers for historical inaccuracies,[56] but that did nothing to diminish the impact of his understanding of how urban geography, politics and theatre came together in the drama. Douglas Bruster's *Drama and the Market in the Age of Shakespeare* (1992), in its concentration on the urban landscape, is directly influenced by Mullaney's work. Bruster, however, gives Mullaney's thesis a new twist by suggesting that while geographically marginal, the playhouses

■ were deeply implicated in a narrative of institutional development which transcended geographical boundaries. It is my argument that to posit a relatively stable and unchanging London against which the Liberties and certain plays seem rebelliously marginal is to underestimate the fluidity of existence and exchange in the early modern city.[57] □

Bruster's approach is what one could call 'materialist'; his book proposes to elaborate 'a poetics of the market' and to suggest that the London public got to see very much what it desired to see in the theatre, which was driven by market forces and therefore provided, as in the alternative title of *Twelfth Night*, 'what you will'.[58] Rather than focus on the telling anecdote in the manner of the early New Historicists, Bruster paints a broad picture of early modern London as a place where the gradual institutionalisation of the theatres goes hand in hand with rapid social change. The emergence of early forms of capitalism in an ever-growing city which provided 'a powerful concentration of artistic talent and pop-ular demand for entertainment' leads Bruster to describe the theatres as 'place[s] of commercial exchange' and to point to the ways in which playhouses and market places – most notably Gresham's Exchange and the New Exchange – were thought to resemble one another.[59] Plays, then, are best viewed as market commodities.

In his consideration of cuckoldry in the genre of 'city comedy', Bruster states his 'belief that, while having proved instrumental in beginning a project which focuses on the political and social aspects of Renaissance drama, the concept of "city comedy" has outlived its usefulness as an aid to understanding plays of the era' – urban dra-mas of the Jacobean period, after all, include tragedies like *Coriola-nus* and *The Revenger's Tragedy*.[60] A figure which keeps re-emerging in early modern urban drama is that of the cuckold, who was turned into an actual London landmark in 'Cuckold's Haven' or 'Cuckold's Point'. For Bruster, the cuckold is an originally rural figure 'with which the playwrights of the English Renaissance projected their eco-nomic vision of London's intensifying social dynamics'.[61] This vision involves seeing sexual intercourse, especially for women, as physical labour or 'drudgery', so that any patient labour – and specifically that of the working husband – becomes tainted with effeminacy. Scenes of cuckoldry play on this emasculation of the husband, but at the same time they also represent 'a carnivalesque celebration of what seems an older and more fertile way of existence'. In the figure of the cuck-olded merchant, the wife's giving away of her body to other customers is one of the ways in which the 'merchant must [...] accustom himself to allowing wealth and commodity to pass from his hands into those of another'.[62] Jacobean comedies, Bruster concludes, use 'the cuck-old myth as a dialectical metaphor capable of reconciling – however uneasily – evolving tensions between country and city, production and reproduction, female and male'.[63] Bruster's materialist reading of economic relations in Jacobean London thus helps us understand the troubling figure of the cuckold as an effect of the larger socioeconomic urban context.

Bruster's emphasis on the economic transactions that are part of the discourse of cuckoldry in early Jacobean drama is symptomatic of the 'New Economic Criticism', whose advent is proclaimed in *Money and the Age of Shakespeare: Essays in New Economic Criticism* (2003), a collection edited by Linda Woodbridge which includes Douglas Bruster's own reflection 'On a Certain Tendency in Economic Criticism of Shakespeare'. For Woodbridge, it is clear that this form of criticism is called for by the plays and the culture of playgoing in early modern London: where other critics have emphasised the ways in which the Southwark theatres were surrounded by brothels, Woodbridge reminds us of the presence of book-keeping schools in the same neighbourhood and argues for the influence of double-entry book-keeping (in which records of debits and credits are kept side-by-side) on the commercial language of the plays. Early modern drama is full of attempts to quantify, measure and value, often with tragic effects. The period, she contends, 'was a shopkeeping age, a bookkeeping age, and an age when despite Polonius's maxims, nearly everybody was a borrower and/or a lender'.[64] Woodbridge's aim, in this volume, is to analyse the intersection between literature and economics in early modern drama in a variety of forms. She accordingly includes essays on nascent capitalism and venture capitalism; commodities, the commodity market and commodity fetishism; gift exchange, value and exchange value; debt, credit, usury, poverty and economic mobility; international trade and mercantile expansion; and, in an overlap with the concerns of gender studies, economic protectionism and the paternal control of daughters and their dowries.

For the purposes of this chapter, however, it is Bruster's contribution which is the most significant, since it takes a metacritical view of a form of criticism of which his own *Drama and the Market* is a prime example. Bruster describes the New Economic Criticism as 'an open unity, an emergent mode of criticism defined by its willingness to treat the economic basis of social interaction both in and out of literary texts, and supporting the production of literature itself'.[65] New Economic Criticism is 'open' because it allows for a vast diversity of methodologies and subject matter. Nevertheless, Bruster argues, we can distinguish, broadly, between two interpretive paths. The first, which he nicknames 'the reckoned', looks at the rational and practical aspects of economic life and is a positivistic form of criticism that is concerned with material objects. The 'reckoned' approach can be contrasted with 'the rash', which analyses the irrational and thematic features of economic life, is largely theoretical in nature and sees commercial exchanges in early modern drama in metaphorical terms. Bruster's point is not that one of these approaches is superior to the other; rather, he wishes to highlight the different ways in which, in recent historical and economic criticism, scholars have dealt with the 'materiality' of material culture. Whereas his own *Drama and the Market* sees the economics of cuckoldry as a metaphor for relations between the city and the country, what he draws attention to is the more positivist and object-oriented approach of critics such as Andrew Gurr. In *The Shakespearian Playing Companies* (1996, see my discussion on pp. 29–30) – a book which Bruster intriguingly categorises as part of the New Economic Criticism, revealing in the process just how subjective such categorisations are both in his chapter and this Guide – Gurr tries to work out the economic logic behind the King's Men's decision to reconstruct the burnt-down Globe theatre in 1613 even though they had a perfectly functional and profitable indoor venue in the Blackfriars. The decision does not make economic sense and leaves Gurr frustrated, revealing the need for Theodore Leinwand's more 'rash' approach to the issue in *Theatre, Finance and Society in Early Modern England* (1999). Confronted with the same problem, Leinwand takes account of the emotional value of the Globe for the King's Men and compares the players to a modern rock-band who will not give up live touring even when CD sales make touring superfluous. Bruster is not entirely satisfied with either approach, though he sees the benefits of both: for him, the 'rash' have as much to learn from the 'reckoned' as the 'reckoned' from the 'rash'. What this involves is for critics to '[read] what we do not ordinarily read; [talk] with those we do not ordinarily talk with'.[66] These conversations, he suggests, are taking place at the moment and promise a new form of economic criticism in which the material and economic culture of early modern drama is seen both as object and metaphor and framed in positivistic as well as theoretical terms.

As is clear from Woodbridge's collection no less than from the studies of Mullaney and Bruster, the main strand of New Historicist criticism has, since Orgel and Goldberg's work on the masque and court culture, moved away from the court into the city. This does not mean that it has, on the whole, stopped being concerned with the public sphere inhabited by men, for the women in the plays and in early modern London remain a blind spot in this work: Mullaney speaks of brothels but not of the prostitutes who work in them, just as Bruster speaks of the 'labour' of the sexually active wife, but does not consider how she is portrayed in the plays and society at large. It took the intervention of feminist scholars like Jean Howard and Karen Newman, whose work will be discussed in the detail they deserve in Chapter 7 of this Guide, to push the women of Jacobean drama into the foreground. It is thanks to the work of such feminist scholars that Woodbridge's collection includes two essays (by Robert Darcy and Natasha Korda) concerned with economic protectionism, dowries and the paternal control of daughters.

I want, at this point, to highlight Jean Howard's revisionist intervention in *The Stage and Social Struggle in Early Modern England* (1994). The book incorporates both her analysis of female play-going which was included in *Staging the Renaissance* (see p. 24 in Chapter 1) and the influential article on cross-dressing I consider in Chapter 7 of this Guide (pp. 121–2). In her discussion of the theatricality and antitheatricality in the drama no less than in puritan tracts, Howard's explicitly 'political analysis' focuses on the ways in which texts perform 'the essential work of ideology, i.e. the naturalization of interested representations of the real'.[67] Howard is most interested in 'the *contradictions* marking not just the theater's representations of theatricality but, in a larger and more general sense, its total role in ideological production': it is in contradictions that she locates the space the public theatre made 'for emergent or marginalized groups'.[68] Howard thus steps away from the avoidance of political statement in earlier New Historicist work and argues for a more politically engaged way of reading early modern drama historically, in which 'incompatibilities' are interpreted not 'as signs of aesthetic failure', but 'as traces of ideological struggle'.[69] Such a mode of reading, she argues, is not well served by the now well-worn 'language of containment and subversion', which 'only flattens and simplifies [the plays'] complex mediations of social change'.[70]

Howard's book is a good example of the strand of historicist criticism that has integrated previous research successfully with an agenda that emerges from work in gender studies and poststructuralist theory. While work like hers does not shy away from bringing theory to early modern studies – and indeed proclaims the need to go on doing so – another powerful strand of historicist criticism now increasingly seeks to engage with the material context of early modern drama 'directly', unmediated by a theoretical framework. Frequently, such work is also devoid of an interest in the 'literary' analysis of the drama. The plays themselves are treated as material artefacts: it is as if the context had eaten up the text. A side effect of this is that the erstwhile dominant figure of Shakespeare is sidelined by the masses of evidence about his period and contemporaries. This is the type of work that can be found in *A New History of Early English Drama*, the collection co-edited by John D. Cox and David Scott Kastan which I have already discussed in some detail in Chapter 2 in this Guide. As I noted there, the collection explicitly seeks to produce 'not more theory but more facts'.[71] Of the anthology's three parts, which cover 'Early English Drama and Physical Space', 'Early English Drama and Social Space' and 'Early English Drama and Conditions of Performance and Publication', it is in the section on 'Social Space', the shortest of the three, that theory resurfaces to some extent. There, it appears for example in Diana E. Henderson's chapter on 'The Theater and Domestic Culture', which builds on the 'new questions and insights of social historians, theater historians, and feminist and queer theorists' alike, or in the contribution of Michael Bristol, whose language, when talking about 'Theater and Popular Culture', is coloured by the Marxism characteristic of his other work.[72] On the whole, however, theory has made way for 'fact' and even Henderson and Bristol concentrate on the material world in their contributions. If there is a keynote to the volume, it is struck by Paul Werstine's concluding essay on 'Plays in Manuscript' which, in revisiting the role W. W. Greg played in (mis)shaping textual criticism, speaks of the 'irreducible historical messiness of the actual manuscripts' which defies and disrupts W. W. Greg's theorisations.[73]

This sidelining of theory is a development that will not have come as a surprise to someone like Howard, who, in 1986, predicted that there was 'a real danger that the emerging interest in history' fuelled by New Historicism '[would] be appropriated by those wishing to suppress or erase the theoretical revolution that has gone on in the last several decades. Ironically, the "new history" may well turn out to be a backlash phenomenon: a flight from theory or simply a program for producing more "new readings" suited to the twenty-five-page article and the sixty-minute class'.[74] The *New History of Early English Drama* fulfils this prediction almost to the letter: it acknowledges its turn away from theory, it substitutes twenty-five-page articles for the fuller narratives that almost all the contributions to *Staging the Renaissance* had been extracted from, and it even uses Howard's term 'new history' in its title. This positivist, 'reckoned' (to invoke Bruster's term), view of history as a place where 'facts' can be found that are not mediated by ideology and interpretation represents a strong reaction against the historicisms of the 1980s and 1990s that had relied so heavily on Foucault and Althusser and had stressed the inseparability of literature from history *and* ideology. It also goes hand-in-hand with the massive and ongoing effort, in a variety of databases such as *Early English Books Online* (*EEBO*) and in print projects such as *Records of Early English Drama* (*REED*), to gather more 'facts' about the period that may be used as 'evidence' for further research in material history.[75]

There is no better example of this new emphasis on facts and data than Peter Lake's *The Antichrist's Lewd Hat: Protestants, Papists, and Players in Post-Reformation England* (2002), a book that is so gigantic that parts of it had to be co-authored with Michael Questier. Lake does not distinguish the drama from its context: if anything, he privileges the latter over the former. The plays themselves are events in an ongoing historical narrative that is characterised by multivocality, indeterminacy and historical contingencies, focusing on the local and specific at the expense of the overarching statement and singular literary reading. Lake notes that the plays contain 'so much social detail, so many references to contemporary social and political and religious "reality" as

[...] to demand what one might term a social and political as well as a formal analysis'.[76] It comes as no surprise to find out that both authors are historians rather than literary critics, and yet their work is a perfect – and brilliantly executed – example of current historicist literary scholarship at its extreme. For Leah Marcus, *The Antichrist's Lewd Hat* is nothing short of 'a model for what literary historicists right now want to be doing themselves'.[77]

Lake's Introduction, in tracing the story of the book's gestation, provides a personal map both of historical investigations of early modern religion since the 1980s and of the various religious forces at play in early modern London and its literature, whether in murder pamphlets and ballads, or the drama which appeared in equally cheap print. Because of the plays' 'inherently dialogic' nature, the subversive visions of disorder and deviance that can be glimpsed in murder pamphlets come to the fore in the drama. There, 'the legitimating moralised and providentialised structures that tended to contain this material in the pamphlets' are challenged by the desire to titillate and entertain the audience rather than edify it.[78] While this argument suggests that Lake is working with the containment-subversion opposition of early New Historicist and cultural materialist thought, it becomes clear on reading the book that he refuses to situate literary texts on this spectrum. For him, the theatre is a

■ playpen in which participants could adopt and lay aside, ventriloquise and caricature, try on for size, test and discard a whole variety of subject positions, claims to cultural authority, arguments and counter-arguments about legitimacy and power. On this view, the theatre, far from being a crucial, much-censored and policed arm of the state ('an ideological state apparatus' in the Althusserian jargon of the late 1970s), in fact represented a sort of festive liminal space in which cultural materials and claims, deployed in earnest and often for the highest stakes on the scaffold and in the press and pulpit, could be played with and critiqued.[79] □

His view of not only the plays, but also the religious situation they depict, as marked by 'instability, conflict and contradiction' is related to Dollimore's quest for the subversion that precedes the tragedies' concluding gestures of containment and to Howard's celebration of contradiction. But where Dollimore and Howard see subversion and opportunities for voicing marginalised views, Lake often prefers simply to note the multivocality and indeterminacy of the evidence – as he puts it, the 'interpretive questions before us are not best conceived as either/or choices'.[80] Rather than align himself with either New Historicism, cultural materialism or more recent hybrid forms within literary studies, Lake tellingly sees his work as 'a history book of an entirely conventional sort – an exercise in what one might term the old cultural history with the politics left in'. The book is explicitly designed to 'administer to new historicist procedures and perspectives a good dose of the revisionist historians' concern with the contingency of events, their obsession with political narrative and their conviction of the absolute centrality of religious and confessional identity formation and conflict to any adequate account of the politics and culture of this period'.[81]

In the body of the book, Lake details a rich and remarkably well-documented context of murder pamphlets, puritan polemic, anti-puritan diatribes, sermons about sinful London known as 'jeremiads', and recusant (i.e., catholic) proselytising in the prisons. These prisons, it turns out, were 'an ideological nerve centre [...] into which a number of persons and groups, discursive modes and religious practices were sucked, associated the one with the other and then pushed out again into the blood stream of the wider social body of catholic England'.[82] Lake's veritable treasure trove of context eventually – after nearly six hundred pages – leads to readings of *The Alchemist* (from which he derives his fabulous book title), *Bartholomew Fair* and *Measure for Measure* that reveal how deeply these plays engage with the religious controversies that marked the Jacobean age. What interests Lake is not the light the context of the rise of puritan and anti-puritan sentiment in London can shed on Jonson's plays, but rather what 'we can learn from Jonson about the nature of puritanism and its relationship to the hierarchies of church, state and society in Jacobean England'.[83] In the diction of Jonson's absurd puritan preacher, Zeal-of-the-Land Busy, Lake finds that 'we may come as close as we ever can to the rhythm and timbre, the feel, of London preachers as they extemporised and improvised on the scriptural or moral themes of their sermons'.[84] By contrast, Shakespeare's portrayal of the 'precise' Angelo in *Measure for Measure* follows the template of contemporary anti-puritan pamphlets. As in so many of the studies discussed in this chapter, *Measure for Measure* features here as a quintessentially Jacobean play that marks James's accession with a reflection on the threat of a wide-ranging 'puritan reformation of manners' that was aimed at combining the powers of the church and the state – for Lake, the play starkly illustrates 'what would happen if power were to be entrusted to the godly'.[85]

The book concludes with Lake sending us back to the sources – historical criticism, in the twenty-first century, begets yet more historical criticism. The middle of the book, by contrast, in a well-hidden cluster of chapters that include a reading of *Macbeth* and *Hamlet* as following the pattern of typical murder pamphlets and of a number of 'city comedies' (*Eastward Ho!*, *The Honest Whore* and *The Dutch Courtesan*), brings to the foreground the topic that will concern us next – that of genre:

■ Just like the murder pamphlets and the domestic tragedies, [the city comedies] seek to process and expel the corrupt impulses, the dreadful sins that they display and glamorise, seeking, as they do so, to resolve the very social, personal and ideological conflicts that they stage. These, however, are comedies, not tragedies; while they share subject matter, ideological terrain and narrative structure with the murder stories, they direct those materials to other than tragic or evangelically explicit ends. If they end, as some of them do, on the gallows or in the prisons, they nevertheless use those locales not so much as thresholds to the next world, but as points of re-entry into this, sites for the festive reintegration of what have been staged in the body of the play as discordant social or moral elements and discourses into a comically rendered but morally and socially refurbished and newly unified version of the social whole.[86] □

Even in this most historicist of books, then, there is an acknowledgement of how powerfully theatrical genres shape their material. It is to criticism concerned specifically with how the festive inclusiveness of comedy overrides tragedy's deadly expulsion of corruption from the social whole that we turn next.

CHAPTER FIVE

The Genres of Jacobean Drama

'$[C]$omedies begin in trouble and end in peace; tragedies begin in calms and end in tempest', Thomas Heywood (1573–1641) wrote in *A Defence of Drama* (c. 1608), clearly distinguishing between dramatic kinds in a way that Shakespeare's Polonius, when losing himself in his listing of 'tragedy, comedy, history, pastoral, pastoral-comical, historical-pastoral, tragical-historical, tragical-comical-historical-pastoral', struggles to match.[1] Both Heywood and Polonius have much to teach us about the genres of Jacobean drama: Heywood's categorical distinction indicates the importance of generic divisions for playwrights and their audiences, while Polonius's muddle reveals the extent to which dramatic genres were, by the end of the sixteenth century, already inflecting each other in ways that defied categorisation and audience expectations. Rosalie Colie explains this paradox: 'the kinds can easily be seen as tiny subcultures with their own habits, habitats, and structures of ideas as well as their own forms. But as subcultures continually melt into or are absorbed by a neighboring culture, so did the kinds in our period melt into one another'.[2] By using specific genres, playwrights could make a statement about previous writers; for Heather Dubrow, genre is a means of 'communication from the writer to his readers' in which he 'is in effect telling us the name and rules of his code, rules that affect not only how he should write the work but also how we should read it'.[3] By the same token, breaking or bridging generic conventions is a means of communicating something essential about how that play must be understood by its viewers. In fact, if we are to believe Alastair Fowler, there is no such thing as a stable genre, since it is 'the character of genres [...] that they change. Only variations or modifications of convention have literary significance', but to grasp that significance, the ability to spot 'family resemblances' and conventions is essential.[4]

In view of the importance of generic distinctions for early modern playwrights, it may seem astonishing that the study of their plays along generic lines was as widely discredited as it was still tacitly practiced in the 1980s and 1990s, the heyday of the study of historical contexts. Because New Historicism sought to bring literary texts into a dialogue with contemporary discourses, it encouraged ways of reading that ignored the embeddedness of a text in a tradition that linked it to other texts of the same and older periods. For historicists, Jean Howard explains, genre critics have 'sometimes seemed to divorce texts from history by implying that texts are generated from similar texts in a hermetically sealed process of imitation and formal transformation, rather than from engagement with what we now rather self-consciously call "the world"'. Such a divorce from history, Howard insists, is not a necessary consequence of genre study; what we need, she argues, is to combine genre study with attention to historical contexts:

> ■ [F]ocusing on generic filiations reveals that literature derives both from other literature (generic indebtedness is powerful proof of that fact) and from deep historical entanglements (registered largely through changes in existing generic forms, through the emergence of new and the decline of formerly popular genres, through the symptomatic contradictions at the heart of particular genres, and through the class and gender interests encoded in them).[5] □

As this statement suggests, the study of genre intersects with many of the concerns that animate the other critical fields I am discussing in this Guide: it affects theatre history and historical criticism as much as it inflects gender studies and the study of race, bodies and performances. Genre study may still seem unfashionable, but it is remarkably central to present-day critical practice.

Tragedy

Ever since Bradley's *Shakespearean Tragedy* (1904, see introduction, p. 16) put the spotlight on the genre, tragedy has been singled out as a genre to study in isolation. His emphasis on 'character criticism' and his application of an Aristotelian framework to Shakespearean tragedies were soon criticised, either implicitly or explicitly, by scholars such as L. C. Knights and Muriel Bradbrook. The latter's *Themes and Conventions of Elizabethan Tragedy* (1935), which reacts against Bradley, still repays careful reading.

As its title indicates, Bradbrook's book is concerned with the genre's governing conventions, which she describes as 'an agreement between writers and readers (or spectators), whereby the artist is allowed to distort and simplify his material through a control of the distribution of emphasis'.[6] Conventions that remained unspoken because generally accepted in the early modern theatre now need to be explained so as to enable the modern reader to understand 'how an Elizabethan would approach a tragedy by Marlowe, Tourneur, Webster or Middleton'.[7] As a result, Bradbrook focuses on what seems alien to us today including, for example, a section on the use of 'double time' schemes whereby the main plot of a tragedy follows a different time line from the subsidiary plot(s). She draws attention to symbolic costuming, allegorical stage effects and patterned action, such as the funeral march that concludes every tragedy.

Bradbrook's emphasis on character types (rather than characterisation) is a direct reaction against Coleridge's and Bradley's forms of character criticism: 'The Elizabethans did not expect every character to produce one rational explanation for every given action; consequently they did not think that characters who offered "inadequate" explanations were monstrous'.[8] But while humorous characters of early Jacobean comedy (especially in plays by Jonson and Chapman) can therefore not be said to have any motivation, matters are more complicated in the tragedies of Fletcher and Massinger, where the 'naïve simplification of feelings' makes way for 'a sophisticated perversion of them'.[9] While Bradbrook's sensitivity to historical difference thus leads her to a much less anachronistic appraisal of the drama than that of her predecessors, the discourse of Jacobean decadence I traced in the introduction to this Guide does contaminate her assessment of the 'perverted' later playwrights even as she is acknowledging their sophistication.

This discourse of decadence is still very much at the heart of Robert Ornstein's approach to Jacobean tragedy in *The Moral Vision of Jacobean Tragedy* (1960). Contrary to what the title suggests, the book does not offer an appraisal of a uniform 'moral vision' along the lines of Tillyard's Elizabethan world picture. Instead, it describes a number of factors that have a bearing on the 'crisis' evident in Jacobean tragedy. The book opens bluntly with the statement:

■ We applaud the Jacobean tragedians but we do not always approve of them. Their poetry seems at times superior to their principles and their sense of the theater more highly developed than their sense of values. [...] Because we cannot find in Elizabethan literature the seeds of Jacobean pessimism, we assume that some fairly sudden shock of disillusion darkened the literary imagination at the turn of the century.[10] □

In the course of the book, Ornstein does not rescind his view of the Jacobeans' lack of principles and values altogether, but he does challenge the idea of there being a 'fairly sudden shock of disillusion' that coincided with the change from the Elizabethan to the Jacobean period. Instead, he proposes that the distinctive mood of Jacobean tragedy comes from being 'caught between old and new ways of determining the realities upon which moral values rest'.[11] The plays show 'an awareness that familiar ways of life are vanishing and that traditional political and social ideals are losing their relevance to the contemporary scene'.[12]

For Ornstein, Bradbrook's emphasis on convention 'seem[s] to rob the dramatists of their individuality and their artistic freedom by creating the impression that even the greatest playwrights were enslaved by the memories and expectations of their audiences'.[13] What is more important than the type of play or plot he is part of, is a character's choice of either action or stoical acceptance of the unavoidable ills that reflect the war-torn reality of early seventeenth-century Europe. The decadence visible in the drama of the first Jacobean decade, its pessimism that speaks directly to the twentieth-century reader who has survived the savagery of World War II, is an expression of the Jacobeans' attempt to 'moralize about [...] political realities' and to 'cling to a traditional moral view of politics even though they sense that medieval ideals are no longer meaningful to their society'.[14] In Jacobean tragedy, the sheer vulnerability of the moral order which the period's moral philosophers saw in the world around them is exposed. The decent man in Jacobean tragedy is weak and ineffectual, but the hope that the plays contain is that there will be 'an inevitable if belated reaction of good, for there is a limit to what even the timid and fearful will bear at the hands of oppressors'.[15]

In the 1980s, Ornstein's focus on the male world of politics and the 'decent man' who belatedly takes on the corruption of the state made way for a number of revisionary studies that brought to the study of early modern tragedy the methodologies and politics of feminist criticism, psychoanalysis and cultural materialism. I have already discussed Jonathan Dollimore's *Radical Tragedy* (1984) and Catherine Belsey's *The Subject of Tragedy* (1985) in my last chapter; here I briefly want to draw attention to Dympna Callaghan's polemical *Woman and Gender in Renaissance Tragedy: A Study of King Lear, Othello, The Duchess of Malfi and The White Devil* (1989), in which thought-provoking statements that turn received ideas about Jacobean tragedy upside-down compensate for the absence of detailed readings of the plays. For Callaghan, there is no doubt that tragedy, as a genre, 'places gender issues in centre stage, and in doing so reveals the precarious status of phallic power'.[16] Because a complex of binary oppositions sets the feminine alongside 'the left, the lower, the dark and the disorderly' (as opposed to the male, right, upper, light and orderly), gender is central to the understanding of the world in Jacobean tragedy, with femininity posing a constant disruptive threat to the established order.[17] In Jacobean society, where the microcosm of the family mirrors the macrocosm of the State, 'the detection of order or disorder at *any* level has implications at *all* analogical levels'.[18] It is thus with matters of state that Jacobean tragedies are concerned when they use some form of female transgression as a catalyst for the tragic action. 'Seen as transgressors', Callaghan points out, the outspoken and sexually active 'female characters cease to be passive victims who exist primarily to embellish the downfall of the tragic hero'.[19]

In her reading, then, the centrality of the male hero is undermined by the heroine, who, while 'often absent, silent or dead', nevertheless has a pivotal function. The silencing of the heroine reveals the greatness of the male need to control and incorporate her: if '[f]emale corpses are constructed as focal points for ocular inspection by other characters on stage and by the audience in a way that male bodies are not', that is evidence of the ways in which the dead female figure is central to the construction of phallic power in the tragedies'.[20]

The dead body is also central to Michael Neill's *Issues of Death: Mortality and Identity in English Renaissance Tragedy* (1997), in which we can see the influence of New Historicism and the new body criticism on the study of tragedy. Instead of femininity, it is death which is seen as a construct by Neill, and tragedy, for him, is one of 'the principal instruments by which the culture of early modern England reinvented death'.[21] In the 'sudden flowering of macabre art towards the end of the fourteenth century', Neill sees the emergence of the 'unmistakable personality' of Death, who is credited with 'tak[ing] a wicked pleasure in parodying, through the lively forms of Death the Antic, sardonic jester, grim summoner, and eldritch lover, the vivid self-exhibition of human identity'.[22] Death – and especially mass death, as in times of plague – brings chaos to 'the painstakingly constructed order of society', epitomised by the city of London.[23] For London theatregoers, tragedy was both a means of confronting death in its appalling levelling authority and a way of 'contain[ing] the fear of death by staging fantasies of ending in which the moment of dying was transformed, by the arts of performance, to a supreme demonstration of distinction'.[24] For Neill, this is what lies at the heart of the tragedies of Webster, where, following the teachings of Montaigne and Senecan stoicism, 'death paradoxically becomes a powerfully individuating experience'.[25] The heroes of Jacobean tragedy shape their ends in a way that declares their mastery over death, and '[t]ragedy's self-reflexive insistence upon its own ability to confer "noble memory" on its heroes [...] needs to be understood in terms of a wider preoccupation with the importance of remembrance in a culture forced to devise new ways of accommodating itself to the experience of mortality' following the Reformation.[26]

Picking up on the work of Jonathan Sawday (see pp. 103–4), Neill argues that tragedy was additionally influenced by the new theatricalised science of anatomy, which saw anatomists performing dissections of criminals' corpses in front of paying audiences. Playwrights made 'capital out of [the tragedies'] physical resemblance to the scene of dissection' by scripting plays that 'activate a pervasive anxiety about the maddening opacity of the human body, which in certain tragedies erupts in shockingly literal displays of anatomical violence'.[27] This explains Gloucester's shocking blinding straight after Lear imagines the dissection of Regan in the Quarto *King Lear* and it also lies at the heart of Giovanni's entrance 'like some derange anatomist to display his sister-lover's impaled heart' in *'Tis Pity She's a Whore*.[28] Less crassly, Neill shows how an anatomical interest in opening up the human body to reveal a hidden interiority also governs the plots of *Othello* and *The Changeling*, which are both 'structured around tropes of opening, discovery, and hidden secrets'.[29] *Antony and Cleopatra* and *The Duchess of Malfi*, meanwhile, are plays that are obsessed with the idea of what constitutes a 'good' death. All these features – the good death, mortuary art, funeral rites and anatomy – can be summed up as a concern with memory and remembrance which is central to *Hamlet* and to the sub-genre of revenge tragedy in general. Revenge tragedy, Neill explains, 'exhibits a world in which the dead, precisely because they are now beyond the help of their survivors, have become practically insatiable in their demands upon the living'.[30] The sub-genre is so well circumscribed in criticism of early modern tragedy that it deserves its own discussion.

Revenge tragedy: a sub-genre

In 1940, Fredson Bowers, in *Elizabethan Revenge Tragedy, 1587–1642*, built on his formidable knowledge of the drama which we saw applied to textual criticism (see pp. 42–3) and provided an overview of the historical and literary background to the sub-genre of revenge tragedy, whose evolution he then traced through readings of a large number of plays. In the theatres, revenge plots had been popular since Kyd's tragedies in the late 1580s, which showed the influence both of 'the villainous characters of the Italian novels' and of Seneca. In characteristic fashion, Bowers sums up the Kydian 'formula for the tragedy of revenge' in twelve numbered points before proceeding to trace this formula through the plays of the 'golden era of the true Kydian revenge tragedy', whose endpoint is marked by *The Revenger's Tragedy* (c. 1607).[31] After this last great Kydian tragedy, whose ending 'removes all possible glamour clinging to a revenger', Bowers paints a familiar picture of Jacobean decline and decadence.[32] The 'new school of tragedy' popular between 1607 and 1620 broke with the Kydian tradition and 'concerned itself chiefly with the depiction of villainy and horrors'. This new type of tragedy was

■ a narrow one, and the drift towards sensationalism and artificiality in the Jacobean age inevitably led audiences to demand more variety with less high seriousness. [...] For the subject matter of the new drama, themes were chosen in which the interest lay in violent, far-fetched, and surprising situations. [...] The violence of these new plays is portrayed for its own sake.[33] □

Things get yet worse after 1620, when the bourgeois disapproval of revenge (following a peak in the fashion for duelling around 1610) leads to revenge tragedies by Massinger, Rowley and Ford. These playwrights not only indulge in the Jacobean love of horror but they also tack on conclusions that are concerned with the ethics of revenge, giving the theme 'a more religious and humane treatment'.[34] Instead of improving the drama, the bourgeoisification of revenge tragedy leads to its corruption, as the motives for revenge are withheld from the audience in order to make sure that it be condemned. By the end of the period, '[r]evenge has lost all power of true inspiration and remains only as an artificial incentive to create and, in turn, to resolve strained and bewildering situations'.[35]

Charles and Elaine Hallett's *The Revenger's Madness: A Study of Revenge Tragedy Motifs* (1980) builds on Bowers' work but restricts the corpus of what they consider to be true revenge tragedies to a few plays that cluster around *Hamlet*, giving privileged treatment to *The Spanish Tragedy*, *Antonio's Revenge* and *The Revenger's Tragedy*. Their analysis of the motifs these tragedies share – the ghost, madness, delay, plays-within-plays, murders and the eventual death of the revenger – results in a typology of the genre that is even more restrictive than Bowers' formula for Kydian tragedy had been, since it leads them to exclude from the corpus of revenge tragedies later plays such as *The Changeling*, *Women Beware Women*, *The Duchess of Malfi* and *The Broken Heart*. While the distinction between the Elizabethan 'golden age' of revenge tragedy and the Jacobean 'decadence' is not quite as stark in the Halletts' study as it had been in Bowers', it remains vital to their understanding of revenge tragedy as a genre that flourished at the end of the sixteenth century, when tragedies 'probe[d] beyond the anger and rage within each of us to investigate the whole question of justice and order in a society that is experiencing a civilizational crisis'.[36]

The Halletts' relatively narrow view of the genre and the privileging of the *Hamlet*-related tragedies that had characterised both their and Bowers' approach is given a welcome counterpoint in Eileen Allman's *Jacobean Revenge Tragedy and the Politics of Virtue* (1999). Allman's book brings to the study of the genre the methodologies of cultural materialism, a feminist agenda and an exclusive focus on the Jacobean period, in which she sees a 'resurgence of misogynist discourse'. This 'can be understood as resulting from very specific historical causes: the king's overt antifeminism, the defensive male response to James's problematizing of heterosexuality, the queen's peripheral participation in political life'.[37] In the mid-Jacobean period, as 'James's struggles with Parliament over absolute authority made tyranny an inflammatory subject', a series of revenge tragedies – *The Maid's Tragedy*, *The Second Maiden's Tragedy*, *Valentinian* and *The Duchess of Malfi*, all written in the narrow time-span of 1610–13 – addressed the joint issues of the tyrant's assumption of absolute authority, the heroism of female characters who refused to stay silent and submissive, and the appearance of male characters who are linked to the heroine and who 'reject the tyrant's sexual and political claim to authority by affirming obedience to the divinely derived principles that, in theory, sanction his dominance'.[38] Allman argues that these four tragedies respond to the misogynistic and absolutist discourses of the Jacobean reign, producing androgynous heroes and heroines who emulate 'the posthumous Elizabeth' in their 'challenge [to] the presumption of male authority'.[39] *The Duchess of Malfi*, while not 'reducible' to the subgenre of revenge tragedy, nevertheless represents the culmination of this trend, as the androgynous Duchess 'offers the play's only alternative to the pathological male authority of Ferdinand and the Cardinal'. In Allman's book, then, the focus has almost entirely shifted from the revenger, who was central to the genre for Bowers and the Hallets, to the heroine: the revengers may 'determine the play's action, but the Duchess determines its meaning'.[40] At the turn of the twentieth century, for critics like Allman and Alison Findlay, '[r]evenge tragedy is a feminine genre'.[41]

Comedy

If the claiming of revenge tragedy as a 'feminine genre' is a recent development, comedy has long been associated with the feminine world of domesticity and marriage, as in Linda Bamber's telling title *Comic Women, Tragic Men: A Study of Gender and Genre in Shakespeare* (1982). This is no doubt to a large extent due to the popularity of Shakespearean comic heroines such as Viola, Beatrice and Rosalind, and indeed the study of early modern comedy as a genre has often taken Shakespeare's romantic comedies as a starting-point. In the important studies of C. L. Barber and Northrop Frye, the comedies of Shakespeare's contemporaries are little more than a convenient contrast that allows the critic to highlight the unique qualities of Shakespeare's comic vision. It is only in studies that focus on the Jacobean sub-genre of 'city comedy' that Shakespeare and his Elizabethan comedies are marginalised and his Jacobean contemporaries become central to the discussion.

The central thesis of C. L. Barber's still influential *Shakespeare's Festive Comedy: A Study of Dramatic Form and Its Relation to Social Custom* (1959) is that Shakespearean romantic comedies are 'saturnalian' and 'festive' not only in atmosphere, but also in structure, following 'the formula, through release to clarification'.[42] Both this formula, and the fact that Shakespearean comedy 'is satiric only incidentally', distinguish it from the comedies of Shakespeare's contemporaries, whose 'satirical comedy tends to deal with relations between social classes and aberrations in movements between them'.[43] By contrast, Shakespearean saturnalian comedy is, for Barber, deeply grounded in the holiday customs and entertainments of 'merry England', which explains the presence of May games and the festive Lord of Misrule in Shakespeare's comic drama. Feste, for Barber, is such a Lord of Misrule, and *Twelfth Night* is Shakespeare's last 'free-and-easy festive comedy', in which 'there is a curious appropriateness in Malvolio's presence, as a kind of foreign body to be expelled by laughter'. Malvolio the puritan and 'man of business', an ambitious social climber who must be understood in the context of the rise of capitalism, is a sign of things to come. Malvolio, in short, is the stuff of Jacobean comedy and Barber reflects that '[o]ne could moralize the spectacle by observing that, in the long run, in the 1640's, Malvolio *was* revenged on the whole pack of them'.[44]

Rather than see *Twelfth Night* as the culmination of Shakespeare's comic writing, Northrop Frye's *A Natural Perspective: The Development of Shakespearean Comedy and Romance* (1964) regards his 'romantic comedies' as the starting-point of a journey that led to Shakespeare's Jacobean Romances, in which his comic vision culminated. For Frye, the key difference between Shakespeare's comedies and those of Jonson is that while 'Jonson writes comedies which [...] maintain a fairly consistent illusion', Shakespeare 'never fail[s] to include something incredible'.[45] Shakespeare's skill in adhering to conventions while giving his imagination full rein is nowhere as evident as in his Jacobean Romances, in which Shakespeare combines an adherence to convention with a sense of spontaneous improvisation. The culmination of his dramatic works in plays that have a strong element of improvisation contrasts starkly with Jonson, for whom 'the logical development [...] was the masque, the abstract dramatic construct which communicates not so much the experience of drama as the symbols of that experience'.[46] For Frye, Jonson is as 'abstract and sophisticated' as Shakespeare is 'childlike and concrete'.[47]

Even though Frye explicitly refuses to attribute more value to Shakespearean simplicity as opposed to Jonsonian sophistication, he does then move on to dedicate the rest of his book to the Shakespearean tradition in a way that suggests that it is superior to its Jonsonian counterpart. A Shakespearean comedy, Frye reminds us, is not necessarily 'a play which ends happily: it is a play in which a certain structure is present and works through to its own logical end, whether we or the cast or the author feel happy about it or not'.[48] All the same, Frye is in agreement with Barber when describing Shakespearean comedy as 'festive'.[49] He furthermore makes a claim for Shakespearean comedy as 'primitive', 'old-fashioned and archaic' in a way that makes it more 'universal'.[50] In this, Shakespeare's comedies approach the status of myth and ritual,

a ritual which is 'reproduced in the typical Shakespearean comic structure' which 'normally begins with an anticomic society, a social organization blocking and opposed to the comic drive, which the action of the
comedy evades or overcomes'.[51] This is followed by a 'period of confusion and sexual licence' in which identities are lost – hence the recurrent
motif of the cross-dressed heroine.[52] The final phase sees the discovery
of social, sexual and individual identity, leading

> ■ to a kind of self-knowledge which releases a character from the bond
> age of his humor. This is not necessarily an introverted knowledge, which
> is of little use to a comedy, but a sense of proportion and of social real
> ity. Humor in this sense is not perhaps a major theme of Shakespeare's
> comedy as it is of Jonson's, but it is an essential minor one.[53] □

In Frye as in Barber, we thus arrive at an understanding of non-
Shakespearean Jacobean comedy – here, Jonson's comedy of humours –
only by reading between the lines of their discussion of Shakespearean
comedy.

By comparison with the enduring influence of both Barber and Frye,
which has entrenched the privileging of Shakespearean comedy, Muriel
Bradbrook's *The Growth and Structure of Elizabethan Comedy* (1955) has
had less impact, even if it is far more foundational for our understanding of Jacobean comedy. It is tempting to conclude that this is because
of its subject matter, since her intimate acquaintance with the broader
early modern canon leads her to consider not only the 'sweet' and
'romantic' 'Shakespearean' comedy of the Elizabethan stage but also the
'bitter', 'satiric' 'Jonsonian' comedy of the Jacobeans. For Bradbrook,
the 'greater Elizabethan and Jacobean comedies' were bred out of 'the
[...] fusion of the popular and learned traditions, [...] two modes which
were not permanently compatible with each other'.[54] Her aim, as in
her book on the tragedies, is to make the comedies more accessible
and intelligible by tracing the conventions of the genre from medieval
drama and school plays through the popular comedies of Peele, Greene
and Nashe up to Lyly's artificial comedy.

Significantly, Bradbrook distinguishes between the legacy of the
popular tradition in the 'sanguine and traditional' comedies of Dekker
and Heywood, the light-hearted 'Comedy of wit, flavoured with satire,
but also with fantasy' of Fletcher and the sub-genre of city comedy.[55]
This latter she describes as 'the kind of play which was popular in the
private playhouses within the city limits, [and which] was very largely
satiric'.[56] The sub-genre gradually evolved from the plays of the 'Poets'
War' of 1598–1601, the years in which the boys' companies at St. Paul's
and the Queen's Chapel entered into a fierce competition. Bradbrook
notes that

■ [t]wo-thirds of this repertory was written by half-a-dozen playwrights – Jonson, Marston and Middleton; Chapman, Beaumont and Fletcher. It was the work of professed poets, who made pretensions both to wit and learning. Conditions of acting in the halls of the City favoured something more like an operatic or concert technique than the style of the open stages; and though most of these playwrights also wrote for the men, yet for the boys they adapted their style.[57] □

Jonson's idiosyncratic comedy of humours developed out of these plays, and while his comedies often remained experimental, his emphasis on the humours and the 'single complex intrigue', his 'manipulation of popular devices and classical traditions, to his own purposes', and his use of comedy as 'a criticism of society and an embodiment of values' eventually led to the birth of 'intellectual drama [...] upon the English stage'.[58] While each playwright gave his comedies a different slant – Marston 'stress[ing] the critical aspect, and Middleton the humours and observation of the London Scene' – the plays have enough of a 'family resemblance', to use Fowler's term, to warrant consideration as constituting a sub-genre with its own ruling conventions.

City comedy: a sub-genre

For Brian Gibbons in *Jacobean City Comedy: A Study of Satiric Plays by Jonson, Marston and Middleton* (1968), the city comedies of Jonson, Marston and Middleton developed out of their reactions 'to each other's successive plays, reshaping, copying, changing emphases, in response to their developing thought about the subject of the city'.[59] Based on the Morality tradition, Roman intrigue comedy, Italian *commedia dell'arte*, and the verse satire and complaint, Jacobean city comedy is notable for the way in which 'high-minded theory confronts low-life experience of the city' in what is a 'profoundly dialectical' approach to the writing of comedy.[60] City comedy is a deeply self-reflexive genre, concerned as it is 'with literary and theatrical fashion, with current affairs and with metropolitan social, political and literary gossip'.[61] The plays present 'a keen analysis in moral terms' of the shortcomings of the urban landscape and its social and economic structures, 'register[ing] a split in the social fabric and an uneasy dissatisfaction with political affairs'.[62] Gibbons singles out the plays of Marston as 'dangerously topical' in the attention they give 'to the dangers of flattery, susceptibility to favourites, luxurious display, irresponsible distribution of honours, and unrestrained ambition for place and rewards' of the early Jacobean years.[63] From the satires of the turn of the century, city comedy gradually evolved into the episodic structure of a 'Comical Satyre' like *Every Man out of His Humour* before finding its maturity in plays like *Volpone, The Dutch Courtesan* and *Michaelmas Term* (all written in 1605), which have 'strong frame plots which in themselves could give critical expression to social and cultural attitudes and energies'.[64] Mostly set in London, mature city comedies satirise the materialism of the city, its sexual mores and its religious extremisms. They debunk the 'hypocritical attitudes of authority' and link 'the damage done by uncontrolled extortionate usury, the anxieties of debt, foreclosure and risky investment, which furnish intrigue plots for the plays [...] to the miseries induced by the law relating to wards and inheritance, so giving a selective emphasis to issues in Jacobean society which [...] have wider historical importance'.[65] Aimed at an audience with a strong component of young law students at the Inns of Court (the four legal societies which have the exclusive right of admitting people to the English bar), these plays make scourging the vices of the city fashionable to such an extent that it leads to an explosion of highly conventional plays by a whole range of dramatists cashing in on the success of the sub-genre.

Alexander Leggatt's decision to structure his argument in *Citizen Comedy in the Age of Shakespeare* (1973) around specific components and types of the sub-genre leads to his consideration of a broader corpus of texts than that covered by Gibbons. For Leggatt, the sub-genre, which cuts across 'the satiric, the didactic, and the simply amusing', is defined by exclusion: city comedies are comedies with an English setting 'which do not deal predominantly with the court or the aristocracy, but with the fluid, often ill-defined area that lies between this and the lowest class of workmen, servants, rogues, and vagabonds'.[66] Money and sex, rather than Shakespearean courtship and romance, are central to these plays, which populate their world with the citizen class. In plot terms, these plays follow the patterns of the classical Roman 'New Comedies' of Plautus and Terence, which were picked up in Italian Renaissance comedies and imitated by Elizabethan and Jacobean playwrights. An important precursor of Jacobean city comedy, for Leggatt, is Dekker's *The Shoemaker's Holiday*, but the crucial difference between this and the later city comedies is its benign vision and 'glorification of citizen life', which contrasts with the 'wry, sardonic wit' and the satirical spirit of Jacobean comedy, with its 'keener awareness of class distinctions'.[67] While citizen comedy in the private theatres between 1604 and 1610 developed in the direction of 'racy comedies in which satire, sex, and financial intrigue are the main ingredients', the adult companies in the public theatres 'offer[ed] comedies teaching moral lessons'.[68] Class issues are less important to the adult companies, and when they are raised, the plays side with the citizens rather than the witty rakes. Ben Jonson is a pivotal figure for Leggatt because of the way in which he bridged both traditions, writing bitter satires for the boys but doing his most important work for the adults, for whom he wrote a 'satire [...] at once more powerful and more universal than that of the private theatres'.[69]

Since 1973, city comedy has not disappeared from the critical landscape – quite to the contrary. Theodore Leinwand's *The City Staged: Jacobean City Comedy, 1603–13* (1986) is another book-length study which was followed by a multitude of books that have treated the sub-genre within contexts other than genre study.[70] Precisely because this sub-genre is so intimately concerned with the mores and vices of the urban landscape, it has lent itself to the investigation of historical contexts, as we saw in the work of Douglas Bruster, who goes as far as to question the utility of defining city comedy as a separate sub-genre. City comedy has also attracted the attention of scholars interested in the body and gender, who, as we will see in Chapters 6 and 7 of this Guide, continue to scrutinise the sub-genre for its representation of sexual politics, domesticity and cross-dressing.

Tragicomedy

The same issues of sexual politics, domesticity and cross-dressing are also central to modern criticism of tragicomedy, the most fundamentally Jacobean of the genres discussed here in that it was generated by a conjunction of events in theatre history (the establishment of boys' companies, the take-over of Blackfriars' by the King's Men) and in literary fashion (the appeal to a more sophisticated audience, the ongoing popularity of romance) that is specific to the early Jacobean period. The genre received considerable attention in the 1950s but thereafter receded in importance for a few decades. Since the late 1980s, however, new approaches in theatre history, historicist and textual criticism have brought the genre back into critical fashion. Tragicomedy, Helen Wilcox noted in 2008, 'is making a comeback'.[71]

Eugene Waith's *The Pattern of Tragicomedy in Beaumont and Fletcher* (1952) starts by acknowledging that the genre, as produced most prominently by Beaumont and Fletcher, is, in the mid-twentieth century, generally dismissed 'as trivial and decadent – a debauchery of what is best in Jacobean drama'.[72] For Waith, the paradox of this dismissal of the genre by modern critics when contrasted with the respect it commanded in its own day is what makes it worthy of critical investigation. The 'pattern of Fletcherian tragicomedy', as Waith calls it, evolved from Fletcher's unsuccessful *The Faithful Shepherdess* (1608) to the collaborative *Philaster* (1609), the first success in the genre, to its apogee in *A King and No King* (1611).[73] Its lack of success notwithstanding, *The Faithful Shepherdess* contains the essence of the new genre: it is

■ neither the mechanical combination of tragedy and comedy that many an earlier English tragicomedy had been, nor is it truly like the pastoral tragicomedy on which it appears to be modeled. The effect of each scene is a fusion of certain effects of tragedy and comedy – what Ellis-Fermor [see Introduction to this Guide, pp. 18–19] singles out as the distinguishing characteristic of Fletcherian tragicomedy – a 'middle mood'. [...] The conflict [between the protagonists] is moving; yet it is a conflict between hypothetical persons – near abstractions. The formal balance of these abstractions removes them still further from reality. What is compelling in *The Faithful Shepherdess* is a distillation of emotion related only incidentally to character or plot and thus, as it were, freed from the laws of cause and effect which govern the narrative and determine the most obvious meaning of the play. Fletcher's new sort of tragicomedy is the product of a refined sensationalism.[74] □

It is precisely what makes Fletcherian tragicomedy distinctive – its abstract nature, formal balance, distilled emotion, blatantly unrealistic plots and refined sensationalism – that made it so popular with its seventeenth-century audiences and made twentieth-century critics such as T. S. Eliot and Muriel Bradbrook find it remote, decadent and uninteresting.

In Waith's description, the plays of Beaumont and Fletcher typically sacrifice consistency of character 'to the undeniable effectiveness of a situation'.[75] The plays are also characterised by the 'formal, declamatory verse, remote from the language of conversation' that brings 'the familiar and the remote' together in the 'intensely emotional speeches'.[76] Intense moments of emotion structure the plays, as scenes of the main plots and subplots alternate to raise and lower the emotional temperature. As exemplified most clearly in *A King and No King*, the pattern of Fletcherian tragicomedy can therefore be summed up as the combination of an imitation of the manners of the familiar world with a remoteness from that world, an intricacy of plot featuring an improbable hypothesis, an atmosphere of evil and a world peopled by protean characters, which gives rise to lively touches of passion that are voiced in emotional language.[77] Waith finds that these features persist in the later plays by Beaumont and Fletcher. Though many of these are not, strictly speaking, tragicomedies, 'the pattern of tragicomedy is often so conspicuous [in them] that the conventional patterns of comedy and tragedy are almost obliterated'.[78]

In the middle section of his book, Waith does discuss the indebtedness of Fletcherian tragicomedy to Battista Guarini (1538–1612), the author of the pastoral tragicomedy *Il Pastor fido* (1585) and of comments on the genre in *Il Compendio della poesia tragicomica* (1601), as well as to the traditions of declamation in Juvenalian satire and Arcadian romance. The best place to look for a discussion of the antecedents of Jacobean tragicomedy, however, is Marvin T. Herrick's *Tragicomedy: Its*

Origin and Development in Italy, France, and England (1955). Herrick aims
to demonstrate the strong links between English pastoral tragicomedy,
which first appeared in the work of Elizabethan playwrights such as
Whetstone and Greene, and its Italian predecessors and French counterparts. Fletcher's *Faithful Shepherdess* once more takes on a key role in this
narrative because it represents 'the author's conscious attempt to follow
Guarini's theory of pastoral tragicomedy even in preserving the nobility
of the principal characters and in eschewing any broad comic effects'.[79]
In trying to trace the limits of the genre, Herrick discusses Marston's
Malcontent (1604) as well as several plays by Dekker and Shakespeare's
romances and his 'problem' comedies *All's Well* and *Measure for Measure*.
He finds that, while these plays do form part of the genre, they do not
form the core of its corpus, which, like Waith, he thinks consists mainly
of the tragicomedies of Beaumont and Fletcher. Herrick, however, provides a corrective to Waith's narrow focus on these authors when he
insists that many of the features of Fletcherian tragicomedy are also to
be found in the plays of other authors. Beaumont and Fletcher 'came
at the climax of [a] gradual development; they could not have produced their particular tragicomedies without the lessons taught by the
earlier writers of tragedies, comedies, histories, pastorals and tragical
comedies'.[80] What Beaumont and Fletcher achieved was to raise the
status of the genre, making it more than the 'mongrel' form deplored
by Sir Philip Sidney.

The criticism of Waith and Herrick is striking for the way in which it
is concerned with stylistic features and source study at the expense of
history and theatre history. More recent studies of Jacobean tragicomedy
have resulted in a significant shift of focus. *Renaissance Tragicomedy: Explorations in Genre and Politics* (1987), a collection of essays edited by Nancy
Klein Maguire, brings to the study of the genre the methodologies of New
Historicism and cultural materialism. The result is a body of essays that
no longer consider the plays as purely aesthetic artefacts, though the first
section, on 'The Generic Context', concentrates on literary criteria and,
in an essay by John T. Shawcross, usefully distinguishes between the
comic *genre* of tragicomedy and its tragic *mode*. Barbara Mowat approaches
the genre from a different angle: for her, Shakespeare's 'problem plays',
which Herrick had already compared to tragicomedies, are Guarinian
tragicomedies, though they differ from these in being wholly tragicomic
and not ending in a clear-cut comic conclusion. The essays in the second
part of the volume largely leave such investigation of generic distinctions
behind and concentrate on the politics of the genre. William Proctor
Williams 'would not want it to appear [...] that Fletcherian tragicomedy is characterized by constantly dealing with political subjects',[81] but
both his and James J. Yoch's essays argue for a reading of early modern
tragicomedy as a genre that engages with the body politic in important

ways. For Williams, Fletcher's 'politics of love' that 'require that men and women conduct themselves in a way which produces a true and legitimate lineage' is linked to James's absolutist claims to divine-right monarchy.[82] Yoch, meanwhile, explains that 'Renaissance tragicomedies illustrated for their audiences right rule of the self and, by implication, of the body politic', as the genre's inherent temperance reflected the sought-for temperance of the body and the state.[83] What unites these essays with the rest of the collection is their sense that while generalisations about the genre should be avoided, tragicomedy was often harnessed to conservative political causes. Thus, Lois Potter shows that between 1641 and 1660, the genre was appropriated by the Cavaliers, who produced tragicomic political satires that 'exploit[ed] the tension between comedy and tragedy'.[84]

Since the publication of Maguire's collection, two more essay collections have covered similar ground and have continued to explore the genre's engagement with its sources and Jacobean politics.[85] Meanwhile, recent work in textual criticism and theatre history has rejuvenated the study of the genre yet further. At this point, it is worth revisiting some of the criticism I discussed in Chapters 2 and 3 with an eye to the ways in which they deal with tragicomedy. Approaching two 'Fletcherian tragicomedies' from the point of view of their print publication, Zachary Lesser, in *Renaissance Drama and the Politics of Publication* (2004), focuses on the publisher Thomas Walkley, who invested in *Philaster* and *A King and No King* and sought to make them attractive to a specific constituency of readers. Lesser notes that '[t]hroughout his forty years in business, Walkley consistently specialized in state affairs, from the conflicts in the early 1620s between the king and his parliaments over the war on the Continent and the proposed Spanish Match, through the divisions of the Long Parliament and the Civil War'.[86] Reading *A King and No King* and *Philaster* in the context of Walkley's publication of the *Parliamentary List* allows Lesser to recognise the plays' concern with '"mixed government," the classical theory, derived from Aristotle and Polybius, that the ideal government consisted of a mixture of monarchy, aristocracy, and democracy – the one, the few, and the many – a mixture that the English at times could attribute to their Parliament'.[87] For Lesser, therefore, *A King and No King* is not the culmination of a decadent genre in which sex takes the place of politics, but rather a play that urgently asks the question of what the relationship between King and Parliament ought to be at a time when this question was a subject of public debate.

Lucy Munro is less interested in the genre's publication history than in its evolution as part of the repertory of a new company of boy players. In *The Children of the Queen's Revels: A Jacobean Theatre Repertory* (2005), Munro suggests that we adopt 'a new way of approaching the old literary-critical standby of source study, not from the point of view of the dramatist alone, but from that of the company'.[88] Noting that 'most of the extant tragicomic plays of the seventeenth century come from the repertories of the Children of the Queen's Revels and the King's Men', Munro compares the tragicomedies produced by these two companies and finds a contrast between the 'romance[s]' staged by the King's Men and the boys' preference for plays, like Marston's paradigmatic *Malcontent*, that were 'more comic and satiric'.[89] The company of the Queen's Revels, she argues, had a far more important role than hitherto allowed in determining not only its repertory, but also the development of the genre of tragicomedy. No longer is the genre seen, in the manner of Waith and Herrick, as a literary phenomenon responding to Italian fashions; in the hands of Munro, the development of Jacobean tragicomedy is inextricably linked to the work and structure of a specific company and its playwrights.

Court masques

Even more so than tragicomedy, the Jacobean masque is closely associated with a specific group of people: Ben Jonson, who wrote the bulk of the scripts, Inigo Jones, who designed and choreographed the masques, and the Jacobean court, whose aristocrats provided both actors and spectators. As we saw in the last chapter, the masque is a genre which has received a lot of attention from New Historicists such as Jonathan Goldberg and Stephen Orgel. Together with Orgel's slim *The Illusion of Power: Political Theater in the English Renaissance* (1975), which I discussed on pp. 58–9, his enormous *Inigo Jones: The Theatre of the Stuart Court, Including the Complete Designs for Productions at Court for the Most Part in the Collection of the Duke of Devonshire Together with Their Texts and Historical Documentation* (1973), which he co-authored with the art historian Roy Strong, forms the foundation of modern studies of the court masque.

The title of Orgel and Strong's book may be as unwieldy as its two volumes, but it is doubly apt: it reminds us of the centrality of designer and spectacle (rather than playwright and script) to the genre and also highlights that the main value of the book lies in the comprehensive way in which it brings together designs, illustrations, scripts and other texts that document the evolution of the genre. Because of the ephemeral nature of performance, the visual and aural impact of the masque is lost to us and must be painstakingly reconstructed from the bewildering array of sources carefully collected, ordered and annotated by Orgel and Strong. Order is also imposed on the sources by four essays that introduce the reader to the spectacle, Platonism, design and politics of the Stuart masque. In 'The Poetics of Spectacle', Orgel links the aesthetic

vision of the Jonesian masque to the didactic and ethical agenda of Ben
Jonson, around whose scripts 'the work of other artists – designer, com-
poser, choreographer – revolved'.[90] The collaboration between Jones and
Jonson led to a conception of the masque in which the visual and the
verbal elements were not antithetical and pictures were read symbolically;
drawing on neo-Platonic philosophy and Italian dramatic theorists, the cre-
ators of the Jacobean masque embraced spectacle as the means of drama
and wonder as its end. It is not surprising, then, that for their first collaboration, *The Masque of Blackness* (1605), Jones's stage design 'subtly changed
the character of both plays and masques by transforming *audiences* into
spectators, fixing the viewer, and directing the theatrical experience toward
the single point in the hall from which the perspective achieved its fullest
effect, the royal throne'.[91] Thereafter, 'illusionistic stages were regularly
used for the masque' in an effort to create wonder in the spectator and
through that wonder allow for an 'apprehension of truth'.[92]

For Jones and Jonson, Orgel explains,

■ Every masque is a ritual in which the society affirms its wisdom and
asserts its control of its world and its destiny. The glories of the transformation scene express the power of princes, bringing order to human
and elemental nature, partaking thereby of the divine. The court and the
aristocratic hierarchy expand and become the world, and the King in turn
is abstracted.[93] □

To create such abstractions, Jones had to construct a stage that would
permit the complicated machinery that created his illusions to work.
In a chapter on 'The Mechanics of Platonism', Orgel details the physical
challenges represented by the Banqueting House at Whitehall, which
had to be fitted up for every performance. Gradually, the older *machina
versatilis*, 'a two-sided setting on a central pivot which, at the moment
of transformation, was turned round from beneath the stage' made
way for the *'scena ductilis*, or "tractable scene." This was essentially a
number of flats or shutters set in grooves on the stage, which could be
swiftly and silently drawn aside to reveal the setting behind' and which
permitted much greater flexibility of settings.[94] Mechanical sets, cloud
machines and flying devices together made the 'Jonsonian masque
[...] an extraordinarily flexible theatrical medium' that allowed Jonson
to stage his radically new hermetic allegories in ways that integrated
settings and text.[95]

Orgel's focus on the Jones-Jonson collaboration is complemented by
Strong's chapter on 'The Arts of Design', in which he traces the evolution of Jones's style. In describing 'his masque visions as pictures with
light and motion', Jones effectively made the masque a vehicle for the
introduction of 'a visual tradition new to England, one governed by the

conventions of Renaissance painting in which the picture frame marked a boundary across which the eye travelled into a world governed by the rules of scientific perspective'.[96] The masque sceneries Jones produced following this scientific perspective were 'used symbolically to represent natural forces unleashed and controlled', allowing every masque to make 'a visual progress from disorder to order, or from order to disorder and back to a higher order'.[97] Jones's scenery thus perfectly complemented the didactic and neo-Platonic aims of the Jonsonian script. Jones emerges from Orgel and Strong's book as an artist who had a decisive role in shaping the Neoplatonic mythology of the Stuart court. The overwhelming sense of visual splendour that is conveyed in the book by the lavish illustrations of stage and costume designs serves as an important reminder to literary critics not to neglect the visual component of the genre.

David Bevington and Peter Holbrook's collection *The Politics of the Stuart Court Masque* (1998), while including three essays on dance and music, gives Inigo Jones a far less prominent role. In the wake of the New Historicist criticism of Orgel and Goldberg (see pp. 58–9 and 61–2) and the work on the genre's marked engagement with issues of race by critics such as Barthelemy, Hall, Floyd-Wilson and Iyengar (see pp. 106–17), the Bevington-Holbrook collection brings together some of the most significant masque and Jonson scholars of the 1990s and, in Martin Butler's opening essay, offers a critical overview of the impact of the New Historicism on the study of the masque. Butler notes that

■ [i]n the developing New Historicist revision of the Renaissance, the masques have come to figure as virtually totemic exemplars of the legitimating functions of culture in the early modern period. Chiming with that resonant Renaissance idea that the state is a work of art, they are now seen as the works of art in which spectacle most emphatically became a tool of state, and as symptomatic of the ineluctable magnetism by which kingly absolutism pulled its age's representational forms into its own orbit.[98] □

The positive influence of the New Historicism generally and Orgel's work in particular on the study of the masque and its ability to reconcile an aesthetic approach with an interest in politics and culture is counterbalanced by the tendency of that criticism to produce 'the masques' ideological significance [...] as, essentially, a matter of their poetic form'. This, for Butler, is problematic, since such readings 'marginalize precisely those elements of contingency and circumstance which each masque was engaged in negotiating'.[99] Not all masques were the same and Butler challenges Orgel's monolithic model according to which 'the only social transaction which [masques] undertook was one of containment'. Instead, 'other kinds of negotiations may also have been hosted by the masques, scenarios which [...] were more in the nature of symbolic transactions between those who were competing for position in and around the courtly arena'.[100] If we take account of court factions, the masque emerges as a more polyvocal genre, giving expression to the interests of different groups at a court where 'the articulation of power at the centre was constantly improvised'.[101]

This recognition of the masque's polyvocality and Butler's advocacy of a model of the masque that acknowledges the strains in Stuart absolutism is key to several of the essays in the collection that differentiate between the various powerbrokers who contested James's absolute authority. For Peter Holbrook, the Jacobean court masque is characterised by 'contested rivalries' between those who endorsed 'James's pacifist and dynastic foreign policy' and those who, embracing a 'romantic-chivalric-Protestant perspective', advocated war with Spain. The masques produced by Samuel Daniel and Ben Jonson for young Prince Henry and Queen Anne and, in later years, for Prince Charles and the Duke of Buckingham, attempt to reconcile opposing factions, so that, for example, in *The Masque of Queens* there is a discernible 'fusion of bellicose form with peaceful content'.[102] Leeds Barroll furthermore energetically argues for an understanding of the masques staged for Queen Anne between 1604 and 1613 as separate from those staged for James. Hugh Craig also notes that the tensions between the complimentary masque and the much more critical antimasque produce a double vision that created a 'dialogue [...] between unruliness and rule'.[103] Focussing on the dance of *Oberon*, Tom Bishop arrives at a similar understanding of conflicting views being presented together. For him, 'Dancing [is] where the real action was' in a genre which often acted as a vehicle for an individual aristocratic performer.[104] Like David Lindley, who contributes a chapter on the political significance of masquing music, Bishop tries to redirect criticism towards an appreciation of 'the central concern of the genre with performance'; for him, the masque must be understood 'as a formal and kinetic event whose politics are not simply uttered, but enacted'.[105]

The Holbrook-Bevington collection is essential reading on the masque not only because it provides an excellent overview of the field at the end of the twentieth century, but also because, in its inclusion of chapters on female masquing and the genre's visual and aural dimensions, it maps out the new directions taken by the most recent generations of critics. Clare McManus's *Women on the Renaissance Stage: Anna of Denmark and Female Masquing in the Stuart Court, 1590–1619* (2002) combines an interest in the visual elements of the masque with a focus on the figure of Anna of Denmark (the spelling she favoured). The queen's masquing and commissioning of masques, McManus reminds us, 'accounted for almost the entirety of the English Jacobean court's female performance in the first two decades of the seventeenth century', and the book sees her performances as part of 'an emerging wider tradition of female performance which would eventually culminate in the appearance of the professional female actor after the Restoration'.[106] The Queen's performances were of necessity silent, since a central convention of the masque was that aristocratic performers were restricted to dancing (professional actors played the speaking roles). What may at first seem like a constraint can also be seen as empowering: the fact that the injunction to silence was shared by aristocratic men and women led to a trumping of gender difference by the demands of status and a greater expectation of physical expressiveness that belied the silence of the dancers. Anticipating Barbara Ravelhofer's *The Early Stuart Masque: Dance, Costume, and Music* (2006), which brings to the discussion a wealth of documentary detail and pan-European historical evidence, an important chapter of McManus's book is therefore concerned with dance and costume as the means of physical expressiveness. McManus concentrates on the ways in which the female bodies of the queen and her women were read: 'The female masquer's body', she notes, 'was the nexus of issues of gender, discourse, the social conception and control of the body, and performance'.[107] Constructed through costume, architecture, and choreography, the female aristocratic body is, in McManus's study, a powerful carrier of meanings 'which did not accord with masculine courtly ideals' and which stood in conflict with the 'elision of physical representation' in the masque text.[108] In the hands of some of the most recent critics of the masque, the focus has thus shifted back towards the spectacle of power discussed by Orgel and Strong in the 1970s, but now this spectacle is no longer attributed simply to the male figures of author and designer and the artistic agency of female patrons and performers is increasingly recognised.

History

Whereas the masque is often treated as a Stuart phenomenon associated with Jonson and Jones, the history play as a dramatic genre is principally seen as an Elizabethan phenomenon that is closely identified with Shakespeare. This is how E. M. W. Tillyard portrays the genre in *Shakespeare's History Plays* (1962), influentially arguing that Shakespeare's two tetralogies essentially propagated a 'Tudor myth' and implying that with the death of the last Tudor monarch, the history play lost its reason to exist.[109] But the genre did survive into the Jacobean period, where it took on a variety of new shapes which ultimately absorbed it.

Not a lot of criticism exists that is specifically concerned with the Jacobean period, though Irving Ribner's *The English History Play in the Age of Shakespeare* (1957; revised 1965) is a good place to start. Ribner notes that defining the history play is difficult because perceptions of what might constitute 'history' in the period included stories we would today describe as mythological. In Ribner's definition of the history play, the purpose of a play is more important than its historical source; Webster's *The White Devil* and *The Duchess of Malfi* are examples of plays based on historical sources which, because they fail to serve the purposes of a history play, cannot be considered part of the genre. These purposes are summed up as follows:

> ■ Those stemming from classical and humanist philosophies of history include (1) a nationalistic glorification of England; (2) an analysis of contemporary affairs, both national and foreign so as to make clear the virtues and the failings of contemporary statesmen; (3) a use of past events as a guide to political behaviour in the present; (4) a use of history as documentation for political theory; and (5) a study of past political disaster as an aid to Stoical fortitude in the present. Those stemming from medieval Christian philosophy of history include: (6) illustration of the providence of God as the ruling force in human – and primarily political – affairs, and (7) exposition of a rational plan in human events which must affirm the wisdom and justice of God.[110] □

Following this definition, *King Lear*, which is based on legendary material but appears 'to have been intended as history' may be called a history, even if, as Ribner readily admits, 'the political concerns of the play represent only one small aspect'.[111] Shakespeare's *Macbeth* and Middleton's *Hengist, King of Kent* are more unambiguously classifiable as histories, though Ribner remarks that the latter's concern with politics disappears after the first act in a way that is commensurate with the fact that by then, 'the English history play had already passed into [a] period of decline'.[112]

   That period of decline is the subject of Ribner's last chapter. 'It is not only that there are fewer history plays' after 1603, notes Ribner, 'but that the ones that are written lack the vitality or artistic merit of the earlier species'.[113] In the Jacobean period, the 'romantic appeal implicit in the careers of kings and nobles and in the fanfare of battles' began to gain the upper hand, resulting in the development of 'romantic drama employing historical figures', such as *Cymbeline* and *Bonduca*.[114] While these plays still carry 'certain secondary political overtones',[115] many such historical romances were devoid of political content and accomplished no historical purposes. The period also saw the evolution of a compound genre, combining history with travel literature. Travel plays like *Dick of Devonshire* or *A Christian Turned Turk* 'have little relation to the problems of history' and are largely fictional; their primary interest lies in the adventure rather than politics.[116] With Shakespeare, too, turning away from the 'proper' purposes of history in *Henry VIII*, we must look to the plays of Thomas Heywood, and in particular to *If You Know Not Me*, for a history play which still does have a 'dominant political purpose', which is 'the assertion of the doctrine of royal supremacy and the refutation of Catholic counter-claims of papal supremacy'.[117] Other than that, the story Ribner traces is one of a genre being gradually absorbed by other genres, including the Roman plays of Shakespeare and Jonson, leading to its extinction towards the end of James's reign.

One of the principal influences on the history play identified by Ribner is John Foxe's *Acts and Monuments* (1563) with its accounts of Protestant martyrdom. For Judith Doolin Spikes in 'The Jacobean History Play and the Myth of the Elect Nation' (1978) and Marsha S. Robinson, in *Writing the Reformation: Actes and Monuments and the Jacobean History Play* (2002), Foxean hybrid plays combining history with biography constitute an important, if under-researched, corpus. Arising from Foxe's conception of the individual life as 'subsumed by an apocalyptic design which gives that life significance',[118] Jacobean history plays perpetuated Foxe's Protestant providential historiography of the struggle between the true English Church and its Roman counterpart, leading from the 'tragedy of earthly persecution' to 'the heavenly apotheosis of the true Church'.[119] As Spikes puts it, the plays are permeated 'by a philosophy which viewed world history as the temporal manifestation of the cosmic warfare, of God's Elect sanctified from all eternity against the irremediably damned followers of Antichrist'.[120] This enabled Jacobean playwrights to substitute a universal view of history for the dynastic and insular 'Tudor myth' that had underpinned the Elizabethan history play. Robinson, on the other hand, shows that plays responded directly to national crises such as the death of Prince Henry in 1613, which was commemorated in the '1613 staging of *Henry VIII*, and the 1612–1613 reprinting of *If You Know Not Me, You Know Nobody, Part I*, *Sir Thomas Wyatt*, *Thomas Lord Cromwell*, and *When You See Me, You Know Me*', new and older plays of diverse political leanings which seem 'to have been read as tracts'.[121] Robinson's innovative approach to the genre allows Elizabethan plays to be read as 'Jacobean' in their printing and reception and thus to grant the history play considerable relevance in the Jacobean period, regardless of the absence of a large corpus of new plays.

The need, for students of the history play in the Jacobean period, to look and think beyond Shakespeare and received accounts of what might constitute a historical drama in the period, is also recognised in Teresa Grant and Barbara Ravelhofer's *English Historical Drama, 1500–1660: Forms Outside the Canon* (2008), whose subtitle finely pinpoints the problem. As the editors acknowledge in their introduction, 'in its own time the "history play" attracted such different labels as "comedy", "interlude" or "show"' and plays which we no longer think of as "histories" were designated as such on title-pages to market them to specific audiences'.[122] Grant and Ravelhofer insist on the genre's role in generating a sense of national identity: by '[r]e-enacting events of the past, a group performs and commemorates collectively. The shared experience creates a feeling of identity, binding the participants together and excluding outsiders'. Their understanding of the genre as constituting 'history-in-the-making shaped by collective memory' thus gives a new spin to Ribner's focus on the political purpose of the history play and its nationalistic glorification of England.[123]

Teresa Grant's essay on Samuel Rowley's *When You See Me You Know Me* (c. 1605) describes that play as deeply involved in such 'history-in-the-making': the play, for Grant, is more than the simple Foxean history described by Robinson. Looked at in the context of Prince Henry's assumption of the patronage of the Admiral's Men, the play can be read as a way of honouring the young militantly Protestant prince, showing us in its portrayal of Tudor Prince Edward 'how Rowley wanted to see Prince Henry: studious, Protestant, chivalric and as the man of the future'.[124] The history that is purportedly about the past is therefore also about the future. It is also about the present in that its representation of the relationship between Catherine Parr and Henry VIII brings royal ecclesiastical policy into the spotlight at a historical moment when James I had entrenched the religious status quo at the 1604 Hampton Court Conference. As history-in-the-making, the play is a political intervention during the 'honeymoon' period of James's reign in which the 'present uses the past to argue for the future'.[125] As presented in this essay as well as in Mark Hutching's discussion of Lodowick Carlell's *Osmond the Great Turk* (1622), the history play is moving towards the sorts of closet drama Ravelhofer discusses in her final chapter: 'play-pamphlets' commenting on the execution of Charles I that are closely allied to journalism in the way in which they 'responded to current historical events in a quasi-dramatic fashion'.[126]

Closet drama

Closet drama (i.e., plays that were never meant to be acted) did not always have the type of journalistic origin described by Ravelhofer. The genre had its own antecedents in Elizabethan translations of Classical and Continental plays that were produced by figures like Mary Sidney Herbert, the Countess of Pembroke, whose *Tragedie of Antonie* (1592–4), a translation of a French contemporary play on the life of Cleopatra, was the first play in English to be published by a woman. It is Sidney's female authorship which provided a model for Elizabeth Cary's *The Tragedy of Mariam* (1613) and which inspired her niece, Mary Sidney Wroth, to write 'Loves Victorie' (c. 1621), a pastoral drama which survives in two manuscript copies. Even though male playwrights like Samuel Daniel, William Alexander and Fulke Greville (all members of the Sidney circle) also produced closet drama, the genre is, for modern critics, closely allied with the issue of women's writing and the female patronage of the arts that flourished in the Sidney family circle and at the court of Anna of Denmark.

Because of the smallness of the dramatic corpus and the emphasis that is often given to Mary Sidney Herbert's Elizabethan *Antonie*, there is not a lot of criticism of Jacobean closet drama that is not specifically focussed either on the Sidney circle or on Elizabeth Cary's *Mariam*, and what there is tends to come in little snippets that form part of a larger argument. A good example of this tendency is Albert H. Tricomi's *Anti-court Drama in England, 1603–1642* (1989), which includes a brief chapter on 'The Not-So-Closeted Tragedies of Daniel and Greville'. Tricomi argues that *Philotas*, the tragedy Daniel revised in 1604, and *Mustapha*, which Greville revised in 1609, in their 'tones of disillusionment and in their concerns with the poisoned relationship between sovereign and subject, [...] manifest strong links to the political tragedies of the learned professional dramatists, Jonson and Chapman'.[127] Tricomi thus draws these political closet tragedies into the orbit of the public theatre, representing the choice of genre as a way of shielding the authors' 'profound indictment of Jacobean political life' from the wrath of the authorities.[128]

Whereas for male playwrights, the choice of closet drama as a dramatic genre is understood as a politic choice to evade censorship, for female playwrights closet drama, as feminist critics have pointed out, represented the only available option of dramatic expression. In a seminal article, '"Profane Stoical Paradoxes": *The Tragedie of Mariam* and Sidnean Closet Drama' (1994), Marta Straznicky furthermore distinguishes between the male-centered closet dramas of Daniel, Alexander and Greville, which portray a stoic ethic in which power is the result of self-conquest and which tended to comment on contemporary politics, and the female-centered plays of Mary Sidney Herbert and Daniel. For Straznicky, the key difference 'between the male-centered and female-centered closet dramas is in the moral value of female characters: while in the former, females are generally the embodiments of unbridled passions, in the latter they exemplify complete self-control'.[129] It is this new female-centred stoicism that *Mariam* draws on, staging 'the reorientation of female desire from earthly to spiritual goods and fashion[ing] this reorientation as the prerequisite for female heroism'. But whereas Cary's female-centred predecessors 'reshaped the masculine stoic ethic into an acceptably depoliticized model of female heroism, *The Tragedie of Mariam* reappropriates for the disempowered female the political power of stoic heroism as an effective means of redress'.[130] Straznicky thus posits Cary's play as the culmination of the Sidnean closet dramas and their preoccupation with stoic ideals of heroism.

A broader view of Cary and women's closet drama more widely
is provided by S. P. Cerasano and Marion Wynne-Davies's *Readings in
Renaissance Women's Drama* (1998), which brings together eight new
and thirteen reprinted essays that represent the state of the field in
the 1980s and 1990s. An extract from Nancy Cotton's *Women Playwrights in England, c. 1363–1759* (1980) traces the evolution of the genre
from Katherine of Sutton's religious plays in the fourteenth century
through to Margaret Cavendish, the Duchess of Newcastle's plays in the
Restoration. Leeds Barroll narrows the focus to the court of Anna of
Denmark, whose household, which intersected with the Sidney circle
and included Lady Mary Wroth, was a hub of cultural and dramatic
activity in the Jacobean period. An extract from Elaine V. Beilin's important *Redeeming Eve: Women Writers of the English Renaissance* (1987) puts
the spotlight on Elizabeth Cary's *Mariam*. Beilin explains that 'Cary
structures the play to make Mariam's conflict between obedience to
and rebellion against Herod's authority the central concern', so that the
play's concentration on female insubordination and self-expression can
be seen to double the playwright's own will to express herself.[131] This
view is echoed by Margaret Ferguson, who also sees the play as giving
voice to both Mariam's and Cary's resistance to the patriarchal order: for
her, the problem addressed by the play 'has to do not only with female
speech in general but also with the play's own mode of material existence, indeed, its *right* to exist in the world'.[132] Barbara Kiefer Lewalski,
meanwhile, sets Cary's choice of the genre in the context of closet plays
written by Mary Sidney Herbert, Samuel Daniel and Fulke Greville: in
her reading, Cary uses the genre like her male peers as 'a recognized
vehicle for the exploration of dangerous political topics'.[133] By contrast,
Lady Mary Wroth's 'Loves Victorie' is read by Margaret Anne McLaren
as a psychological drama of courtship which approaches sexual relationships obliquely and which reflects 'the special experience of a woman
writing in Jacobean England'.[134]

Karen Raber's *Dramatic Difference: Gender, Class and Genre in the Early
Modern Closet Drama* (2001), a book with an overt feminist agenda, is
an excellent complement to the Cerasano/Wynne-Davies collection and
represents the fullest modern discussion of the genre, covering both
male and female dramatists. For Raber,

■ closet drama offered early modern writers of both sexes the opportunity to interrogate their culture's investment in drama and performance.
For women writers, closet drama offered more: a form of dramatic writing
that allowed their participation in the discourses of dramatic representation, but a form that also, through its distance from the stage and other
public domains of theatre, allowed reflection on women's tenuous and
marginal relationship to theatrical domains.[135] □

Furthermore, the genre is distinctive and important because of its class associations: based in the aristocratic household, closet drama exposes tensions between public and private modes of writing and between court and theatre. As presented by Raber, the genre's liminality, its blurring of boundaries between the household and public life, is what made it such a powerful tool in the hands of aristocratic women, who used it to interrogate their class and individual identities. The genre, which Raber shows to have been well established by the time Mary Sidney Herbert appropriated it in the 1590s, is 'politically, culturally, and socially dynamic', registering 'historical shifts in the construction of gender and class difference' and 'provid[ing] a form for examining – and in some cases intervening in – the evolution of ideology'.[136]

What makes Raber's study so useful is the fact that in order to argue her case about the genre's ideological interventions in debates about the theatre, gender and class, she sets female and male, as well as public and private playwrights side-by-side. In a chapter on Fulke Greville, Raber contrasts Sidney's successful manipulation of the structures that link domestic and political life in *Antonie* with Greville's inability to achieve the same impact: Greville's 'status, his gender, and his lack of domestic ties place him outside the networks that made Sidney's success possible' and where, 'for Mary Sidney, the family is a source of strength and authority', 'for Greville it is in contrast the locus of failure, distortion, and corruption'.[137] While for men, closet drama provides only a 'fantasy of successful literary intervention in politics', for women writers like Elizabeth Cary, the genre made possible a critique of the constraints on women's speech. In *Mariam*, Cary builds on the plays of her Sidnean predecessors to create a tragedy which responds to James I's claims to absolute authority through the depiction of the despotic and paternalistic Herod, who is defied by a heroine who refuses to perform. For Raber, this refusal is typical of the genre: closet drama constructs 'dramatic identities that resist, in various ways, performance and theater' creating a new form of 'closeted identity' which she associates with the bourgeois self under construction in the period.[138] In Raber's book, closet drama is not merely the only option available to the woman dramatist: it engages with contemporary politics, domesticity, the construction of gender, identity and the body in ways that demand the attention of future researchers.

CHAPTER SIX

Body and Race Scholarship

Bodies

'Body scholarship', an approach to texts that focuses on their representation of the human body, is a way of looking at the drama which has had a significant impact on the discipline and which originated in studies of the medieval body, medical discourses and anatomical treatises that did not, at their inception, have the analysis of Jacobean drama as their aim. The field is sometimes also referred to as 'historical phenomenology', which refers to a way of looking at representations of the body in early modern texts which 'reconstruct[s] early modern thinking about self-experience, so that interpreters of literature can interpret representations of the interior life with greater sophistication'. The goal of this scholarship is not to create 'rigid and static taxonomies for explaining human personhood', but rather to bring an understanding of early modern conceptualisations of the body to literary analysis of texts that communicate the experience of embodiment, and the relationship between the corporeal grounding of the soul and the emotions, in the early modern period.[1] The choice of specific scientific discourses to explicate the feeling of embodiment in the early modern period, as we will see, has a significant impact on the feelings and embodiment stipulated: whereas Thomas Laqueur's study of Galenic medicine in the early modern period results in an understanding of the body that challenges the modern conception of sexual difference, the anatomies studied by Jonathan Sawday condition his notion of the body's competition with the soul. Meanwhile, the Galen-influenced medical and midwifery texts Gail Kern Paster analyses underpin her understanding of the early modern body as governed by humours that determine the corporeal expression of emotions.

Mikhail Bakhtin's *Rabelais and His World*, an analysis of folk humour in the Middle Ages and the early modern period, pre-dates the historical phenomenology whose thinking it informs: it was first submitted as a thesis in 1940 but did not have an impact on Anglo-Saxon early modern studies till the publication of its English translation in 1968. Since then, it has become hugely influential and has, as mediated by Peter Stallybrass and Allon White in *The Politics and Poetics of Transgression* (1986), altered the way in which we look at early modern bodies and culture.[2] In his Introduction, Bakhtin describes laughter and carnival festivities and rituals, with their inversions of and liberation from the established order, as a kind of safety-valve that allowed that order to re-establish itself while giving an outlet to disruptive forces within society within 'the popular sphere of the marketplace'.[3] In a society in which rank was normally insisted on, carnival festivities created an exceptional sphere of equality. Bakhtin describes carnival as a spectacle in which everyone participates 'because its very idea embraces all the people'.[4] The logic that rules carnival is that of the 'inside out', 'of the "turnabout", of a continual shifting from top to bottom, from front to rear, of numerous parodies and travesties, humiliations, profanations, comic crownings and uncrownings'. The festive laughter provoked by carnival is ambivalent, for while it is shared by and directed at everyone, including those who laugh, it is also 'gay, triumphant, and at the same time mocking, deriding. It asserts and denies, it buries and revives'.[5]

Festive laughter, Bakhtin goes on to explain, finds its focus in what he terms 'the material bodily principle', which is essential to 'grotesque realism'.[6] The degradation of the body that is part of carnivalesque inversion is not destructive but regenerative and life-affirming. Carnival celebrates the grotesque body, which Bakhtin describes in the following influential terms:

■ [T]he grotesque body is not [...] a closed, completed unit; it is unfinished, outgrows itself, transgresses its own limits. The stress is laid on those parts of the body that are open to the outside world, that is, the parts through which the world enters the body or emerges from it, or through which the body itself goes out to meet the world. This means that the emphasis is on the apertures or the convexities, or on various ramifications and offshoots: the open mouth, the genital organs, the breasts, the phallus, the potbelly, the nose. The body discloses its essence as a principle of growth which exceeds its own limits only in copulation, pregnancy, childbirth, the throes of death, eating, drinking, or defecation. This is the ever unfinished, ever creating body.[7] □

Bakhtin argues that this grotesque body, associated with medieval festivities and a pre-modern regime, increasingly had to make way for a more recognisably modern conceptualisation of the body as closed. The closed, 'classical' body, Bakhtin explains in his chapter on the grotesque image of the body, is no longer a communal body, no longer focussed on the lower bodily strata. Instead, it is an individual body that is 'finished', clearly delineated and self-sufficient.[8] It does not celebrate rebirth and excess but connotes death and Lenten restraint.

Bakhtin's distinction between Carnival and Lent, the grotesque and the classical body, has become central to early modern studies. His influence is evident in Thomas Laqueur's *Making Sex: Body and Gender from the Greeks to Freud* (1990). This seminal work caused a major paradigm shift in late twentieth-century perceptions of early modern representations of the body, unsettling the modern assumption that the sexed body is an ahistorical 'fact'. Laqueur's revisionary grand narrative has since then been challenged, including by the most recent generation of 'body critics' such as Valerie Traub, Gianna Pomata and Maurizio Calbi,[9] but it is used productively even by these critics and continues to have a palpable effect on our understanding of the gendering/sexing of bodies on the Jacobean stage. Put simply, what Laqueur's research reveals are two things that fundamentally affect the early modern conception of the gendered bodies: firstly, that it was a common belief that women must have an orgasm in order to conceive; secondly, that female and male anatomies were thought to be essentially the same, different only in degree rather than kind. This latter conceptualisation of the human body is described by Laqueur as the 'one-sex model', a way of looking at anatomical sexual difference that derived its principles from Aristotle and Galen. The 'one-sex model' was only replaced by the modern 'two-sex model', in which male bodies and female bodies are conceptualised as essentially different, during the Enlightenment. This reconceptualisation served a moral, cultural and political purpose: from the eighteenth century onwards, the dominant view has been 'that there are two stable, incommensurable, opposite sexes and that the political, economic, and cultural lives of men and women, their gender roles, are somehow based on these "facts"'.[10] Laqueur's study powerfully exposes the political foundation of science, which rationalises and legitimises 'distinctions not only of sex but also of race and class, to the disadvantage of the powerless'.[11] In highlighting this, the book itself constitutes a political intervention.

What must interest students of Jacobean drama is Laqueur's stipulation that the pre-Enlightenment conception of the sexed body saw it as secondary (he refers to it as an *epiphenomenon*, an additional feature), 'while *gender*, what we would take to be a cultural category, was primary or "real"'. As a consequence, 'it was precisely when talk seemed to be most directly about the biology of two sexes that it was most embedded in the politics of gender, in culture. To be a man or a woman was to hold a social rank, a place in society, to assume a cultural role, not to *be* organically one or the other of two incommensurable sexes'.[12] In his second chapter, Laqueur shows how this view of the body was reflected in what anatomists *saw* when they looked at male and female genitalia. Galen and his followers saw female anatomy as an inversion, and hence less perfect, version of male anatomy; women 'have exactly the same organs but in exactly the wrong places': the ovaries correspond to the testes, the womb to the scrotum, the vagina to the penis.[13] Sexual difference itself was seen as porous and mutable: there are 'hirsute, viral women – the virago – who are too hot to procreate and are as bold as men; and there are weak, effeminate men, too cold to procreate and perhaps even womanly in wanting to be penetrated'.[14] A change in the body temperature could even lead to a woman's transformation into a man (as her genitalia were pushed outward by her masculine heat). Sex, within this system of belief, was 'a shaky foundation' for social differentiation. 'Changes in corporeal structures [...] could push a body easily from one juridical category (female) to another (male). These categories were based on gender distinctions – active/passive, hot/cold, formed/unformed, informing/formable – of which an external or an internal penis was only the diagnostic sign.'[15] What Laqueur's work thus reveals is how precariously the seemingly rigid gender hierarchy of early modern Europe was based on a physiological distinction between men and women that was anything but absolute.

Physiological distinctions are also the subject of Jonathan Sawday's *The Body Emblazoned: Dissection and the Human Body in Renaissance Culture* (1995), which considers the anatomic conceptualisation of the human body across early modern Europe and a whole variety of artistic forms, from art to poetry to architecture. Sawday, who critiques Laqueur's 'one-sex' model for taking the metaphorical language of early modern scientific discourse too literally,[16] shares Laqueur's fascination with early modern anatomy. He sees early modern culture as 'a culture of dissection' in which the arts no less than other forms of social and intellectual life were governed by the logic of division and anatomisation and in which science in the modern sense was yet to emerge.[17] For him, the early modern period is a moment of paradigmatic change from a body which, while in constant struggle with it, could not be imagined separately from its soul, to a vision of the human body as a soulless machine. According to Sawday, this shift, which took its full effect towards the end of the seventeenth century, had profound implications for the ways in which the body could be invoked for political and ideological uses: whereas the conception of body and soul as indivisible had authorised metaphors of the body politic, the body as a representation of hierarchical power and monarchical authority, such metaphorical uses of the body could not survive the objectification of the mechanical body.

Of particular relevance to students of Jacobean drama is the early modern conception of the body as inextricably connected with the self and the soul, which found widespread expression in what Sawday calls the '"fashion" for anatomy in the Renaissance'.[18] Sawday is interested in the two-way exchange between early modern anatomists and early modern culture. His readings of key texts which include *Coriolanus* and

The Atheist's Tragedy show how anatomy pervades early modern literature, including the male Petrarchan lover's masochistic fantasy of anatomical surrender to his cruel mistress, the homosocial poetic fashion for 'emblazoning' and thus erotically dissecting the female body, and the plays of Shakespeare and his contemporaries. As Hillary M. Nunn has since shown in *Staging Anatomies: Dissection and Spectacle in Early Stuart Tragedy* (2005), anatomical spectacles and metaphors are in fact widespread in a whole range of Jacobean plays. Playwrights, poets and painters all seem to have used the language of anatomy to express ideas about the human body as much as anatomists relied on rhetorical tropes gleaned from poetry to describe what they saw.

For Sawday, a particularly important intersection of art, culture and anatomy is embodied in the figure of Medusa, who 'stands for fear of interiority; more often than not, a specifically male fear of the female interior',[19] and whose myth 'is immediately appropriate to any description of the potentially transgressive gaze of the subject who studies his or her own bodily interior'.[20] Because of the taboos surrounding the violation of the dead human body, it was the corpses of executed criminals that were used for anatomical research, where the posthumous dissection was seen as an extension of the punishment. Both the execution and the anatomisation were like 'two acts in a single drama' performed in front of an audience eager for spectacle.[21] The opening up of the criminal's body in an anatomical theatre had the effect of 'feminising' it, rendering it an alien region, a Bakhtinian grotesque body to be investigated, colonised and dominated by an implicitly male gaze. No wonder then, that opening up a female body, whether figuratively or literally, was an act with particularly strong ideological implications: it was 'a voyage of scientific discovery, but it was also to trace [...] the rebellious nature of womankind'.[22] In the anatomy theatres' iconographic representations of Adam and Eve, the reason for the need to control rebellious womankind was invoked in the very place in which the anatomists' dissection of female bodies revealed – and in revealing, mastered – their monstrous, grotesque, quasi-autonomous wombs 'which lurked, like [Spenser's] Acrasia in her bower, ready to transform heroic masculine rigour into luxurious sensual excess'.[23]

Like Sawday, Gail Kern Paster, in *The Body Embarrassed: Drama and the Disciplines of Shame in Early Modern England* (1993), picks up on Bakhtin's grotesque body and Laqueur's account of Galenic medicine to look at the body as described by early modern scientists and artists. But where Sawday focuses on anatomy, Paster concentrates on 'humoral theory, a system of explanation of the body's composition and functioning which held sway for centuries from the classical period until the start of a slow and incomplete disintegraton in the seventeenth century'.[24] This she finds expressed in key medical treatises, late seventeenth-century midwifery manuals, conduct books, jest books and in a broad range of Jacobean plays. Paster brings a complex and sophisticated combination of modern theoretical approaches, including Lacanian psychoanalysis, feminism and New Historicist methodologies, to bear on these texts. In her readings, she pays especially close attention to moments that reveal the operations of shame as a control mechanism that seeks to regulate bodily functions and the associated expressions of emotion. More often than not, the body that is thus embarrassed is female: it is the Bakhtinian grotesqueness of female menstruation, lactation and urination that is the most obsessively regulated in patriarchal early modern culture and that stands at the centre of Paster's analysis.

The early modern body, in Paster's description, is a Galenic body that is governed by the four humours of blood, phlegm, choler (yellow bile) and black bile – 'real' bodily fluids that had to be kept in a state of balance for the body and the associated emotions to be in a state of health. It is a porous, semi-permeable body, 'able to be influenced by the immediate environment' and subject to changes according to 'such variables as age and gender', the weather (which influenced body temperature, with a hotter body more soluble and male and a cooler body more sluggish and female) or even the intake of food and air.[25] The excretions and emissions that Bakhtin had seen as grotesque are necessary for the humoural body to regulate itself by releasing excessive vapours, internal winds and fluids.

Emotions, which we habitually psychologise and often conceive of as separate from physiological processes, are within humoural theory inextricably connected to the body and its humoural dynamic and imbalances. Thus attached to the body, emotions are quite detached from the mind: the internal organs which regulate the humours have an 'agency, purposiveness, and plenitude to which the subject's own will is often decidedly irrelevant'.[26] Among these emotions, shame holds pride of place in Paster's book because it is crucial to the influential contention by Norbert Elias, a cultural historian, that the civilising process, which led to the evolution of a bourgeois subject, was contingent on an expansion of the threshold of shame in the period. This 'emergent ideology of bodily refinement and exquisite self-mastery' thus stood in direct contradiction to the need for humoural evacuation and, in particular, to the intrinsic 'leakiness' of the female body.[27] Shame, the emotion resulting from this contradiction, while deeply corporeal, is also a social and even theatrical emotion, since it hinges on the perception of the self as scrutinised by an audience.

Unlike the other body critics discussed here, Paster actually concentrates her literary analyses on Jacobean plays in particular. She takes as her starting-point the incontinent and embarrassed 'leaky' women in Jonson's *Bartholomew Fair* and Middleton's *Chaste Maid in*

Cheapside. Like a number of proverbs, emblems and treatises, these plays 'construct the female body as effluent, overproductive, out of control'.[28] What is noteworthy in these plays is the way 'biological need' is represented 'as engendered joke': only women, the weaker vessels, were represented as leaky, subject to incontinence of bladder and sexuality.[29] Paster also provocatively analyses blood, excrement, and the linked processes of birth and breastfeeding in a number of Jacobean plays. While blood in itself is not an embarrassing fluid, its gendered manifestation as menstruation is demonised as bodily waste and bleeding; like 'the other varieties of female incontinence – sexual, urinary, linguistic', it is constructed as an effect of an embarrassing lack of self-mastery.[30] When, at the end of *The Changeling*, blood flows into the sewer, this is a blood-letting of Beatrice-Joanna's superfluous, diseased blood, and for Paster the bleeding male bodies in Shakespeare's Roman plays also express an anxiety about these bodies' resemblance to leaky women. The scatological quarrel between Face and Subtle in *The Alchemist*, on the other hand, is considered against the background of the enemas to which children were routinely subjected. Finally, Paster reads the images of wet-nursing and/or weaning in *The Winter's Tale*, *Antony and Cleopatra* and *The Witch of Edmonton* as expressions of 'ambivalent cultural fantasies of rejection and return'.[31] Paster's book is thus a prime example of how historical phenomenology can be utilised to illuminate Jacobean drama. No wonder that her work has had a pervasive influence, affecting not only gender studies, but also the study of race in early modern drama.

Race, ethnicity and Islam: Othello, Cleopatra and beyond

The desire, within mainstream Shakespeare studies, to understand the racial politics of *Othello*, *Antony and Cleopatra*, *Cymbeline* and *The Tempest* has had a surprisingly positive effect on the study of Jacobean drama, for it has opened up an increasingly animated debate around the representation of race, non-Christian religion (mostly focussed on Islam) and ethnicity in a whole range of early modern dramatic texts. Most of these are Jacobean and engage specifically with the Jacobean political context and the accounts of the New World that were circulated and published in the period. The most important of these travel narratives and other early modern non-dramatic texts concerned with racial difference are helpfully anthologised in Ania Loomba and Jonathan Burton's *Race in Early Modern England: A Documentary Companion* (2007), an anthology whose introduction provides an excellent overview of the field and is a good place to start one's research.[32]

The debate about the significance of Othello's race and hence about the perception of blackness in Jacobean England was kick-started in 1967 by G. K. Hunter's influential lecture 'Othello and Colour Prejudice'. Hunter argues that by producing 'a daring theatrical novelty – a black hero for a white community', Shakespeare deliberately thwarts audience expectations when the stereotypical 'Moor' they are expecting to see – a stereotype built up through the identification of Africans with either Cain or Ham in Biblical tradition – turns out to be not only a Christian but a defender of Christendom, to boot.[33] He contextualises this insight by explaining that the dominant view of 'Moors' as barbarous was challenged by alternative travel narratives that stressed the natural innocence of non-white races. Shakespeare's tragedy, then, can be seen to move from one end of this axis to the other: Othello starts out as the natural innocent and ends up fulfilling audience expectations when he 'becomes what Iago and the society to which *we* belong assumes him to be'.[34] In Hunter's reading, the audience is thus crucially implicated in the creation of Othello as a fulfilment of their predictions about the correspondence of outward and inward 'blackness'. The play, however, ends not so much in a confirmation of the stereotypical association of blackness with sinfulness as in the recognition that, in Othello's remorse and suicide, 'the Christian reality reasserts its superior position over the pagan appearance'.[35] Blackness, for Hunter, is largely an iconographic device (a way of indexing sinfulness) and a means of manipulating and challenging the early modern and, indeed, the modern audience's assumption of Africans' sinfulness.

Anthony Gerard Barthelemy's *Black Face Maligned Race: The Representation of Blacks in English Drama from Shakespeare to Southerne* (1987) picks up on Hunter's attempt to gain a better understanding of the term 'Moor' and the prejudices of an early modern audience and creates a typology of most of the English dramatic texts featuring a black character. Biblical tradition, Barthelemy explains, identified the colour white with salvation and black with damnation and took the story of Noah's sinful son Ham as a foundation myth explaining the origin of African races, which were seen as intrinsically sinful, bestial and lustful. Even though there is evidence that 'Black Africans probably first arrived in England in 1554', no distinction was commonly made between different African races and non-Christian religions. The word 'Moor' was used for many different races and religions, as it could signify 'non-black Muslim, black Christian, or black Muslim. The only certainty a reader has when he sees the word is that the person referred to is not a European Christian'.[36] Because Islam represented both a religious and a military threat, 'Moor' furthermore became an 'economical way of rendering the blackness of these Islamic enemies of Christianity', whatever their actual skin colour or racial origin – hence the 'popularity of the term *white Moor*', which

also had the effect of uncoupling, to some extent, the automatic association of the word 'Moor' with black skin.[37]

In the drama, Barthelemy finds that the characterisation of black
characters is largely stereotypical. His methodology is to identify dramatic texts that contain black characters and to expose the ways in
which these figures conform to prevailing stereotypes. Jonson's *Masque
of Blackness*, for example, 'really is a play about salvation [...] and
blackness really does signify separation from grace, in this case the sav-
ing grace of James I'.[38] Speaking of all masques featuring black characters, he explains that '[i]n the world of the masque, to be black is
to be denied everything that the learned tradition has canonized. It
is to be outside an imitation heaven, outside the Elysian Fields. To be
included requires being washed white, but that is impossible except
for those who can invoke the privileges of masking'.[39] Much the same
is true of the plays Barthelemy discusses, in which he finds that 'the
overwhelming majority of black Moors [...] endorsed, represented, or
were evil'.[40] The 'nonvillainous Moors' Barthelemy lists as precursors
and successors of Othello do not really alter the stereotype, since '[b]y
demonstrating virtue, these few honest Moors offer further valida-
tion of the more common, harmful, and denigrating representations
of black Moors because they prove that it is possible to resist the call of
evil, though most unusual'.[41] It is only in the Lord Mayors' Pageants
staged between 1585 and 1692 that Barthelemy finds a variation on
the theme, for here 'the economics of colonialism play an essential role'
for the first time.[42] Sponsored by rich merchants, these civic pageants
contained mute black figures in exotic costume whose emblematic role
was in part to 'increase the air of extravagance surrounding a particular pageant car' and in part to 'serve as visible reminders of British
success in trade and exploration'.[43] These characters therefore can be
seen to 'endorse ideas upon which British colonialism was founded and
expanded'.[44]

For his reading of *Othello*, Barthelemy follows Hunter by reading
Othello's race not within such a proto-colonialist context but against the
background of common expectations about stage Moors. Shakespeare
distributes the traditional attributes of the black man (jealousy, lascivi-
ousness, villainy) among white characters. The play, for Barthelemy,
tracks Othello's movement towards the stereotype, until he finally identifies himself with the devil. The audience's 'sympathy for Othello [...]
is sympathy for his struggle to escape his fate, not sympathy for what
he is fated to be'.[45] Shakespeare may have been manipulating the stereotype, but 'Othello remains identifiable as a version of that type'.[46] Barthelemy is far less willing than Hunter, it seems, to see Shakespeare's
play as a questioning of the automatic association of blackness with
evil, and the spectators in his view remain secure in their sense of what

Othello is fated to be. Only the hero is allowed to entertain, for a little while, the hope that he may not be a stereotype after all.

Ania Loomba's *Gender, Race, Renaissance Drama* (1989) picks *Othello* up once more and adds gender, class and the contemporary Indian classroom to the equation. For her, the play has to be made sense of against a background of wife battering in India's urban areas and a postcolonial heritage. In her work, *Antony and Cleopatra* becomes a central text for postcolonial investigation: Cleopatra is considered a threat not only because of her theatricality and position of power, but also because she 'is the non-European, the outsider, the white man's ultimate "other"', who 'embodies all the overlapping stereotypes of femininity and non-Europeans common in the language of colonialism'.[47] *The Tempest*, too, is considered as a play in which colonial relations are played out. Alongside these Shakespearean texts, all the 'big' Jacobean tragedies, from *The Duchess of Malfi* and *The White Devil* to *Women Beware Women* and *The Changeling*, are also analysed for their relevance to the study of English literature in an India for which these texts have become part of the cultural heritage. In all these plays, 'women who are the targets of violence [...] threaten the class and race limits of patriarchal societies *through their wayward sexuality*' and suffer punishment for this.[48] Through her analysis of these tragedies, Loomba aims to show how the 'processes by which women and black people are constructed as the "others" of white patriarchal society are similar and connected, and [how] they also reflect upon other sorts of exclusion such as that based on class'.[49] While these 'others' are thus constructed by patriarchy, they are also 'subversive of this authority': stereotypes, in her view, are no more monolithic than dominant discourses ever are, and stereotyped figures 'are not entirely contained, or harnessed by and useful to, those who produce them'.[50] Influenced by materialist and feminist criticism of the mid-1980s, as well as by the postcolonial theories of Franz Fanon and Edward Said, Loomba thus brings to the field a sense of the potentially subversive dynamism of racial and gender stereotyping and, concomitantly, a sense of political agency that goes beyond the Jacobean texts to address the contemporary world.

It is Loomba's rebellion against 'institutionalised readings of Renaissance tragedy' and her outrage at the way Jacobean drama seems to thrive on the oppression of 'others' which still lends her study an irresistible energy. In an important chapter on sexuality and racial difference, Loomba attacks standard readings of *Othello* which negate the effects of race and gender to turn the play into a tragedy of love. She historicises the racism and misogyny inherent in these readings, which she traces back to early modern attitudes while being careful to distinguish between different histories of racism in particular. For Loomba, 'Othello moves from being a colonised subject existing on the terms of white Venetian society and trying to internalise its ideology, towards being marginalised, outcast and alienated from it in every way, until he occupies his "true" position as its other'. Once he has reached that position, he becomes a near schizophrenic hero whose last speech expresses his split identity – he becomes simultaneously the Christian and the Infidel, the Venetian and the Turk, the keeper of the State and its opponent. At the same time, Desdemona passes from being his ally who would guarantee his white status to becoming his sexual and racial 'other'. She, too, is a split, inconsistent subject and is the 'other' to Othello and to the Venetian patriarchy. 'The "central conflict" of the play then, if we must locate one, is [...] between the racism of a white patriarchy and the threat posed to it by both a black man and a white woman'.[51] Since this black man and white woman are themselves caught up in a web of sexual and racial tension, with Desdemona's status veering from the privilege of whiteness to her oppression as a woman, the result is a far more complex and dynamic picture of the play than that outlined by Loomba's predecessors. Importantly, too, 'race' no longer refers simply to blackness but is a lens through which whiteness, too, may be analysed.

Loomba's dual attention to race and gender left its mark on the race criticism of the 1990s, which saw the publication of Margo Hendricks and Patricia Parker's collection of essays *Women, 'Race,' and Writing in the Early Modern Period* (1994) and Kim F. Hall's *Things of Darkness: Economies of Race and Gender in Early Modern England* (1995). Together, these two books push forward Loomba's agenda of studying racial and sexual oppression as different but interrelated. In the Hendricks/Parker collection, essays by Lynda Boose and Jyotsna Singh revisit the representation of race and gender in *Othello*, and, in Boose's essay, link this to the unrepresentability of the racial status of Cleopatra: while early modern plays can imagine the coupling of a white woman with a black man, the opposite alignment of race and gender remains unrepresentable. Singh's essay, on the other hand, attacks 'Western feminist engagements with race which, in trying to chart the complexities of the relation between race and gender oppressions, implicitly *collapse* the categories of difference by assuming a common history of marginalization'.[52] Her influential article is best read in tandem with Karen Newman's *Fashioning Femininity* (see pp. 126–9), which she identifies as representative of such feminist work.

Kim Hall's book, on the other hand, shares Loomba's sense of political activism. Hall also follows Loomba in demonstrating how blackness and whiteness stand in a binary opposition constructed by mutually reinforcing tropes: there are marvellous chapters here on jewellery, paintings, travel narratives and dark ladies in Petrarchan sonnets. As a black feminist scholar, Hall's agenda is both an investigation of early modern representations of Africa and Africans and a rethinking of black feminist methodology. The latter is the subject of her provocative concluding chapter in which she reflects on the 'almost mutual exclusion of Renaissance studies and black feminist criticism'.[53] There, she argues against reading early modern references to race as embedded in a European aesthetic tradition. Instead, she insists that darkness and lightness are not simple markers of aesthetic or moral categories but 'became in the early modern period the conduit through which the English began to formulate the notions of "self" and "other" so well known in Anglo-American racial discourses'.[54] It is therefore wrong to question 'the viability of "race" as a term in cultural or literary studies' and to gloss over the racism of early modern discourses, which are marked by cultural anxieties 'about complexion, miscegenation, control of women, and, above all, "Englishness"'.[55] To indulge in 'the luxury of *not* thinking about race' results in a critical practice that 'maintain[s] white privilege in Renaissance studies' and is therefore itself racist.[56] Hall's readings repeatedly and assertively *resist*: her methodology uses traditional literary criticism and New Historicist methodology while 'refus[ing] to accept both the authority of the writers [she] work[s] with and [...] resist[ing] the hegemony of white male knowledge in the academy'.[57]

The context in which Hall sets her investigation of 'tropes of blackness' is that of the English connection 'to the traffic in slaves and the opening of heretofore unknown sections of Africa', which began in the 1550s.[58] James I's creation of the Company of Adventurers of London Trading into Parts of Africa in 1618 played an important part in English competition 'for the crucial rights to the slave trade that would provide the necessary labor to buttress their other colonial ambitions' in the later seventeenth century.[59] In travel narratives such as Hakluyt's *Principal Nagivations* (1589), which attempt to inscribe order on native cultures, such order is organised according to race and gender, with the containment of women emerging as one of the central criteria according to which alien cultures were judged. Against the background of James' I's desire to bring England, Scotland and Wales together into a single political entity/union/marriage, women's bodies in the drama

> ■ become the site of a struggle between, on the one hand, the need for both colonial trade and cultural assimilation through union and, on the other, the desire for well-recognized boundaries between self and other. Many Jacobean plays generally indict interracial or 'racialized' couplings in ways that very often become a castigation of the female as well as an expression of attitudes about race.[60] □

The plays Hall concentrates on are *The Tempest* and *Antony and Cleopatra*, which she reads alongside Jonson's masques of *Blackness* and *Beauty* and

Webster's *The Devil's Law-Case*. What is important about Hall's treatment of these plays is the way she situates them within the Jacobean court and its fascination with blackness, marriage and colonial expansion. In a court where all women were 'black' because in a position of intrinsic inferiority, women themselves, as Hall shows through her analysis of the figure of Cleopatra in the poems and plays of Jacobean women authors, used blackness and the aesthetics of white beauty as a way of 'strengthen[ing] their own rhetorical and social positions at the expense of more marginalized groups'.[61]

Twenty-first-century race criticism: new avenues

Since the turn of the millennium, the study of race has diversified and some of the key assumptions underpinning the work of earlier race critics have been challenged. Mary Floyd-Wilson's *English Ethnicity and Race in Early Modern Drama* (2003) is a book which controversially runs counter to the principles established by Hall, Loomba and Barthelemy. Influenced by Gail Paster's work on the humoural body, Floyd-Wilson uses the framework of early modern 'ethnological geo-humoralism',[62] an explanation of racial difference as an effect of the humoural body's geographical origin, to re-interpret plays by Marlowe, Shakespeare and Jonson that fashion English ethnicity in relation to racial 'others'. Floyd-Wilson takes issue with her predecessors' use of the biblical figure of Ham as a way of explaining the association of blackness with sinfulness and is dissatisfied with their reliance on the opposition between black and white. Instead, she concentrates on the way classical, medieval and early modern texts on regional identities work with a classical tripartite scheme in which Africa is located in the South, England in the North, and Greece and Rome lie in the privileged central temperate zone. Southern and Northern locations and racial/ethnic identities are thus decentred, underprivileged and considered barbarous. The extreme climates of the North and South, Floyd-Wilson argues, are thought to influence the inhabitants of these zones: the martial prowess of the Scythians in the North and the wisdom and spirituality of the Ethiopians in the South are seen as the effect of their geographical/climatic location. Because of a 'logic of inversion', she explains, 'the white northerner and the black southerner' are furthermore fixed 'in an interdependent relationship: if the southerner is hot and dry, then the northerner must be cold and moist; if the southerner is weak and wise, the northerner must be strong and witless'.[63]

According to Floyd-Wilson, the English belief in such 'geographical determinism' was at the heart of their perception of themselves as intrinsically intemperate in their bodies and of their culture as 'borrowed and belated'.[64] No wonder, then, that a great effort went into revising such an unflattering model, leading to a conceptual shift that saw the reorganisation of 'early modern ethnology along newly nationalist lines', which incidentally also facilitated the Atlantic slave trade.[65] The shift is registered in *Othello*, where Desdemona's classical humoural perception of Othello's race is juxtaposed with and defeated by Iago's 'nascent racialism'.[66] Gradually 'the classical tripartite structure is translated into an English binary of the northern self and the southern Other'.[67] Eventually, this new English ethnic identity was consolidated by the rejection of the belief in the Trojan genealogy of Britons (whereby Brut, the son of Aeneas, was seen as the founder of Britain) in favour of William Camden's account of how 'the English people's native barbarism had been purged by the Roman conquest'.[68] Ethnic barbarism is here acknowledged and embraced at the same moment as it is denied.

In her readings of *Cymbeline* and *The Masque of Blackness*, Floyd-Wilson argues that the perception of English identity as 'peculiar' and 'pure' in the texts of William Camden and Richard Verstegan, who embraced English barbarism, combined with the Union of England and Scotland under King James to create complex ethnological fantasies of origin. *Blackness*, for instance, 'stages a mythopoetic solution to the English fear that uniting with its northern neighbor would move England further from the origins of civilization and the civility of temperance'.[69] What the masque achieves 'may not be the deferred transformation of the Ethiopians' skin' – which is what Barthelemy's interpretation had emphasised – 'but the presentation of a genealogy of people who transmitted southern wisdom and culture to a region [James's Scotland] that eventually granted them external whiteness'. Through the agency of the sun/the Jacobean government, the Ethiopians' 'inner qualities of wisdom, civility, piety, constancy, and a contemplative nature' are incorporated in white Britannia.[70]

Repeatedly, in this way, Floyd-Wilson turns her attention away from blackness and the deeply engrained racism of early modern representations of blackness and produces readings that not only implicitly negate this racism, but that furthermore use such representations to investigate the fraught creation of a specifically English – *white* – ethnicity. Although she does acknowledge the history of slavery and of the oppression of black races, Floyd-Wilson's reading of Jonson's Ethiopians as embodying positive features that must be incorporated in white identity comes dangerously close to denying the masque's racism. *English Ethnicity and Race* tends to gloss over racial oppression to privilege whiteness in a way that critically re-enacts the early modern white-washing of the Ethiop. Reading English ethnicity as 'barbarous' and 'marginal' and as a northern equivalent of southern blackness makes blackness and whiteness equivalent and problematically elides the history of racial oppression in the name of an investigation of race.

Published in the same year as Floyd-Wilson's book, 2003, Daniel Vitkus' *Turning Turk: English Theater and the Multicultural Mediterranean, 1570–1630* takes a very different approach, and one that is informed by an understanding of postmodern and postcolonial criticism that is as sophisticated as Floyd-Wilson's grasp of humoural theory. As the title indicates, Vitkus' study is concerned not with Englishness but with the ways the English theatre mediates encounters with racial, cultural and – crucially – religious Others. What he does share with Floyd-Wilson is a perception of the early modern English as less secure in their colonial dominance than has been commonly assumed: in fact, one of the central tenets of his book is the notion that this period is one that can be categorised as 'before Empire', and even before Orientalism (as described by Said). In Jacobean England, the '"colonial" discourse was merely the premature articulation of a third-rank power' and must therefore be described, at most, as a 'proto-imperialist discourse'.[71] Vitkus explains:

■ The English encounter with exotic alterity, and the theatrical representations inspired by that encounter, helped to form the emergent identity of an English nation that was eagerly fantasizing about having an empire, but was still in the preliminary phase of its colonizing drive. English subjects understood themselves by comprehending their difference from outsiders, but their identities were also changing as their outlook and behavior were affected and altered by foreign practices that they were learning to emulate.[72] □

Vitkus criticises Hall's *Things of Darkness* for overemphasising the imperialist expansion of the Elizabethan and Jacobean periods. Instead of the binary world stipulated by much postcolonial criticism, and without replacing this binary with the tripartite world stipulated by Floyd-Wilson, Vitkus describes the Mediterranean as 'an extensive network of "contact zones"',[73] in which divergent cultural and religious groups encountered each other as a result of fledgling trade relations. It is through traders and their intelligence-gathering activities that a body of knowledge about the Mediterranean was produced. The various groups encountered on missions motivated by 'profit and plunder' 'were defined by an overlapping set of identity categories, including race, religion, somatic difference, sexuality, and political affiliation', as well as behaviour.[74] It is through contacts with these groups that, on the one hand, English identity took on an increasingly capitalist form and, on the other hand, notions of racial identity became more rigid, a rigidity which is registered in the anxiety about 'turning Turk'.

This is the anxiety which Vitkus finds embodied again and again on the London stage, where the dynamic of attraction and repulsion resulted in portrayals of alien figures as often heroic but also potentially transgressive. Importantly, alien characters allow for transformation, reflecting the way the 'space of "trade" in the early modern Mediterranean is an "in-between space" of liminality and hybridity, where transformation takes place'.[75] Vitkus' conception of alterity stresses its fundamentally dynamic nature, as in 'English representations of the Mediterranean, various binarisms (English-foreign, friend-enemy, black-white, Christian-infidel) are broken down and deconstructed as often as they are upheld'.[76] The London stage is conceptualised here as a site of cultural production, driven by the desire for economic gain, which mediates for its paying audience the Mediterranean sphere of economic and cultural exchange. To satisfy the audience's desire for exotic display, playwrights and players 'were mapping out an imaginary geography that was culture-bound, partial, and selective' and that made of the stage 'an important site for ideological adaptation and reaction to invasive new economic practices that were transforming English society'.[77] In the early seventeenth century, these economic practices began to go beyond the Mediterranean to include voyages to the New World in which explorers, for the first time, could begin to assume an imperial identity, so that a fantasy of colonial and imperial identity began to coexist with the widespread fear of the might of the Ottoman empire.

In his chapter on *Othello*, Vitkus situates the play within the context of Protestant anxieties about conversion to Roman Catholicism or Islam (both of which were 'considered a kind of sexual transgression or spiritual whoredom'), foregrounding the way the play 'exhibits a conflation of various tropes of conversion – transformations from Christian to Turk, from virgin to whore, from good to evil, and from gracious virtue to black damnation'.[78] Amid real fears about the domination of the Ottoman empire, Othello's identity as a 'Moor' becomes readable as a shorthand for 'Turk', itself a shorthand for 'Muslim'. The promise of military conflict with the Turk of Istanbul in the first act is conveniently displaced onto the erotic plot in the remainder of the tragedy. There, Othello forgoes his Christian identity in the murder of Desdemona in which he transforms himself 'into a version of the Islamic tyrant', anticipating Thomas Goffe's *The Couragious Turke, or Amurath the First* (c. 1613–18).[79] Vitkus reads Othello's suicide as a confirmation of his now Turkish identity and his self-punishment for his conversion: his suicide is a faithless act of despair in which the hero's self-cutting re-enacts the circumcision that marks him as a Turk. Othello, in this reading, is 'double-damned' for backsliding from his conversion to Christendom into a re-conversion 'to a black, Muslim identity, an embodiment of the Europeans' phobic fantasy: Othello has become the ugly stereotype'.[80]

The same emphasis on Turkish and Muslim identity is also brought to bear on a number of other conversion plays of the Jacobean period, including Robert Daborne's *A Christian Turned Turk* and Philip Massinger's *The Renegado*, which arguably form a 'coherent subgenre and [are] linked together by a shared set of references to conventional plots and characters that represent Christian-Islamic relations in the Mediterranean'.[81] In such plays, whose plots revolve around Christian women enslaved by lustful Muslims or the heroic rescue and conversion of a virtuous Muslim woman by a Christian man, Islamic culture is represented as powerful and erotically alluring. Dramatic tension is created out of the pervasive fear of conversion, resulting in portrayals of Christians converted to Islam as 'villains, dupes, or tragic victims'. Contact with Islam in itself, even if it does not lead to conversion, is represented as contaminating, as Christian characters 'become "Turkish" in their willingness to change identity and serve or emulate Muslim masters'. These plays, Vitkus argues, expose an anxiety not only about individual conversion to Islam, but also about a more generalised, insidious 'turning Turk' of the whole of English society, which 'was adopting new procedures and identities that were based on a Mediterranean experience defined by an instability of identity and a questionable moral and religious status'.[82] Provocatively, Vitkus concludes by taking this metaphorical conversion through contact with alien cultures one step further: he suggests that not only Turkish characters, but also Italian Machiavels and Jewish merchants embodied the types of 'Other' that English subjects were afraid of turning into. Vitkus thus keeps insisting on the fluidity of identities and the necessity of resisting the fixed binaries of Self and Other that stand in contradiction to the more complex dynamics created by early modern multicultural traffic in the Mediterranean.

I want to end this chapter with a brief pointer to two more recent studies whose approaches differ from each other and their predecessors in significant ways. Sujata Iyengar's *Shades of Difference: Mythologies of Skin Color in Early Modern England* (2005) might be attacked for its lack of a coherent narrative of how racial difference was understood in the early modern period. Such a criticism, however, would be to misunderstand her project, which is precisely concerned with avoiding grand, 'overarching statements of early modern beliefs about skin color and human differences' and replacing them with the 'shades of difference' of her title, attending to 'material contexts and discursive networks' in order to see a whole spectrum of colours and racial identities (without a *necessary* link between colour and race) where others only see black and white, dark and fair.[83] The closest she comes to providing an overarching statement is her deliberately vague and 'non-systematic' assertion that the 'alignment of various non-systematic xenophobias – mythologies of color, nationality, religion, class, and gender – into a coherent mythology of race is an emergent structure of feeling in the sixteenth century'.[84] In an implicit critique of Hall, Iyengar insists that 'the terms *race* and *racialism*' (terms which she helpfully defines in her Introduction) 'cannot and should not be treated as pure or hermetic categories'. She also resists her predecessors' 'imposition of a straightforward historical trajectory "toward" racialism or "toward" color-prejudice' and instead views the early modern period as polyphonic, with different discourses competing against one another.[85]

In keeping with the period's polyphony, Iyengar's methodology often involves reading a variety of texts, both dramatic and non-dramatic, alongside each other to demonstrate how texts that are connected by a specific theme fluctuate in their understanding of skin colour and often also of gender. Her third chapter is particularly relevant: it provides a reading of five Jacobean masques in which Iyengar compares the representation of black Africans to that of the Irish and Native Americans because they were all seen as potential subjects of colonisation. She returns to dramatic forms in her reading of Webster's *White Devil* that tracks the way Vittoria's blushes are painted out of existence by the 'men who wish to control her sexuality'.[86] In rogue literature, and a number of Jacobean plays, she shows how 'the early modern discourse of Gypsydom reveals the ambiguous and uneven process by which several modes of difference become racialized: clothing [...], resistance to labor [...], unsanctioned geographical mobility, a supposed autonomous governing structure [...], theatricality, and dark skin'.[87] Race, in Iyengar's description, is a far more complex compound than in the work of twentieth-century critics.

Finally, Virginia Mason Vaughan's *Performing Blackness on English Stages, 1500–1800* (2005) importantly takes us back to the physical representation of blackness in the theatre, probing both how 'black' characters were staged and how these stagings reflected and produced cultural changes. Vaughan's book is the most recent in her substantial and influential body of work concerned with *Othello, The Tempest* and the representation of racial difference on the Jacobean and twentieth-century stages and screens. Her analysis, while free of jargon, is both informed by critical theory and thoroughly historicised. The book ranges from early representations in which blackness was primarily used 'as a marker of religious difference' and linked black characters to the devil, to the Jacobean period, where the representation of black figures as more 'real' reflected increasing contact with Africa, and the Restoration, when the actor's blackened face denoted his or her status as a slave.[88] Importantly, Vaughan warns us off considering plays as evidence of real-life cultural encounters: 'the black characters that populated early modern theatres tell us little about actual black Africans; they are the projections of imaginations that capitalize on the assumptions, fantasies, fears, and anxieties of England's pale-complexioned audiences'.[89] Again and again, Vaughan's book insists on the *theatricality* of the figures she discusses: for her the notion of white-washed Ethiops, when voiced by an actor in blackface, does not refer to geohumoural connections between Scots and Ethiopians, nor does it denote the figure's separation from grace as embodied by the King. Instead, blackface performance undercuts the proverbial white-washing: 'even though the audience may be caught up in the play's theatrical illusion, the repetition of this proverb creates a fissure in the mimesis'.[90] Arguably, such fissures are points of resistance, moments when the ideology governing the representation breaks apart.

Apart from her slim chapter on *Othello*, which supplements her extended treatment of the play in *Othello: A Contextual History* (1994), the sections of Vaughan's book that are especially useful for a study of Jacobean drama are the 'Preliminaries', which trace the shift from religious to racially defined discourses of identity and include a fascinating account of the make-up techniques, leather-and-velvet masks and messy-sounding tinctures used to produce blackface, as well as Chapters 4, 5 and 7. These chapters survey an impressive number of plays, which she subdivides into 'Black Kings and Queens', 'Bedtricksters' and 'Europeans disguised as Black Moors'. The latter two are especially interesting: Vaughan groups together a surprisingly large corpus of Jacobean plays featuring a black-faced Moorish servant who is substituted for a white master or mistress, allowing 'fears and fantasies of sexual pollution' that were a correlative of New World and Mediterranean trade to be given expression on English stages.[91] Black substitute bedmates like Kate in Fletcher's *Monsieur Thomas* channel illicit male desire, competition and intrigue away from white heroines such as Mary, who can, as a result, pursue their own marriage choices freely. Finally, in late Jacobean and Caroline plays performed in elite theatres such as the Blackfriars and featuring characters who use blackface as a disguise, Vaughan detects the first stirrings of a cultural anxiety about racial boundaries in noble households: 'the pattern of the disguised Moor', she argues, 'may reflect growing anxiety among aristocratic Londoners about the black servants in their own households, including fears that when masters and servants lived in such close quarters, the boundaries between "white" and "black" might become permeable'.[92] The resolutions of these plots play on the topos of the white-washed Ethiop in novel ways: because these female Ethiops *are* washed white on stage, 'the ineluctable connection between whiteness and virtue is reified before [the audience's] eyes'.[93] The anxiety generated by the middle of these plays is thus abated by their resolutions, and the portrayal of female figures in blackface disguise (arguably, a form of 'cross-dressing') betrays a complex compound of attraction and repulsion which deserves further scholarly investigation, using the methodologies not only of race criticism but also of gender studies, to which I will turn next.

CHAPTER SEVEN

Gender and Sexuality

Cross-dressing in shakespeare's romantic comedies and jacobean city comedy

If 'body scholarship' can still be described as an 'emerging field',[1] this is no longer the case for work on gender and sexuality in the early modern period. In the 1980s feminist work on Shakespeare, whose focus, as in Juliet Dusinberre's popular *Shakespeare and the Nature of Women* (1975), had often been to reclaim his female characters as inspirational proto-feminist figures and co-opt Shakespeare as a fellow combatant in the quest for gender equality, came into contact with New Historicism and cultural materialism. As a result, the representation of female characters and gender relations has been reappraised across the canon. In the 1980s and 1990s, these reappraisals often put the question of the cross-dressing of boy actors at the centre of their investigations. Three especially influential arguments will have to stand in here for a much larger, more complex, debate.

Lisa Jardine's *Still Harping on Daughters: Women and Drama in the Age of Shakespeare* (1983) was written out of the author's irritation with the limitations of a feminist criticism that tended either to see Shakespeare's female characters as 'mirror[ing] in a perfectly reflecting glass the varieties of womanhood in contemporary society' (she names Dusinberre as a representative of this view) or to judge 'Shakespeare's work as out-and-out sexist' and seek to 'uncover his prejudices to the reader'.[2] What worries Jardine in both these types of approach is the failure to see female characters as just that: characters. To counter this mode of reading, Jardine considers specific cultural issues of the early modern period which provide useful perspectives on the treatment of women in the drama. Thus, she reappraises the influence on women's status of Protestantism, humanist education, and marital partnership; the wealth and independence of widows that leads to the perception of 'strong' women in Jacobean drama as inherently culpable; the importance of sumptuary law for the maintenance of class and gender boundaries; and the ideology that saw a woman's tongue as both her weapon and a sexual instrument, thus allowing for an easy slippage from accusations of

scolding to accusations of sexual insatiability. Jardine aims to show
that 'the strong interest in women shown by Elizabethan and Jacobean
drama does not in fact reflect newly improved social conditions', but that
it 'is related to the patriarchy's unexpressed worry about the great social
changes which characterise the period'.[3] The first and most important of
the patriarchy's worries that she chooses to unpack is that provoked by
the figure of the 'boy-player – the "play-boy" – who takes the woman's
part and represents femaleness, but who is the object of Elizabethan
erotic interest in his own male right'.[4]

In *Still Harping on Daughters*, as in most discussions of cross-dressing,
Shakespeare's *As You Like It*, with its boy-actor playing a girl disguis-
ing herself as a boy who pretends to be a girl, serves as a touchstone
of the interpretation (Jonson's *Epicoene* is another key text). Jardine
reads the play in the context of John Rainoldes' anti-theatrical tract
Th' Overthrow of Stage-Playes (1599) and compares it to a variety of
Elizabethan and Jacobean plays. Contrary to Dusinberre, who saw the
fact that women's parts were played by boys as empowering because it
highlighted the performativity of gender roles, Jardine refuses to see
theatrical cross-dressing as innocuous and to accept straightforwardly
the cross-dressed actor as a 'woman'. She points to the anti-theatrical
literature which referred the readers to the Bible, where cross-dressing is associated with 'sodomy, homosexuality [...], dress-swapping,
male marriage, and sex between father and son'.[5] For her, Rosalind's
adoption of the name of 'Ganymede' in *As You Like It* is highly significant: the name is that of Jupiter's boy-lover and was commonly held
to be a 'homosexual prototype'. (We will see, in the last part of this
section, why Jardine's anachronistic use of the term 'homosexual'
may be considered problematic.) Jardine argues that this choice of
name alluded to the character's 'erotic androgyny'.[6] Moralists like
Rainoldes objected to the way in which 'the boy player's female dress
and behaviour' made him into an 'erotically irresistible' hermaph-
roditic figure. The boy actor, Jardine claims, was not only seen to
'kindle homosexual love in the male members of his audience', but
could also provoke heterosexual and homoerotic desire in women.[7]
Spectators remained aware of the actual sex of the boy beneath the
double disguise, and it is this perception of transvestism that was dis-
turbingly alluring: 'It does not matter that the coy seductiveness of
the boy player is for plot purposes being appreciated by a woman.
[...] "Playing the woman's part" – male effeminacy – is an act for
a male audience's appreciation'.[8] Implicit in Jardine's argument is
a notion that heterosexual desire between 'real' women and men
is marginalised on the early modern stage and that anti-theatrical
polemicists were right in viewing cross-dressed actors as the cause of
an 'unhealthy interest' on the part of the beholder.[9]

Five years later, Jean E. Howard influentially reconsidered this subject in 'Crossdressing, The Theatre, and Gender Struggle in Early Modern England' (see also my discussion of her book, p. 68). Howard approaches the question of cross-dressing from the vantage-point of historical women's transvestism in early modern England and the outrage this provoked among preachers and polemicists, suggesting 'that the polemics signal a sex-gender system under pressure and that crossdressing, as fact and as idea, threatened a normative social order'.[10] Central to Howard's argument is that the potential subversiveness of cross-dressing 'could be and was recuperated in a number of ways'. Her focus is therefore on the 'gender struggle' of her title, or, in the terms of the materialist feminism she espouses, on the struggle between sub-version and containment as articulated through a variety of often con-tradictory discourses about gender. Howard is interested in finding out how the behaviour of real-life cross-dressing women 'was ideologically processed or rendered intelligible in the discourses of the time'.[11] Real-life cross-dressing created a gap between the woman's actual social status and gender and her appearance (importantly, cross-dressing results in a transgression of both gender *and* class boundaries), showing the social order to be mutable. Because of the existence of the one-sex system (see my discussion of Laqueur, pp. 102–3), the early modern need for the 'idea of two genders, one subordinate to the other, to provide a key element in its hierarchical view of the social order' had to be satisfied through an ideological rather than physiological production and policing of gender boundaries – hence the legislative intervention of sumptuary laws and the labelling of cross-dressed women as whores.[12] For Howard, the increased disciplining of women in this period is a sign of the 'con-siderable instability in the gender system' that was a result of the period's vast social changes which led, paradoxically, to both 'a strengthening of patriarchal authority in the family and the state' and to the production of 'sites of resistance and possibilities of new powers for women'.[13]

It is within this context of historical gender struggle that Howard examines theatrical cross-dressing, asking whether the theatre's 'many fables of crossdressing' also formed 'part of the cultural apparatus for policing gender boundaries' or whether, to the contrary, it served 'as a site for their further disturbance'.[14] Howard is not concerned with the audience's erotic interest in the cross-dressed boy actor; instead her focus is on the relationships between the cross-dressed characters and the figures with whom they interact within the theatrical fiction. The comedies Howard analyses – *As You Like It* and *Twelfth Night* of course, but also *The Merchant of Venice*, *Epicoene*, *The Roaring Girl* and *The City Madam* – all 'play a role in producing and managing anxieties about women on top, women who are not "in their places" [...] and in managing anxieties about the fragility of male authority'.[15] Although

Howard finds that most plays strive to contain threats to traditional hierarchies, some significantly do not.

For Howard, Jonson's *Epicoene* is at one extreme end of this spectrum. Through the inclusion of the unruly 'masculine' collegiate ladies and the domineering Mistress Otter, *Epicoene*, Howard explains, registers the manner in which 'the emerging metropolis offers new opportunities for women to be other than chaste, silent, and obedient'.[16] The play's misogyny finds its mouthpiece in the miser Morose, whose nephew gets a cross-dressed boy to perform the part of Morose's silent and obedient bride Epicoene. While the use of cross-dressing exposes the fact that this image of female perfection is a masculine construction, Howard criticises the way 'the problem of the complexities of right rule in marriage – in the urban setting of London – is sidestepped' through the revelation that the 'wife' is really a man. 'In this instance', Howard concludes, 'male crossdressing becomes a way to appropriate and then erase the troubling figure of wife [sic]'.[17]

At the opposite extreme of Howard's spectrum are plays, like Shakespeare's *Twelfth Night* and Middleton and Dekker's *The Roaring Girl*, which, 'through their fables, enabled changes in the way gender identities and gender relations were discursively constructed in the period'.[18] Unlike the other plays Howard discusses, *The Roaring Girl* is both based on a real-life figure (the transvestite Moll Frith) and 'traversed by discourses of social protest' against various kinds of injustice. Moll uses male clothing not as a disguise but 'to signal her freedom from the traditional positions assigned a woman in her culture'.[19] The play's support for its protagonist's freedom, Howard contends, is evident from its insistence on her chastity, as this represents 'an interruption of that discourse about women which equates a mannish independence with sexual promiscuity'.[20] *The Roaring Girl* is exceptional because it does not result in 'strengthen[ing] notions of difference by stressing what the disguised woman *cannot* do, or by stressing those feelings held to constitute a "true" female subjectivity', as Shakespeare's transvestite heroines tend to do.[21] The gender struggle Howard identifies in Jacobean society is thus mirrored in the plays, whose scripts defend a whole range of ideological positions.

Stephen Orgel revisits this territory in *Impersonations: The Performance of Gender in Shakespeare's England* (1996), where he expands on his earlier provocative argument in 'Nobody's Perfect, or Why Did the English Stage Take Boys for Women?' (1989).[22] As this question shows, it is the convention of cross-dressing itself that Orgel scrutinises. Citing evidence from sources that range from the early Tudor years up to Stuart England (a methodology which arguably flattens out historical changes during this somewhat baggy conception of what constituted 'Shakespeare's England'), Orgel suggests that the convention was not as uniform as 'standard history' suggests, since some women did, in fact, appear on early modern English stages. Theatre history has accepted that women performed in court masques, but Orgel adds evidence that figures such as a 'virgin' in 1583, Moll Frith in the Jacobean period and Madame Coniack and Mistress Shepard in 1632 also appeared on public stages.[23] In his consideration of the work arrangements for actual boy actors, Orgel furthermore draws attention to the important fact that there is insufficient evidence to support the idea that these apprentices were actually being trained for adult roles: only seven boys can be shown to have gone on to adult roles. Significantly, however, Orgel's attempt to oppose the notion that only cross-dressed boys performed women's roles in the early modern English theatre, like his similar endeavour to demonstrate that women could work as apprentices, be members of guilds and even run their own businesses (all part of an argument that it was not actual prohibitions or structural problems that kept women off the stage), is based on very few cases of exceptional individuals which collectively work to confirm the rule rather than challenge it.

In his detailed exploration of the actual practice of theatrical cross-dressing, Orgel's argument moves closer to Jardine's than to Howard's. Relying on Laqueur's work on the one-sex model and feminist philosopher Judith Butler's theorisation of the performativity of gender roles,[24] Orgel explains that gender difference was constructed in the period and boys had to be 'trained' as men once they were breeched.[25] The resulting pervasive fear that men would be effeminate was exacerbated by Puritan insistence on the Biblical prohibition of the adulteration of the sexual 'essences that God has given us'.[26] The danger stage transvestism represents for antitheatrical writers is that 'what the spectator is "really" attracted to in plays is an undifferentiated sexuality, a sexuality that does not distinguish men from women and reduces men to women'.[27] This is, Orgel argues, the kind of eroticism generated by cross-dressed 'eroticized boys' who 'appear to be a middle term between men and women' and invite the desire of both.[28] Building on the work of the queer historians I discuss later (pp. 131–9), Orgel argues that early modern culture was not otherwise marked by 'a morbid fear of homoeroticism as such' and saw homosexual love as compatible with heterosexuality and marriage.[29] Boys, like women, were acceptable objects of men's desires, and women, Orgel contends, would have gained satisfaction from seeing a cross-dressed boy because 'in a culture as patriarchally stratified as that of Renaissance England', this 'might be to disarm and socialize [the transvestite youth] in ways that were specifically female, to see him not as possessor or master, but as companionable and pliable and one of them – as everything, in fact, that the socialized Renaissance woman herself is supposed to be'.[30] The female playgoer stipulated by Orgel was seduced by the boy's ability to adopt a feminine role while remaining male: at heart, her desire was heterosexual. In a study that is strongly marked by queer studies, this conclusion is somewhat surprising in its reduction of erotic possibilities to male homoeroticism and heterosexuality, a view of early modern eroticism that was to be challenged by Valerie Traub (see pp. 137–9).

Beyond cross-dressing: gender and sexuality in feminist revisions of Jacobean drama

The beginning of feminist re-vision of the early modern period can be conveniently pinpointed as the publication in 1977, by Joan Kelly-Gadol, of an essay which provocatively asked 'Did Women have a Renaissance?'[31] In asking this question, Kelly-Gadol was picking up on the unease, among feminist scholars such as Jardine, about the all-too-easy assumption that the achievements of humanism and the Reformation had a uniformly positive effect on men and women alike and was suggesting that women, in fact, did not 'have a Renaissance'. Feminist critics responded by re-assessing the evidence and providing revisionist readings of early modern theatre that paid particular attention to gender, sexuality and the position of women within political and social structures.

In the year of Howard's article on cross-dressing, Mary Beth Rose published *The Expense of Spirit: Love and Sexuality in English Renaissance Drama*, a book which compares 'dramatic representations of love and sexuality with those in contemporary moral and religious writings on women, love, and marriage', with the goal of demonstrating how these texts 'combine to create, interpret, and transform a dominant sexual discourse'.[32] Rose shows that the happy, and deeply conservative, resolutions of Elizabethan romantic comedy came under increasing pressure as Jacobean drama began to register 'the complex process of conducting economic and social relations in a newly forming urban environment'.[33] The result is the development of new and the evolution of old dramatic genres that allow for a more aggressive exploration of sexuality: Jacobean city comedy, tragedy and tragicomedy.

Echoing Dusinberre and Jardine, Rose sees the Protestant doctrine of marriage as a decisive factor influencing conceptions of both private and public spheres. But where Jardine had emphasised the manner in which Protestant emphasis on marriage and the family probably had the practical outcome of women having 'a *diminished* ability to influence their own lives' (emphasis in original),[34] Rose is closer to Dusinberre in seeing, in Jacobean drama, a reflection of a move towards a greater valorisation of women and their private and public roles. She accordingly

argues that Jacobean city comedy, in managing to combine 'satiric critique and festive celebration', 'brings into the light of representation
precisely those dissociations and contradictions in English Renaissance
sexual ideology which [Elizabethan] romantic comedy evokes but seeks
to reconcile and contain'.[35] Arguing that sexual disguise, on the Jacobean stage, is used to expose anxieties surrounding increasing social
mobility, Rose describes *Epicoene* as the prime instance of city comedy's
persistent association of sexuality with social disjunction and sin.
Through the portrayal of the collegiate ladies, who challenge the traditional order, as hermaphroditical, 'Jonson associates social mobility
with sexual monstrosity and sexual monstrosity with women's attempt
at equality'.[36] The play calls attention to the romantic convention of a
conclusion in marriage by inverting it, since the comedy concludes on
the dissolution rather than celebration of a marriage and Morose's declaration of impotence rather than a promise of consummation. Rather
than a celebration of the performativity of gender roles, the title character's sexual disguise is furthermore ultimately reductive: 'as it turns
out, the only possible silent woman – the best woman – is, simply, a
man'.[37] For Rose, '[t]he heroic solution to reconciling eros with city
life' is provided not by the male wits' homoeroticism but by Dauphine's
'harsh repression of sexual desire' altogether: in this play, 'it is not eros
that will guarantee the perpetuation of society, but acquisition, secrecy,
and wit, all exercised in service of preserving traditional rank and hierarchy'.[38] Rose's focus on sexuality rather than gender emphasises that
the threats to the sex-gender system in the play are countered by the
conservative hero's asexuality – sex is so debased in Jonson's London
that the only guard against it is its renunciation.

Rose contrasts *Epicoene* with *The Roaring Girl*, which she reads in the
context of the *Hic Mulier*/*HaecVir* pamphlets published in 1620, roughly
ten years after the composition of the play. The play and pamphlets
reveal the deep-seated ambivalence about gender equality and wom-
en's independence in Jacobean England. Although Moll's cross-dressing
is initially associated by the playwrights 'with erotic appeal and illicit
sexuality',[39] Rose, like Howard, points out that she is ultimately defined
through her sexual innocence. The play 'dramatizes the specious logic
involved in connecting Moll's unconventional male attire automatically
with whorish behavior'.[40] By making Moll the touchstone that allows
the other characters to be 'defined as social and moral beings according to their responses to her', the playwrights join 'those who, like the
author of *Haec-Vir*, were beginning to call for greater freedom for women
and equality between the sexes'.[41] But the cost of this call for greater
equality is, as in *Epicoene*, a renunciation of sex. Unlike Shakespeare's
traditional disguised heroines, and her foil Mary Fitzallard, Moll does
not provide the reassurance that she will return to female garb and

heterosexual marriage at the end of the play. The price of Moll's free-dom is her exclusion from the happy resolution in marriage and the question of where exactly she fits into established structures remains unresolved at the end of the play.

Whereas the comic endings of the city comedies barely manage to contain the anxieties provoked by the female characters' challenge to patriarchal structures, the Jacobean tragedies Rose subsequently concen-trates on are even harsher. In contrast with Elizabethan tragedies, whose political concerns tended to consign 'women, eros, and sexuality to the periphery', *Othello* and *The Duchess of Malfi* 'emphasize a heroism of per-sonal endurance, creating tragedies of private life that [...] focus on the consequences of corrupt or unorthodox sexuality in a dark and narrow world increasingly devoid of possibility'.[42] The Jacobean tragedies' focus on the private sphere 'bear[s] witness to a particular historical moment when private life was beginning to be assigned as much dignity and sig-nificance as public life and to be related analogously, rather than hierar-chically, to public affairs'.[43] The tragedies give expression to the anxieties caused by this shift, Rose argues, by granting their female characters greater prominence and allowing them to enact the 'heroics of private life' only to defeat them more brutally in the end. *Othello* registers the evolution from the Elizabethan to the Jacobean model by putting the old-fashioned 'hero of action' Othello side-by-side with Desdemona's newer 'heroics of marriage',[44] with the tragedy resulting from the clash of these conflicting forms of heroism.[45] *The Duchess of Malfi*, on the other hand, makes its heroine's erotic identity central to its concerns and attempts to confer equal distinction on the public and private domains. This attempt, however, is also doomed to fail: the tragedy's conclusion removes its her-oine from 'the active resolution of the conflicts of the play' and relegates her to being 'an unattainable ideal'.[46] The play's ending is overwhelmed by the fundamentally 'conservative and nostalgic' bent of Jacobean trag-edy, in which the need for a future is articulated through the destruc-tion of and subsequent mourning for the past.[47] It is only in Jacobean tragicomedy, a genre that 'mediat[es] between future and past dramatic forms', that a radical vision comes into being.[48] For Rose, 'Fletcherian tragicomedy displays a new willingness to dismiss the cultural formations of the past' and permits chivalry to be renounced for the sake of mar-riage.[49] Rose's book thus traces the evolution from the wish-fulfilments of Elizabethan romantic comedy through the harsher visions of Jacobean city comedy and tragedy to Fletcherian tragicomedy, which responds to social change by 'chang[ing] the terms of dramatic conflict, moving toward redefining the relation between public and private life as separate but equal spheres'.[50]

Like *The Expense of Spirit*, Karen Newman's *Fashioning Femininity and English Renaissance Drama* (1991) combines a New Historicist methodology with a feminist sensibility. Using deconstructive methodologies, Newman's accessible book seeks to elucidate the origins and workings of early modern gender ideology. The central questions she poses are: 'What is the relationship of gender to power and the state? How was femininity fashioned and deployed in early modern England?'[51] For Newman, 'female subjectivity' is both 'the construction of the gendered subject and the ideology of women's submission or subjection to men', and she insists on understanding 'identity, sexual difference, and even sexuality itself' as constructions.[52] She is therefore as wary of feminist critics who focus on women without displaying an awareness of the constructedness of this category as she is of historicist critics who unquestioningly accept the prescriptions of conduct literature and sermons as a reflection of actual women's experience.

Newman begins by exploring the fashioning of the category of 'femininity' through the vast variety of printed texts through which 'ideologies of femininity' in the period were widely disseminated. Covering some of the territory of the 'body' critics (see pp. 100–18), Newman argues that anatomical texts formed part 'of a rhetorical disciplining of the female body by fragmenting it', a strategy which she finds is also characteristic of poetry (through the blazon), marriage sermons and conduct manuals. Together, such texts fashioned a notion of femininity that tended to conflate a woman's open mouth with her open genitals (a point also made by Jardine), and that represented her body as inherently corruptible, fragile, and in need of masculine control. At the same time, in a characteristic move, Newman points out how in these texts the attempt to fragment the female order in order to control it undermines itself, as this fragmentation 'not only masters by dismembering but also threatens such mastery through that very dispersion and the semiotic instabilities it sets in motion'.[53] Similarly, in her analysis of the increasingly restrictive view of women's role within Puritan 'companionate' marriage and the 'skimmingtons' that punished transgressive couples, Newman asserts:

■ Though there is no question that Renaissance discourses of femininity advanced social controls and the policing of female behavior, they also enabled opposing discourses, which though they often speak with the same vocabulary and from the same categories, were nevertheless tactically productive. [...] On stage, women are frequently represented transgressing conventional social roles, but not necessarily punished for doing so.[54] □

Newman thus emphasises women's resistance to male control and seeks to reveal the instabilities within dominant ideologies that allowed women to resist repressive definitions of femininity and 'proper female behaviour'.

Newman claims that the anxieties provoked by social changes in the period and in particular by 'the challenges to traditional ideals of womanhood' led 'to a displacement of anxiety on to the woman', which resulted, in turn, in the 'criminalization of women, the labeling of old behaviors in new ways'.[55] Accusations of witchcraft were therefore on the increase. Once on trial, however, the women accused of witchcraft were paradoxically given the opportunity to speak out as part of their confession on the scaffold. These speeches were 'a means of self-fashioning', 'an opportunity to deploy the powers of representation to which they were often denied access'.[56] (What Newman somewhat glosses over in her reading of these scaffold confessions is that the women paid for their empowering ability to 'self-fashion' with their lives.) If the witches in *Macbeth* and other Jacobean witchcraft plays are particularly known for their equivocations, that is because, on theatrical and judicial scaffolds alike, witchcraft dramatised 'the spectacle of the production of subjectivity in both senses: the being subject to another and the becoming the subject of discourse'.[57]

Fashioning Femininity contains particularly influential readings of *Othello* and *Epicoene*. In the chapter on *Othello*, which Jyotsna Singh has powerfully used as the basis of her postcolonialist critique of feminist readings of the play (see p. 110), Newman describes how the 'union of Desdemona and Othello represents a sympathetic identification between femininity and the monstrous [the black man's supposedly monstrous sexuality] that offers a potentially subversive recognition of sexual and racial difference'.[58] She sees Othello as deeply conflicted in that he 'embodies not only the norms of male power and privilege represented by the white male hegemony ruling Venice', a world predicated on 'the denial of difference, but also the threatening power of the alien'.[59] The threatening, monstrous alien is closer to home and immediately recognisable as female in *Epicoene*, which Newman analyses within the context of sumptuary laws, the development of fashion, and the 'burgeoning consumer culture Jonson and his contemporaries identify as feminine'.[60] The discourses linked to these developments resulted in femininity being perceived as 'something to achieve rather than something natural or given'. Consequently the femininity of the cross-dressed boy playing Epicoene 'is foregrounded as masquerade or "hyperfemininity"'.[61] In this figure, no less than in the pieced-together faces of the collegiate ladies, Jonson focalises his ambivalence toward consumerism, social mobility and urban growth. Newman's genuinely unsettling contribution to the criticism of this play is her implication of the audience and the modern reader and critic in Jonson's conservative anxiety about female talkativeness and consumerism: if the play 'works' for modern audiences and readers and we understand its satire, that is because we share its 'assumptions about behavior appropriate to women'.[62] Newman thus ends up questioning – and critiquing – the way femininity is fashioned today.

The study with which I want to conclude this discussion of gender and sexuality is a deliberately quirky choice. Wendy Wall's *Staging Domesticity: Household Work and English Identity in Early Modern Drama* (2002) was described by Barbara Hodgdon as 'Easily the most engaging, most thoroughly enjoyable study' of its year.[63] Wall describes herself as 'join[ing] an ongoing project aimed at refining feminist criticism of Renaissance culture so as to take into account gains made by queer theorists, social historians, and materialist critics'.[64] Wall concentrates on the nitty-gritty of domestic life and the power relations obtaining in the middle-class home. Noting that according to humoural theory, diet was a crucial way of maintaining physiological equilibrium, Wall introduces her readers to the medical remedies housewives concocted and administered. The sheer rhetorical verve with which manuals described the slaughtering of animals to be used as ingredients leads Wall to suggest that '[p]art of the pleasure of housework [...] might involve the fantasy of taming, displaying, barbing, and splatting bodies'.[65] There is a disconcerting gap between the cookbook's blood-stained woman and the meek creature imagined by conduct manuals. Such a gap also exists between the husband's sovereign position in the household and the fact that he had to submit to his wife's and servants' medical ministrations: official patriarchal ideologies thus run counter to domestic practice, creating tensions that find their expression onstage. The household was simultaneously familiar and reassuring, and alien and threatening. Wall's principal argument is that '[t]he drama of the period fuses these two representations to show how domesticity, in part because of its disorienting character, paradoxically enabled people to imagine new identities and subject positions'. Political agency and identity, in this study, are situated at the hearth rather than at court, as 'Englishness' is more a matter of oscillation of feelings of alienation and belonging to the home 'with its vexed cultural and economic concerns' than a sense of where one belongs within the social hierarchy.[66]

Following the division of early modern housework into the five principal tasks of wet-nursing, housecleaning, cooking, medical care and butchery, Wall relates each of these tasks in turn to specific plays. Of particular interest are the introduction, in which Wall outlines a methodology which could be applied to any number of plays, and the first chapter, in which she discusses a wide range of texts relating to the domestic sphere in which domesticity was variously 'framed as nostalgia, relegated to a country past, linked to a culture of expertise, tied to foreignness, eroticized as secret delights, championed as the backbone of national culture'.[67] Wall's penultimate chapter is dedicated to the Jacobean *Knight of the Burning Pestle*. For Wall, Nell's identity as a housewife complicates the play's apparently straightforward attack on middle-class taste, enabling an exploration of 'cultural fantasies of dependency, familiarity, and nationality'.[68] Specifically, Nell's desire to help the actors with a variety of homely remedies is an inappropriate act that is obliquely related to all her other transgressive impulses. Nell seeks to exoticise the world represented on-stage while 'anchor[ing] everything to the reality principle that she embodies for her culture'. Her presence gives rise to the articulation of 'domestic desires and fears that the play doesn't completely disavow'.[69] As Wall demonstrates through an analysis of a series of early modern advisory texts, 'the housewife was nervously agreed to be the ultimate authority on common ailments',[70] an authority over the body which provoked all sorts of anxieties, especially since it seems to have commonly taken the form of – by the sound of it – extremely painful and uncomfortable remedies (e.g. hot boiled eggs applied to the anus, steaming urine on a breast). Cultural anxieties about the physical dependency of adults on the administrations of the housewife are concentrated on Nell's inappropriate domineering over boy actors both because such boys were dependants within a particularly 'vague structure of mastering' and because they were seen as titillating in their gorgeous costumes and position as the Queen's 'minions'. Hence, Wall argues, Nell's strange investment in the simultaneous eroticisation and infantilisation of the boy actors, 'revealing a free-floating and potentially polymorphous erotics of service that could underwrite household work, theatre relations or dramatic spectacle'.[71]

Wall concludes with an analysis of Heywood's *A Woman Killed with Kindness*, which she reads against a background of everyday butchery: for her, the play trades on perceptions of both animal and human bodies as precariously subject to dismemberment and recycling. Houswifery is here shown to be shared among a number of domestic workers, including male servants such as Nick, who functions simultaneously as the play's ethical barometer and an indication of the tensions existing within the hierarchical early modern household. In Wall's reading, the play 'demonstrates that the early modern domestic world revolved around communal supervision', a supervision which in this case is exercised upon the household's mistress.[72] Meanwhile, the tragedy's 'emphasis on separable and cannibalized body parts [...] raises the specter of household relations as an ever-shifting set of dissected corporeal exchanges'.[73] Seen in this context, Frankford's incorporation of Wendoll as his servant/companion can be read as a creating an excessive homoerotic bond of servitude which exposes and threatens existing lines of dependency; Wendoll's sexual penetration of Frankford's wife merely extends his prior metaphorical invasion of Frankford's own body. This, then, turns out to be a tragedy that attacks the excessive bond between master and servant more than it does the wife's adultery, though it is she who has to die in order for 'proper' male alliances to be re-established once the gentleman-companion has been expelled. In her final chapter, Wall's focus on the *household* thus lays a greater stress on Jacobean drama's 'queerness', in the two senses of 'explicitly homo-erotic relationships and the non-normative potential of early modern domesticity generally'.[74]

Queer studies and Jacobean drama

Wall's comfortable description of the early modern family as potentially 'queer' and of 'explicitly homoerotic relationships' is only possible as a result of the work of 'queer' critics who have comprehensively redrawn the map of early modern sexualities and 'erotics'.[75] The occasional antagonism towards feminist critics in the work of some male queer critics arises from their desire to distance their work and their focus on masculinity and male-male relations from the traditional agenda of feminism, which sought (and still seeks) to correct the misogynist bias of most pre- and much post-1970s criticism and which, in doing so, has sometimes ended up reproducing the marginalisation of homosexual desire evident in patriarchal discourses. Nevertheless it is indicative of the strong interdependence of feminism and queer studies that Heather Findlay finds that the path taken by gay scholarship

■ has duplicated in miniature the path taken by feminist literary criti-cism. If [...] feminist criticism began with 'gynocriticism', which focuses on women authors and characters, and expanded into 'feminist critique', which focuses on the role of gender in texts by male and female authors [...], similarly, gay scholarship in the Renaissance has moved from iden-tifying, explicating, and legitimating homosexual authors and characters to analyzing the function of sexuality in texts by various writers, not just those who appear to have been drawn sexually to members of their own sex or imaginatively to homosexual themes.[76] □

The playwrights most susceptible to being 'outed' by early queer critics were Marlowe and Shakespeare, with the latter a privileged target not only because of the homoeroticism of the *Sonnets* but also because of his 'timeless' and 'universal' status in popular imagination. In this section, I want to concentrate on the one hand on the beginning of queer investi-gation of early modern literature and on the other hand on more recent formulations that look beyond Shakespeare, repress the urge to 'out' any playwrights and more productively, I think, analyse a wide range of representations of homoerotic desire in Jacobean drama.

Modern 'queer' investigation of the early modern period kick-started in 1982 with *Homosexuality in Renaissance England*, a slim volume by the historian Alan Bray, published by the Gay Men's Press, which was to have an impact well beyond its specialist markets. Bray wants to get rid of anachronistic views of early modern sexualities and argues that the late nineteenth-century 'invention' of homosexuality has coloured popular perceptions of the early modern period as a time where artistic and sexual freedoms went hand-in-hand. He proposes a return to early modern perceptions and terminologies and a differentiated appreciation of sexual behaviours in the terms of the period. Though we may easily identify descriptions of certain sexual acts as 'homosexual', Bray contends that we need to understand these acts against the background of the early modern deep abhorrence for anything that could be described as 'buggery' or 'sodomy'. He warns that these terms actually 'carry other meanings as well: the concepts involved are broader'. Thus 'buggery' could be used both for homosexual acts and for bestiality, while 'sodomy' could signify both homosexual and heterosexual 'sins'.[77] In fact, Bray explains that what we now call homosexuality was part of the dissolution of the created order and therefore

■ was not a sexuality in is own right, but existed as a potential for confusion and disorder in one undivided sexuality. Hence the absence [...] of any satisfactory parallel for the contemporary use of 'homosexuality' in the sense of an alternative sexuality. What sodomy and buggery represented – and homosexuality was only part of these – was rather the disorder in sexual relations that, in principle at least, could break out anywhere.[78] □

This crucial insight explains the association of sodomy with Roman Catholicism and witchcraft, as both of these were figured as a threat to order in the world.

Bray's book then turns to a consideration of the portrayals of 'ganymedes' and 'catamites' in late Elizabethan and early Jacobean satires and finds that such texts consistently describe the stereotypical sodomite as 'a young man-about-town, with his mistress on one arm and his "catamite" on the other; he is indolent, extravagant and debauched'.[79] He contrasts this representation with historical fact and concludes that the satirical representation of the sodomite depended largely on political and literary traditions (especially the influence of Juvenal) rather than on observed fact. The danger, when looking for early modern 'homosexuality' in the period's satires is 'that what we are seeing is not Renaissance London but second-century Rome at one remove'.[80] Because the satires are intended to hurt and therefore must had some basis in reality, the satires are nevertheless still valuable documents for Bray.

The reality, which Bray reconstructs from tiny fragments in literary texts, Quarter Sessions records and other documents, is one in which there is a wide gap between people's actual sexual acts and their perception of these acts. The cultural abhorrence of sodomy was such that even men who, from a modern point of view, were clearly engaging in sexual acts that could be categorised as 'homosexual', did not perceive them as being sodomitical. What we now call homosexual relations took place not between strangers but rather between people who knew each other well. In an environment in which premarital heterosexual intercourse was rigorously policed, unmarried servants could find homosexual relations an appropriate alternative sexual outlet, which was facilitated by the common practice of male servants sharing beds. There is also 'considerable evidence [...] of homosexual as well as heterosexual relationships being common between masters and servants'.[81] At universities, too, college fellows and their students shared rooms, so much so that Bray describes 'homosexuality' as 'institutionalised' in learning environments.[82] Furthermore, there seems to have been a tacit toleration of homosexual prostitution in London. Another type of prostitution, Bray claims, 'existed in connection with the London playhouses', where 'at times an actor's relationship with his patron could have overtones of homosexuality and prostitution'.[83] The 'crucial realisation' which Bray wants us to come to is that an economic and social power differential between the men involved is common to all these forms of 'homosexual' relations. As long as an act of this kind did not 'disturb the peace or the social order, and in particular so long as it was consistent with patriarchal mores, it was largely in practice ignored'.[84] Homosexual activity was not 'tolerated' in the modern sense, but it remained invisible as long as it did not upset established hierarchies.

The idea of sodomy as a disturbance of order and upsetting of hierarchical relations is central to Jonathan Goldberg's *Sodometries: Renaissance Texts/Modern Sexualities* (1992), a landmark study in which Goldberg, whom we encountered earlier as an important proponent of the New Historicism (see pp. 61–2), belatedly entered the arena of queer studies. Here, Goldberg combines his historical interest in the early modern period with a modern political agenda and a mix of deconstructionist and psychoanalytic methodologies. Goldberg's preoccupation with the status of homosexuals in US culture at the end of the twentieth century is perceptible everywhere and nowhere more so than in the preface and introductory chapter. Picking up on Bray, on whom he relies heavily, he describes sodomy as an 'utterly confused category' and proposes the use of the term 'sodometries' in a dual effort to be historically pertinent to the texts under discussion and to invoke its 'nonce-word suggestiveness, as if sodomy were a relational term, a measure whose geometry we do not know, whose (a)symmetries we are to explore'.[85] Sodomy/sodometry, Goldberg suggests, is an act which can be understood in relation to George Puttenham's description of the rhetorical figure of the *histeron proteron* or 'the preposterous', a mode of speech that introduces disorder of a social or sexual kind (it designates an inversion of order, of which 'to put the cart before the horse' is the classical example). Typical of the merging of modern sexualities and early modern texts Goldberg promises in his title is his explanation of 'the preposterous' with reference to a Gulf War propaganda image which superimposed Saddam Hussein's head on the anus of a camel (putting the head behind what should be in front), identifying the Iraqi head of state as both a sodomite and a target of sodomitical aggression. Jumping from Puttenham to Saddam Hussein may seem preposterous, but in Goldberg's hands it enables sharp insights and allows him elegantly to deconstruct modern figurations of homosexuality, whether in war propaganda or the Law.

In his chapter on the transvestite stage of Marlowe's *Edward II* (1592) – as important a play for queer studies as *As You Like It* is for feminist analyses of cross-dressing – Goldberg is careful to distinguish between gender and sexuality. He uses the play to question the way in which Gaveston is often identified with cross-dressing because of a reference to the 'lovely boy in Dian's shape' in his opening monologue. The point of the play, Goldberg insists, is that Gaveston merely '*rehearses* one powerful way Marlowe's culture had for stigmatising theatrical and sexual practices, defining in advance precisely the kind of theatricalization *Edward II* will not offer, the sexual sphere in which the play does not operate. Neither Gaveston nor Edward wears dresses. The familiar linking of boy and woman is disarmed, summoned up to be put aside' (emphasis added).[86] The shocking thing about the relationship between Edward and Gaveston is not its sexual nature but rather the fact that the lovers transgress boundaries of class as the king raises his minion to his level. Sodomy, as Bray had argued, only becomes visible when the male/male relations threaten established order. The fact that one of the men involved is the king makes that disorder more threatening: in Marlowe's play, the 'figure upon which all systems of relationship between men depend, whether conducted through women or not, is the figure who, in the very exercise of his prerogatives, violates the law that he is supposed to found'. It is in this way that Edward's is a 'sodomitical regime' and that all the behaviour in the play can be described as sodomy: disorder is just as present in Mortimer's usurpation and Isabella's adultery.[87] Sodomy blatantly 'is not homosexuality tout court, nor are male/female relations of alliance', such as Edward's marriage to Isabella and his desire to see his minions married well, 'the same as heterosexuality'.[88]

Although Goldberg does not actually discuss any Jacobean play in detail, his book is still indispensable for the field because of its pervasive influence on all subsequent 'queerings' of early modern drama and because his analysis of *Edward II* is the occasion for a reconsideration of the figure of the cross-dressed boy actor in the criticism of the 1980s. There is at times a defensiveness in this book which, on occasion, turns ugly when he indulges in intellectual mud-throwing against peers, or equates the 'incipient heterosexuality' embodied by Shakespeare's Hotspur with 'misogyny and an incipient homophobia'.[89] A blind spot in his work, as in Bray's, is that in studies that insist on alternative sexual possibilities, the possibility of female/female forms of sexual desire is neglected. Such a bias is openly acknowledged in Mario DiGangi's *The Homoerotics of Early Modern Drama* (1997), which completes *Sodometries'* move away from a narrow focus on 'sodomy' and towards a looser consideration of a range of erotic practices. If DiGangi chooses to concentrate on male/male homoeroticism (a term he prefers to the more ideologically charged and emotive 'sodomy'), that is, he explains, because it was crucially different from female/female homoeroticism both in legal and social terms.

DiGangi is worried about the tendency, in queer criticism, to focus on Shakespeare on the one hand and on the other hand to see Marlowe's *Edward II* as 'the *locus classicus* of homosexuality in Renaissance drama'.[90] While the former 'may have the unfortunate consequence of establishing [Shakespeare's] depictions of homoeroticism as culturally "representative"', the latter is problematic because, in the age of AIDS, any narrative which ends with the killing off of the overt homosexual might read as 'realistic' and somehow 'right' (thought-provokingly, DiGangi contrasts this with the common view of the ending of the heteroerotic tragedy of *Othello* as feeling 'wrong').[91] As a result, he casts his net more widely and offers re-readings not only of the usual suspects Shakespeare and Marlowe, but also of Jonson, Chapman, Middleton and Fletcher. These Jacobean authors, DiGangi asserts, 'often present a fuller picture of the early modern household and the same-sex relations enabled by its particular functioning and composition' than do Shakespeare's plays.[92]

In an important critical intervention in genre studies, DiGangi organises his material according to types of homoeroticism that can be identified with specific dramatic genres. The trajectory he plots starts with the 'homoerotics of marriage' in Shakespeare's romantic comedies, which are based on the Ovidian myths of Ganymede, Hylas and Orpheus 'in which male homoerotic desire actively disrupts marital (hetero)sexuality';[93] it moves through Jacobean city comedies focussed on master-servant relations and historical tragedies concerned with the king's relationship with his favourites and arrives at the 'incompatibility of heteroeroticism and masculinity' in Fletcherian tragicomedy.[94] To give a flavour of DiGangi's mode of thinking while offering a point of comparison with the feminist studies outlined above, I will concentrate on his interpretation of *Epicoene*.

'The homoerotics of mastery in satiric comedy' is a chapter which pays detailed attention to master-servant relationships in both canonical and non-canonical Jacobean city comedies, with a particular emphasis on Middleton's homoerotic economies in *Michaelmas Term* and *No Wit, No Help Like a Woman's*, Chapman's *The Gentleman Usher* and Jonson's *Every Man Out of His Humour*, *The Alchemist*, *Volpone* and *Epicoene*. DiGangi begins by questioning why, in city comedies, the wit's exposure of the gull's/ass's folly so often focuses on the ass/arse and concludes that the ass/arse is the site of a 'convergence of servitude and eroticism that becomes particularly meaningful within the early modern discourse of male service'.[95] Significantly, the figure of Epicoene her/himself is not central to DiGangi's reading; instead, he asks us to consider 'the particularly homoerotic dynamics of Dauphine's mastery over other men' and to pay attention to the 'sodomitical effect' (a very useful concept) of Morose's violations of the social order.[96] Dauphine arranges his uncle's sodomitical marriage with his servant boy Epicoene (with whom Dauphine may or may not be having a sexual relationship) and humiliates the fops/asses and even his friends without ever being 'compromised by or suspected of sodomy'. Morose, on the other hand, even though it is clear that his marriage with Epicoene has remained unconsummated, is sodomitical because

■ his public confession of sexual disorder confirms and tersely represents his many violations of social order: his unnatural humors and his mistreatment of his nephew, servants, and wife. Epicoene's presence thus brings into the arena of sexuality – as unnatural frigidity, or, after her unmasking as a boy, unnatural sodomy – the disorder Morose has promoted throughout the play.[97] □

In this way, the play allows us to distinguish between the *orderly*, unremarkable homoeroticism of Dauphine and the *disorderly*, sodomitical homoeroticism of his uncle. As in Jonson's other satirical comedies, the 'implied ideal society' in *Epicoene* turns out to be 'constituted not through orderly courtship and marriage rituals between men and women, but through the homosocial fellowship of aggressive male wits' like Dauphine.[98]

Homosocial fellowship is also at the heart of Mary Bly's *Queer Virgins and Virgin Queans on the Early Modern Stage* (2000), which is narrowly focussed on the repertory of a relatively obscure company, the King's Revels. Even though the plays Bly discusses will not be relevant for many readers, what makes the book irresistible is not only the sheer fun of Bly's argument, but also the way it uses the methodologies of theatre history and the insights of textual critics to make an important intervention in queer studies. Bly, in fact, takes issue with the assumption of DiGangi, Goldberg and Bray, which takes its origins in Foucault's *History of Sexuality* (1988–90),[99] that there was no such thing as a homosexual or even 'sodomitial' identity before the creation of so-called molly houses (homosexual brothels) in Restoration London. By focussing her study of the King's Revels' repertory between 1607–8 on 'silenced laughter: on puns whose acrobatics no longer please, and indeed are hardly intelligible' to modern ears,[100] Bly manages to contest this assumption and to demonstrate that there may indeed have been a group of playgoers whose laughter at the 'queer' puns which were characteristic of the company's plays and their 'lewd and essentially unmarriageable' heroines gave them a group identity.[101] This identity was not 'homosexual' in the modern sense of the word as 'an identity that controls a person's subjectivity', but crucially, Bly argues that the puns 'inscribe a place within early modern culture in which homoerotic double talk is both erotic and celebratory, funny and profitable'.[102] The writers of these plays, too, seem to have been part of this community, as many of them were amateurs and seemed to collaborate in a way that 'signals the presence of a constraining authority governing the tenor of the plays'.[103] There is, thus, a 'space for identification as a sodomite in early modern culture', and that space is inextricably linked to the performance and enjoyment of plays.[104]

Valerie Traub's vast, erudite and theoretically sophisticated *The Renaissance of Lesbianism in Early Modern England* (2002) makes no equivalent claims for 'sapphic' communities in the Jacobean period. Because, in her account, a recognisably 'lesbian' identity only emerged as a result of developments in the Restoration and early eighteenth century, she shares instead DiGangi's attention to relationships that are not marked as sodomitical but are unremarkable because of their orderliness and the way they uphold dominant ideologies. In her book, finally, the bias of queer studies in favour of male/male homoeroticism is questioned and corrected. One by one, Traub revisits the most important debates and sources on which body criticism, gender studies, postcolonial studies and queer history and queer criticism have concentrated. The scope of this cultural and literary history of female/female desire from the mid-sixteenth century (when the clitoris was 'discovered') into the eighteenth centuries (the beginnings of lesbianism as an erotic identity) therefore goes far beyond drama and the Jacobean period, but it is the foundational text for any investigation of Jacobean drama that pays attention to articulations of same-sex erotic activity among women.

Traub puzzles over the paradox that whereas 'women's erotic desires for other women were considered improbable, implausible, insignificant', such desires did exist and were practiced and represented.[105] More often than not, she demonstrates, representations of female homoeroticism leaned on classical antecedents, and like DiGangi, Traub finds that Ovid was a particularly popular source of mythological pre-texts. Traub contends that desire among women, as a discursive phenomenon, was fashioned principally out of the classical 'medico-satiric discourse of the tribade', the (often foreign, exotic) woman endowed with an abnormally big clitoris which she was said to rub and use as a penis.[106] While tribadism was viewed with abhorrence throughout early modern Europe and women did get convicted of sodomy and were executed as a result, the evidence Traub has gathered suggests that the prosecution of women for sodomy was exceptional and only occurred when the woman's sexual activities had in some way usurped male prerogatives (e.g. passing as a man, using a dildo). Female/female sexual acts which did not overtly disturb patriarchal authority seem to have escaped prosecution, allowing all sorts of sexual acts that did not involve penetration ('the only socially intelligible form of erotic congress') to happen between 'chaste' girls and women.[107] This 'chaste' female/female desire relied not on the classical antecedent of the tribade but on the 'literary-philosophical discourse of idealized friendship' or *amicitia*/amity which was available to Western, white women to describe their orderly intimate relations.[108] As her tracing of this dual heritage shows, Traub's work repeatedly insists on the historical difference of female/female desire in the early modern period and the need to be sensitive to the ways in which sexual acts between women were perceived and conceptualised in this period. Hence her italicisation of *lesbianism* throughout the book: her hope is that this will act as a reminder of the 'epistemological inadequacy, psychological coarseness, and historical contingency' of the term, since 'to use the term lesbian when discussing early modern texts is prematurely to unify concepts that only began to come into contact, jostle, and intersect late in the period'.[109]

Turning to the early modern stage, Traub notes how lust is routinely displaced from men onto women, who are branded whores in tragedies and whose supposed infidelity is in the comedies expressed through 'the figure of the comic whore, cuckold jokes, and rituals of female humiliation'.[110] In all these figurations, the danger women represent seems to be *hetero*sexual in nature; where female/female desire is expressed, this desire is significantly *in*significant, invisible, as a threat to social and sexual order. This carries into the domain of cultural representation the invisibility of '*lesbianism*' in English law, which in all its shapes seemed to 'either ignore or refuse to admit the possibility of female-female sex'.[111] Traub illustrates this insignificance with an attentive reading of

A Midsummer Night's Dream, whose 'repeated, if tantalizingly brief, allu-sions to female intimacies' (Helena/Hermia, Titania/votaress, Hyppolita, the 'fair vestal' untouched by Cupid's arrow) she uses 'to lift the curtain on occluded practices within early modern culture'.[112] Shakespeare's play is typical of a substantial corpus of comedies that show the neces-sity for a female-female bond (here that between Hermia and Helena) to be dissolved to allow the play to be resolved by a patriarchal marriage.

In her central chapter on 'The (in)significance of *lesbian* desire', where she analyses a range of early modern plays that repeat the pattern of *A Midsummer Night's Dream*, Traub takes issue with the common perception of cross-dressing as the primary site for female homoeroticism in early modern drama. This perception raises a number of problems:

■ First, to the extent that transvestism seems the *only* means of access into female erotic intimacy, other points of access are overlooked. Second, social orthodoxy, which would condemn female masculinity if, at the conclusion of the narrative, the character's 'real femininity' fails to shine through, continues unchallenged. [...] And third, insofar as cross-dressing implies that homoeroticism has to be physically disguised to be articulated, it unwittingly brings to bear the 'epistemology of the closet', to invoke [queer theorist and author of *The Epistemology of the Closet* (1990)] Eve [Kosofsky] Sedgwick, on a world prior to closets.[113] □

Instead, Traub draws our attention to the many articulations of desire among female characters that are securely gendered female and des-tined for a heterosexual union. The 'femme-femme' love of these female characters, as Traub demonstrates with a close reading of Emilia in *Two Noble Kinsmen*, is both 'idealized and portrayed as a foil to male-female antagonism; at the same time, these bonds are repre-sented as temporary, firmly located in childhood and adolescence, and necessarily giving way to patriarchal marriage'. Thus, Traub argues, 'female homoerotic desire simultaneously is acknowledged *and mas-tered* by male writers'. Routinely confined to the rhetorical register of an elegiac pastoralism, this female homoeroticism is 'granted sig-nification only in such terms that would render it insignificant'.[114] It is no small measure of Traub's achievement that what the plays thus portray as unremarkable can now no longer be ignored by critics investigating the representation of either gender or sexuality in early modern drama, though a lot more work needs to be done in this area. It is also a sign of the achievement of the critics discussed in this chap-ter that much of the work in performance studies, the youngest of the approaches discussed in this book to which we turn next, is inflected by concerns about the performance of gender and sexuality on stages and screens in the twentieth and twenty-first centuries.

CHAPTER EIGHT

Performance Studies

From Shakespearean performance criticism to Shakespearean performance studies

It is perhaps fitting, for a book which is partly designed to map out avenues for further research, that the last chapter should be dedicated to a field which is still in the process of consolidating. Although the study of Shakespeare in performance has now become part of the mainstream, with academic journals, conferences, edited collections and monographs dedicated to the subject, this is not true of the study of the plays of his contemporaries in performance. Indeed, as Sarah Werner remarks, '[o]ur knowledge and theories of performance are shaped nearly entirely by Shakespeare's drama and not by those of his contemporaries'.[1] This is so in spite of the inclusion of non-Shakespearean plays in the repertoire of Shakespeare's Globe, the Royal Shakespeare Company's (RSC) 2002 and 2005 seasons of mainly non-Shakespearean texts in the Swan theatre, the efforts of the Red Bull Theatre Company in New York, which stages plays by Shakespeare's contemporaries and which hosts readings of lesser-known plays,[2] and the release of three 'Jacobean' films around the turn of the millennium (Marcus Thompson's *Middleton's Changeling* (1997–8), Mike Figgis's *Hotel* (2001) and Alex Cox's *Revengers Tragedy* (2002)), which seemed to herald a renaissance of Jacobean drama.

Within Shakespeare studies, the modern study of performance began in the 1970s. In 1971, Roger Manvell published *Shakespeare and the Film*, the first attempt at a comprehensive history of the genre. This was followed in 1977 by Jack Jorgens's *Shakespeare on Film*, which analyses classic international film adaptations and influentially distinguishes between theatrical, realist and filmic modes of film adaptation. The publication of J. L. Styan's polemical *The Shakespeare Revolution* in 1977 was even more important.[3] Earlier calls for a consideration of how the study of modern performances could teach us something about early modern texts had been made by scholar-practitioners such as William Poel and Harley Granville-Barker, but it is with Styan that the study of Shakespeare in the modern theatre entered the mainstream.

Styan traces the line of descent of his book back to the growing interest in 'Elizabethan' playing conditions in the wake of the discovery of the de Witt sketch of the Swan theatre in 1888 and W. W. Greg's publication of the *Diary* and *Papers* of Philip Henslowe at the beginning of the twentieth century, leading to E.K.Chambers's seminal work *The Elizabethan Stage* (see my discussion of this book on pp. 12–14). The study of modern theatrical performance of early modern drama thus began with theatre history and early modern performance: for both the literary scholar and the director, Styan believes, the 'secret of what [Shakespeare] intended lies in how he worked'.[4] That secret, he argues, can be discovered either through historical study or – and this is where Styan marks a branching off from traditional theatre history – by looking at how the plays 'work' in the modern theatre. This had become possible in the 1970s thanks to the efforts of theatre practitioners such as Tyrone Guthrie (1900–71), whose design (together with Tanya Moiseiwitsch (1914–2003)) for the stage at Stratford, Ontario in 1953 influenced 'new theatre-building throughout America and England'. The resulting buildings sought to reproduce early modern playing conditions and thus encouraged a non-realistic approach to the drama, culminating in 'Peter Brook's landmark production of *A Midsummer Night's Dream* at Stratford in England in 1970'. For Styan, this production showed how even when using 'apparently non-Elizabethan devices', performances could help us understand Shakespeare better.[5]

Styan's belief that 'the best practitioners' seek 'to be loyal to their author' is typical of the discourses of fidelity and authenticity prevalent in the early days of performance criticism.[6] Twenty years later, in 'Shakespeare's page, Shakespeare's stage: performance criticism', an incisive chapter on the evolution of the field and its continuing use of Shakespeare as an authorising figure, William B. Worthen was to criticise the way in which, for Styan, 'the historical particularity of the modern stage and of the various avant-gardes […] is reduced to a single Shakespearean essence – non-illusionistic representation'.[7] Styan's concerted effort to search for this Shakespearean essence in modern performances makes of the modern stage 'a site of interpretation, rather than a place of production, a place where meanings are found, not made'.[8] Performance criticism as practiced by Styan sees the performance as always already inferior to the text, which authorises all the meanings that can be 'discovered' in performance.

It took a few more years for performance criticism to free itself (more or less successfully, depending on the critic) from the tyranny of a search for authenticity and 'faithfulness' to the Shakespearean text and to mature, under the influence of cultural studies and the development of drama departments in British and American universities, into a study of how theatre practitioners *create* meaning through performance. The influence of Michel Foucault's interrogation of the concept of authorship and the consequent rethinking of what constitutes a 'text' within textual criticism coincided with an increased self-reflexivity and push towards a theorisation of the field. Gradually, traditional Shakespearean performance criticism evolved into Shakespearean performance studies. This is a broader, more theoretically informed field, whose concern is how modern 'performances' of Shakespeare – whether theatrical, televisual, filmic, or digital – use Shakespeare's works as a pre-text for the creation of meanings relevant to contemporary culture. As Terence Hawkes explains in *Meaning By Shakespeare* (1992):

■ We *use* [Shakespeare's plays] in order to generate meaning. In the twentieth century, Shakespeare's plays have become one of the central agencies through which our culture performs this operation. That is what they do, that is how they work, and that is what they are for. Shakespeare doesn't mean: *we* mean *by* Shakespeare.[9] □

Significantly, Hawkes's book is not a performance study but is concerned with a wide variety of ways in which twentieth-century culture appropriates Shakespeare to reflect its own concerns. The fact that his statement nevertheless so succinctly situates the concerns of performance studies from the 1990s onwards shows how strongly this field is invigorated by cultural studies and materialist criticism.

A key figure who emerges in the 1990s is Barbara Hodgdon. In the first chapter of *The End Crowns All: Closure and Contradiction in Shakespeare's History* (1991), Hodgdon almost incidentally sets out the agenda for performance studies and, crucially, insists on the need for a proper theoretical underpinning of the field. Hodgdon sees the Shakespearean play as 'one part of a larger intertext' which performs different kinds of 'cultural work' now and in the early modern period.[10] Programmatically, she states,

■ since I consider that a Shakespearean play exists in multiple states – as the words constituting the playtexts, as the readings based on those texts, and as their concrete, historically particular theatrical representations, or performance texts – my project encompasses all these forms of textuality or, to put it another way, several different 'Shakespeares'.[11] □

In every line of this statement the influence of recent developments in textual criticism can be felt: the insistence on textual multiplicity, instability and the view of 'Shakespeare' as a Foucauldian author-function. More than any other kind of 'Shakespearean' text, Hodgdon reminds us, theatrical performances are time-bound and context-bound and are 'invariably geared to historically determined cultural or critical preoccupations'.[12] Hodgdon quarrels with critics who seek in performances for a Shakespeare familiar from their study of the text. Such 'textual fidelity' is an illusion, since performances 'fracture such ideal constructs into multiplicity, diversity, heterogeneity, and, often, discontinuity, especially when they venture into unknown territory that may shatter readers-turned-spectators' notions of textual integrity'.[13]

Drawing on the work of theatre historians, Hodgdon seeks authority for her view of performance as a medium at least equivalent, if not superior, to the printed text in the fact that in 'Elizabethan and Jacobean theater practice [...] the staged representation not only preceded but certainly had primacy over the "play as text"'.[14] Hodgdon's awareness of the 'conceptual illusion behind the term "text"' leads her to develop an influential terminology that is subtler than the simple opposition between 'text' and 'performance':

> ■ When I refer specifically to the words that are traditionally construed as 'Shakespeare's play', I generally use the term 'playtext', both to convey some sense of their indeterminacy and to differentiate them from other, more determinate, textual categories. To further destabilize both the ideal of an established, authoritative text of a Shakespearean play and the notion that the written word represents the only form in which a play can possess or participate in textuality, I refer to theatrical representations as 'performance texts', an apparent oxymoron that freely acknowledges the perceived incompatibility between the (infinitely) flexible substate(s) of a Shakespearean play and the (relative) fixity of the term 'text'. □

This terminology significantly does not privilege either the playtext or the performance text, but allows the two modes of textuality to exist in an equal relationship of 'intertextual complementarity'.[15] Performance text(s) and playtext(s) can enter into a dialogue with each other, mediated by the figure of the critic herself, who refuses to hide behind a collective 'we' and insists that her readings of playtext(s) and performance text(s) are 'necessarily the textual construction of a singular, historically and culturally determined reader and spectator'.[16] This is not theatre history that pretends to be objective: in Hodgdon's hands, the very subjectivity of the critic's response is a crucial element in the re-creation of performance in the medium of print.

Whereas in *The End Crowns All*, Hodgdon concentrates on the theatre work of the RSC, her critical practice then and now is far broader and encompasses film – arguably a more stable mode of textuality that needs to be integrated into her theoretical framework[17] – and 'texts' as varied as production photographs, literary criticism, a Barbie doll modelled on Liz Taylor's Cleopatra and Shakespeare-themed souvenirs from Stratford-upon-Avon.[18] Her ability to bring all these different forms of text into dialogue with one another and with contemporary culture makes her one of the most influential figures in Shakespearean performance studies. This position has been consolidated by her guest editorship, in 2002, of issue 52:2 of *Shakespeare Quarterly* dedicated to Shakespeare on screen and by her co-editorship, with William B. Worthen – the author of two important metacritical books on the subject – of the weighty *Companion to Shakespeare and Performance* (2005). The avowed 'theoretical heterodoxy of Shakespeare performance studies' as represented by the thirty-four essays by leading scholars in this volume shows that this field is still fresh, vibrant and far from having found a single, unifying voice.[19] For the purposes of this introductory sketch, however, I wish to concentrate instead on two other books, by Carol Chillington Rutter and Diana Henderson, that arguably exemplify the two principal strands of contemporary Shakespearean performance studies and that interpret performances of Shakespeare's plays in ways which may be adapted, with some re-thinking, for a consideration of non-Shakespearean drama in performance.

Carol Rutter's mainly stage-centred monograph *Enter the Body: Women and Representation on Shakespeare's Stage* (2001) engages with the Jacobean context and works within the paradigms established by performance studies, cultural studies, feminist criticism and the study of race. What distinguishes Rutter is her interest in the 'work' bodies – and especially women's bodies – 'do' both in contemporary performance and the early modern theatre. Her book signals a circumscribed return to an attempt 'to recover something of early modern performance practice' through performance criticism. But this is not a naïve search for some Shakespearean authority that might become apparent in modern performance. Rather, Rutter's return to the early modern period relies on 'calling as witness a variety of contemporary texts that help [her] understand' the 'body consciousness' of Shakespeare's culture: 'documents, letters, playhouse accounts, portraits, tomb effigies, official and unofficial notices'.[20] Rutter's performance study is thus informed by her proven skills as a theatre historian as well as by the work of the anthropologist Clifford Geertz, who introduced the notion of 'thick descriptions' into the critical arena in the 1970s.[21] By creating a dense narrative out of her evidence and memories, Rutter wants to 'produce the kind of archival record of [her] own viewing [of performance] that remembers it accurately for subsequent readers – even as [she] acknowledge[s] its inaccuracy'.[22]

I want to concentrate on Rutter's chapter on 'Shadowing Cleopatra: Making Whiteness Strange'. This is where she most provocatively engages with the Jacobean dramatic context, and where her methodology and thinking about non-Shakespearean (con)texts are especially stimulating. Starting from a consideration of four RSC production photographs of Cleopatra with her 'girls' in 1953, 1972, 1982 and 1992, Rutter notes how white Cleopatras always seem to be surrounded by black (or blacked-up) actors playing 'her sidekicks and servants'.[23] Setting each production in its own historical and cultural context, Rutter traces a narrative of paradoxical erasure and foregrounding of black bodies on the RSC stage which, in view of the imperial narrative Shakespeare constructs with his opposition of black and white bodies, has political implications. For example, Rutter contrasts the 1992 main-house production, in which blonde Clare Higgins' Cleopatra was shadowed by black actor Claire Benedict's Charmian, with the same company's staging, in the more marginal Swan, of Marlowe's *Tamburlaine*, in which Benedict played Zenocrate. Rutter's comment on this juxtaposition has important implications for the study of non-Shakespearean drama in performance:

■ As Marlowe's epic tale of sex, war, empire and betrayal has it, Zenocrate, taken captive by Tamburlaine, captivates him Cleopatra-like. If anyone noticed that Egyptian queens were playing on alternate nights in playhouses standing side by side, they might have made something of the coincidence that cultural-outsider Marlowe's queen was black, insider Shakespeare's was one of 'our' girls, (lily) white.[24] □

The relationship between Shakespeare and the drama of his contemporaries is thus racialised, with Shakespeare, as late as in the 1990s, identified with imperialist white culture and set against the Orientalist discourse associated with the drama of his contemporaries. The contemporaries' association with transgressive sexuality, femininity and exoticism, adds gendered and racialised connotations to the time-worn opposition between Shakespeare's wholesome genius and Jacobean decadence.

In the last part of her chapter, Rutter turns to the specifically Jacobean contexts that conditioned the ways in which Shakespeare could conceive of putting a 'black' Cleopatra on-stage. Significantly, this return to the Jacobean period is motivated by Rutter's rage against the supposedly 'authentic' casting of 37-year-old Mark Rylance as Cleopatra for the 1999 production at Shakespeare's Globe (as if he were a 'boy' actor). Rutter's comments once more situate Shakespeare at the cultural and geographical centre and make of Shakespearean casting a larger issue in terms of racial, sexual, gender and class politics:

■ Let us, for one thing, be under no illusion that arguing 'authenticity' is harmless antiquarianism. Rather, it's a tactic of legitimation whose end is political, for it leaves Shakespeare in the sole possession of white male actors, gay or straight, Shakespeare's only 'authentic' players. What this means is that at a time when Shakespeare in Britain is being opened up pluralistically in companies like

Talawa, Northern Broadsides, Cheek by Jowl and the English Shakespeare Company to cross-race, cross-gender, cross-class and cross-cultural casting (and viewing), Shakespeare is likewise being claimed as the exclusive property of 'authorized' Shakespeare playhouses like the Globe and the RST: 'our Bill', it seems, must be located at the 'centre'. □

Cheekily, Rutter's politically motivated battle for the casting of a black woman as Cleopatra on a British mainstream stage therefore takes the shape of a search for historical 'authenticity': 'if Cleopatra's 'tawny front' stands a chance of being reinvented in mainstream representation, arguing her 'authenticity' is the imperative strategy for recovery'. Setting *Antony and Cleopatra* side-by-side with *Othello* and Jonson's *Masque of Blackness*, Rutter reads 'Cleopatra not just as a nostalgic homage to Elizabeth, a queen of "infinite variety", but [as] a tribute to yet another "wrangling queen", Anna of Denmark'.[25] Rutter's Jacobean Cleopatra is a composite of the 'black gipsy' of folk tradition, the queen of 'a black nation managed by women' of 'frank sexuality' which Shakespeare could have found in Herodotus, and the black daughter of Niger played by the conspicuously fertile and extravagant Anna of Denmark in *Blackness*.[26]

Rutter's book offers a stimulating model for the study of non-Shakespearean Jacobean drama in performance, embedding *Antony and Cleopatra* in the Jacobean period while productively situating it in the gender and race politics of the present day. Crucially, her work provokes questions about the cultural politics of Shakespearean and non-Shakespearean production that urgently demand to be addressed in criticism. What is at stake when Jacobean plays are staged by Shakespeare-identified companies such as the RSC or Shakespeare's Globe? How do such productions differ from Jacobean drama staged in fringe and provincial venues? If Rutter manages to map out the opposition between Shakespeare and Marlowe in terms of race, can the same be done, for example, in terms of class? Is there a distinction to be made between the 'authenticity' sought for a production of Shakespeare and that sought for the staging of a play by another playwright?

Quite different questions are provoked by Diana Henderson's *Concise Companion to Shakespeare on Screen* (2006), whose essays were commissioned to 'demonstrate the rich variety of possible roads into the study and interpretation of Shakespeare on screen' and are designed to 'provide a snapshot of this moment's "state of the field"'.[27] The volume's importance lies in the way it enables us to transfer to the study of Jacobean drama the distinct critical angles its contributors were asked to 'model' in their essays so as to provide 'the vocabulary and resources to help readers apply various methodologies to productions of their own choosing'.[28] In his examination of Michael Almereyda's *Hamlet* (2000), for example, Robert Shaughnessy probes the question of why the film replaces the military and political framework of the play with an economic framework (Alex Cox's *Revengers Tragedy* begs the same question). Moreover, his preoccupation with Almereyda's substitution of a film-within-the-film for the play-within-the-play speaks to the striking self-reflexivity of Mike Figgis's *Hotel*, whose plot is loosely structured around *The Duchess of Malfi* and which incorporates a film-within-the-film of *Malfi*. Peter S. Donaldson also ponders the issue of Almereyda's metacinematic strategies and furthermore makes observations about his *Hamlet*'s use of grainy digital video technology that are equally true of *Hotel*'s prominent use of digital cameras. My point is not simply that *Revengers* and *Hotel* stand in an interesting intertextual relationship to Almereyda's *Hamlet*, but that the kind of thinking and theoretical framework that Shaughnessy and Donaldson employ is transferable. Shaughnessy's remark that 'for increasing numbers of spectators (and critics), Shakespeare films are read in relation to other films (Shakespearean and otherwise), rather than to – and even instead of – literary or theatrical versions of the text' is an important warning against considering film adaptations only in relation to their original playtexts and stage productions of those texts.[29] Shaughnessy's thinking about the theatricality of older *Hamlet*s, furthermore, should be essential reading for anyone exploring the available screen versions of Jonson's *Volpone*, which share a strong element of theatricality.

Other 'transferable' thinking can be found in Barbara Hodgdon's reflection on the role of 'R. P.' or 'received pronunciation' in making the Shakespearean actor's voice 'both author-itative and authentic', which is thought-provoking in relation to the conspicuous use of local accents in *Hotel* and *Revengers*. Her discussion of how the 'disjuncture between voice and body' is negotiated in the 'overtly postmodern milieu' of 'Luhrmann's *William Shakespeare's Romeo + Juliet* [1996]' speaks to the clumsily ostentatious postmodernity of Marcus Thompson's *Middleton's Changeling*.[30] Moreover, her assessment of the 'psycho-physiological mode of acting', which is 'currently the dominant paradigm' in acting Shakespeare on screen, can be contrasted with the deliberate use of distancing devices in contemporary Jacobean films.[31] Conversely, my own chapter on sex and violence maps out ways of looking at violence and the representation of masculinity that can be useful for a consideration of the male body in Jacobean film. Meanwhile, Mark Thornton Burnett's appraisal of the 'ultimately "glocal" appearance' characteristic of various adaptations of *Hamlet* and *Macbeth* is relevant for the defiantly Liverpudlian setting of *Revengers*. Particularly suggestive, here, is the idea of the 'deploy[ment of] the local to confront Shakespeare and, in particular, his global status as transnational voice'.[32] Finally, the first essay in the collection, by Elsie Walker, returns to the vexed question of 'authenticity' and 'faithfulness' to the 'original' text. Walker demonstrates that the directors' claims about the fidelity of their films often mask their 'more complex, playful and/or painful confrontation with Shakespeare'.[33] An important question raised by Walker's essay is that of the significance of Shakespeare's contemporaries in our cinematic culture. If 'even those making the most self-consciously postmodern Shakespeare films speak of the restorative power of the endlessly enduring, immediate, and relevant Shakespearean text',[34] then what is invoked when Shakespeare's contemporaries are brought onto our screens? What is their 'authority', and what cultural work do they perform? These questions all urgently need answers.

'Jacobean performance studies': founding a new critical field

The questions implicitly raised by Walker begin to be addressed by Susan Bennett's *Performing Nostalgia: Shifting Shakespeare and the Contemporary Past* (1996), a superb but lonely pioneer of Jacobean performance studies. There *are* earlier studies of Jacobean plays in performance, of course, but even valuable performance criticism like Michael Scott's *John Marston's Plays: Theme, Structure and Performance* (1978) and Christina Luckyj's *A Winter's Snake: Dramatic Form in the Tragedies of John Webster* (1989) does not have the conceptual sophistication of modern Shakespearean performance studies.

Bennett's *Performing Nostalgia* in its very structure advertises the cross-fertilisation that brings a solid theoretical framework from Shakespearean performance studies across to Jacobean drama, for its starting point, once again, is Shakespeare. Bennett notes 'how often Shakespeare performs the role which links the psychic experience of nostalgia to the possibility of reviving an authentic, naturally better, and material past'.[35] Nonetheless, she wonders whether there are ways in which performers can ever escape being bound to tradition and do more than merely 'fantasize the possibility of the new' in their productions of old texts. Importantly, her project is concerned with performances that challenge 'tradition' and 'Shakespeare' and seek to articulate transgression rather than nostalgia. It is out of this quest for the performance of 'transgressive knowledge' that Bennett's chapter on Jacobean drama, 'Not-Shakespeare, Our Contemporary: Transgression, Dissidence, and Desire', arises.[36]

Bennett is arrested by the increase in the number of productions of non-Shakespearean early modern drama on English stages in the 1980s and early 1990s. She sees this upsurge as a theatrical parallel to the 'obsession with the "radical" in critical inquiry' in the same period.[37] 'The Jacobean', for Bennett, is a signifier which refers to 'both more and less' than simply the plays produced during the reign of James I. In her flexible usage, 'the Jacobean' denotes 'many kinds of cultural production (deriving from any number of historical moments) which share some of the values that characterized the primary generic forms of Jacobean drama, the city comedy and the revenge tragedy'.[38] This use of the term opens up films like Peter Greenaway's *The Cook, the Thief, His Wife and Her Lover* (1989) and Derek Jarman's *Edward II* (1991) to her 'Jacobean' enquiry. Instead of troubling the waters, Bennett's loose use of 'the Jacobean' clarifies the important role these films played in the emergence of non-Shakespearean drama as a major cultural, theatrical and critical phenomenon from the 1980s onwards. 'All of these productions', Bennett asserts, to some extent 'appropriate a Jacobean text as novelty. More importantly, they appropriate these texts because these are novelties that sell', even if they only sell because audiences seek in Jacobean plays more Shakespeare, but with an added twist of 'psychopathic violence and deviant desires'. Whereas the nostalgia associated with revivals of Shakespeare is relatively straightforward in its conservatism, the nostalgia activated by Jacobean revivals during the Thatcher years is more complex:

■ [T]he Jacobean as performance realizes an intention to have the audience visualize the past in the present: to see its resemblance to our own world and to nourish our psychic desires for the past itself. Unlike the idealized authenticity and authority of Shakespeare's (great) texts, these Jacobean revivals point to a less than perfect past, but nonetheless one which can help us legitimise our own defective present. The designation's function, even as it marks transgression and dissidence, points to a continuous and repetitive history, the inevitability of which we can do no more than accept.[39] □

Here lies a provisional answer to some of the questions about the performance of non-Shakespearean drama raised in Walker's essay on Shakespearean authority: staging the Jacobeans may amount to little more than a bit of 'radical chic' with which to mask conservative impulses.[40]

Not all Jacobean revivals of the period, however, participate in this nostalgic justification of present dysfunction through reference to a comfortingly defective past. As Bennett demonstrates in the second part of her chapter, 'the Jacobean' can, in some instances, be 'one site where the contradictory impulses of nostalgia perform themselves in a disruptive and occasionally emancipatory mode'.[41] Bennett's reading of Jarman's *Edward II* is particularly interesting, for it provides a useful framework for looking at the three Jacobean films that were about to appear when her book was published. Bennett finds that Jarman's film, 'has a clearly articulated dissident politics' that arises from its gay director's fight against official homophobia. Especially evocative, when thinking of the 'queer' sexualities that emerge so consistently in the three recent Jacobean films, are Bennett's remarks on how the opposition between Shakespeare and his contemporaries can be mapped according to sexuality and even nationality: 'Marlowe's plays [...] are explicitly marked as not-Shakespeare (and, apparently, by association not-English) and designated thus on an identification of sexual identity. Actual sexual preferences and practices of the authors are neither important nor stable for the efficiency of this designation'.[42] A different way of mapping Jacobean drama in opposition to Shakespeare is hinted at with an analysis of productions of Jacobean plays by fringe companies such as Red Shift and in venues such as the Royal Court Theatre; more marginal companies and venues, Bennett suggests, are instrumental in offering an alternative view of Jacobean drama to that promoted by the dominant, Shakespeare-identified, RSC and Shakespeare's Globe theatres.

Putting down Bennett's book and picking up Martin White's *Renaissance Drama in Action: An Introduction to Aspects of Theatre Practice and Performance* (1998) is an unsettling experience. This is not only because White's implied reader is a student whereas Bennett's is an academic, but more so because its methodology is derived from theatre history and performance criticism. 'Performance text', in White's usage, does not refer to contemporary performance-as-text; rather, it refers to what Hodgdon would call the 'playtext', but a playtext which is inherently geared towards theatrical performance, whether in the Jacobean or the modern theatre. The interest of White's book lies in his down-to-earth observations about the difficulties inherent in approaching Jacobean drama, whether on the page or on stage.

White's discussion of the theatrical conditions pertaining in early modern London is punctuated by case studies of modern performances. Here, in an essay by Harriet Walter on her performance of the title role in *The Duchess of Malfi* for the RSC in 1989, we find a rare example in print of a modern performer's attempt at finding a Stanislavskian 'character' in a Jacobean playtext. Walter offers insights into the play which are hard to gain for anyone who does not share the performer's obsession with her/his own character. One such insight is the shift the Duchess undergoes from being an active subject to becoming, increasingly, an object: 'it gets harder as after her arrest she *does* less and less, and more and more is done to her [...]. Increasingly, as her power to act diminishes, so her words become her actions'.[43] A rich diachronic dialogue between early modern and twentieth-century performance practices is created by juxtaposing Walter's essay with White's close reading of the final scene of *Malfi* that relates it to Adrian Noble's 1980

Manchester Royal Exchange production of the play and with White's detailed description of indoor playing spaces and theatre practice in Jacobean and Caroline London.

White also includes a revealing case study of a production of *'Tis Pity She's a Whore* in the Wickham Theatre, the University of Bristol's reconstruction of a 'Jacobean' private theatre. It is this sort of work that White excels in, as is also evident from his *Chamber of Demonstrations* (2009), a book in the shape of an interactive DVD and website that allows the viewer to see the lighting conditions and staging possibilities afforded in the Wickham Theatre (see also pp. 28–9).[44] White's primary concern, in *Chamber of Demonstrations* even more than in *Renaissance Drama in Action*, is with using modern performance, and especially student productions, as a 'test-bed', as 'work arising from a critical and historical study of the plays, as practical examples of how they relate space and language and action'.[45]

By contrast, Roberta Barker's *Early Modern Tragedy, Gender and Performance, 1984–2000: The Destined Livery* (2007), while showing a debt to White and making clever use of Walter's 'case study', is a vigorous attempt to bring the methodologies of performance studies to non-Shakespearean drama. Her introduction, accordingly, thoroughly references the work of Hodgdon, Worthen, Bennett, Aebischer and Rutter at the same time as she repeatedly endeavours to 'ground' her book in the early modern context, whether by using early modern conduct manuals or talking about the significance of cross-dressing. Barker wants to know whether modern female actors performing roles written for boys are 'simply reproducing oppressive early modern images of gender' or whether they can adopt modes of representation – and spectators can adopt modes of viewing – that allow the performances to be read both for their 'inscriptions of binary gender constructions and for [their] potential power to challenge or complicate those constructions'.[46] Barker's corpus of nine performances is deliberately small and she mostly does not attempt to probe the ways in which productions of non-Shakespearean plays may be seen to be in a dialogue not just with earlier productions of the same texts, but also with each other and with stagings of Shakespeare's plays (no comparisons of Cleopatra with Zenocrate here). Instead, her interpretations of two productions of *The Duchess of Malfi* and of Juliet Mitchell's staging of *A Woman Killed with Kindness* (the only 'properly' Jacobean plays analysed by Barker) are particularly 'thick' descriptions. The creation of Barker's personal archive of her viewing (to borrow Rutter's term) is combined with a critical assessment of how the productions' more or less qualified use of naturalistic staging methods had an impact on the representation of gendered identities and subject positions. In its critical integration of Walter's essay into a consideration of modern performances of Jacobean drama that is informed by critical theory and that applies the methodologies of Shakespearean performance studies to Jacobean drama, Barker's book is a milestone in Jacobean performance studies. Meanwhile, her consideration of Jarman's *Edward II* sets the stage for Jacobean performance studies to take on the medium of film.

Jacobean drama on film

The corpus of Jacobean drama commercially available on film is very small indeed. It consists of four French films based on *Volpone*. Maurice Tourneur's *Volpone, ou l'amour de l'or* (1941) and Jean Meyer's *Volpone* (1978) both use Jules Romains' translation of Stefan Zweig's German-language adaptation of the play. Francis Perrin's *Volpone ou le Renard* (2002) uses Jonson's text in a translation by Jean Collette and Toni Cecchinato, while Frédéric Auburtin's 2003 *Volpone*, starring Gérard Depardieu, largely relies on Eric-Emmanuel Schmitt's translation, to which it adds a lengthy opening sequence. The French *Volpone*-corpus is complemented by Jaques Rivette's New Wave adaptation of *The Revenger's Tragedy* as *Noroît* (1976), starring Geraldine Chaplin. Rivette's French-language plot revolving around two rival gangs of female pirates, loosely based on the Jacobean play, integrates a play-within-the-play which uses some of the English text of *The Revenger's Tragedy*. In its bizarre use of anachronisms, its refusal to conform to mainstream forms of cinematic narrative and its free play with the Jacobean pre-text, *Noroît* is the ancestor of the more recent three English feature films of revenge tragedies which I have referred to repeatedly in this chapter: Marcus Thompson's *Middleton's Changeling*, Mike Figgis's *Hotel* and Alex Cox's *Revengers Tragedy*.

Volpone on English stages and French screens

Of all non-Shakespearean drama, it is *Volpone* which has seen the largest number of still available film adaptations and has had the most success on the Continent. But even with a play that has had such unusually ample theatrical, filmic and critical exposure, the task of writing about its performance history is fraught with difficulties, as Ejner J. Jensen notes in *Ben Jonson's Comedies on the Modern Stage* (1985):

■ it is important to recognize that [...] the shadow cast by Shakespeare makes our perception of Jonson rather imperfect. When theatrical reviewers approach a Shakespearean production, chances are good that they have seen other versions of the play. Moreover, it is likely that their knowledge of past performances and indeed of the entire production history of the play will condition their expectations and focus their attention. And this is to say nothing of their knowledge of the critical heritage. [...] Such familiarity cannot be expected by those who assess productions of Jonson's comedies [...]. Thus any account of Jonson's stage fortunes is bound to differ in important ways from the various efforts to record the production history of the plays of Shakespeare.[47] □

It is therefore not only because R. B. Parker's 'Volpone in Performance: 1921–1972' (1978) and Jensen's stage history predate the inception of modern performance studies that their accounts of the play's stage fortunes in the twentieth century read distinctly differently to performance criticism of Shakespeare's plays: the dissimilarity is inherent in the kinds of material traces performances of Shakespeare's contemporaries leave behind. Parker's solution is to concentrate on how directors of Volpone dealt with various problems of staging (décor, casting, the relation of the main plot to the subplot, the play's metatheatricality and the tone of its dénouement). Jensen, on the other hand, strives to establish whether Jonson's plays can ever be more than museum pieces. The very fact that this question needs asking pinpoints the problem at the heart of Jacobean performance studies.

Because Jensen's focus is on the theatre, he has little to say about the Zweig/Romains/Tourneur Volpone, the only one of the three available films to have received any critical attention. Jensen merely acknowledges that 'Zweig's work had an undoubted influence on the reception of Jonson's Volpone in this century' and that '[b]y supplying an updated and in some ways more accessible version of Jonson's dramatic fable, it has sometimes, like a rude child, shouldered its parent from view'.[48] A similar resentment of the film is perceptible in James M. Welsh's 'Shades of Ben Jonson and Stefan Zweig: "Volpone" on Film' (1974): for Welsh, 'there can be no doubt that the play Volpone has been violated, foreshortened, and diluted both in structure and effect'.[49] Although Welsh thus ranks himself among those who seek in performance signs of authenticity and faithfulness to the text, his essay ends with an attempt to move beyond simple condemnation to a suggestion that the 'film should be accepted on its own terms' because of its 'technical perfection' and 'the extraordinary skill of its actors'.[50]

Two more recent articles convey a more positive view of Zweig and Tourneur. Karen Forsyth, in 'Stefan Zweig's Adaptations of Ben Jonson' (1981), concentrates on Zweig's text and, while acknowledging that '[l]ack of solid scholarship was always one of the vulnerable points of Zweig's literary ventures',[51] gives an appreciative account of Zweig's Volpone (1926) and his version of Epicoene, which he turned into a libretto for Richard Strauss's comic opera *Die schweigsame Frau* ('The Silent Woman') in 1935. Forsyth detects a pattern in Zweig's versions of Jonson which is compatible with the Austro-Bavarian tradition and Strauss's late Romanticism: 'A simpler plot is extracted from a Jonsonian web, a moral hero (or heroes) is drawn forth out of a less glamorous prototype, an erring individual is encouraged to return to the harmonious fold, and above all a need for conciliation and reconciliation softens the contours and ensures a happy outcome'.[52] Forsyth's focus on the text is complemented by Hanna Scolnicov's attention to the film in '*The Merchant in Volpone*: Narrative and Conceptual Montage in Maurice Tourneur's Film' (2001). She argues that Jules Romains inserted elements of Shakespeare's *The Merchant of Venice* into Tourneur's script. Her use of film studies terminology enables her to give a sophisticated account of how 'the film blends the Shakespearean elements into the Jonsonian intrigue to create a conceptual as well as narrative montage'.[53] Scolnicov describes the film as 'the last in a series of steps leading from Ben Jonson's Jacobean interpretation of the Roman legacy-hunting theme up to the twentieth-century adaptation to the new medium, crossing languages and cultures on the way', and her reading emphasises the contributions each of the adapters made to combining disparate texts and disparate shots into a single aesthetic product.[54]

Jacobean tragedy on film

Moving from the *comédie française*-style French *Volpone*s and the mostly conservative criticism they have provoked to *Noroît* and the three British turn-of-the-millennium film releases of Jacobean tragedies requires a change of gear. It is as if the filmmakers had assumed that all the 'straightness' available had already been taken over, in the cultural sphere, by Shakespeare and had embraced the 'decadence' of his Jacobean counterparts as something positive. This, of course, is in close accord with Bennett's insight about the ways in which 'the Jacobean' signifies excess and it also chimes in with Rutter's observations about the troubled relationship between Shakespeare and his Jacobean 'others', who are defined according to a binary opposition of gentle/violent, heterosexual/homosexual, white/black. It does not matter, for this distinction, that critics have long argued for a reconsideration of Shakespeare's work as controversial, fraught with political and individual violence, implicated in proto-colonialist discourses, and particularly appropriate for queer readings, or that the performance tradition of Shakespeare's plays is far from being as 'straight' as is implicitly assumed.

As I argue in 'Renaissance Tragedy on Film: Defying Mainstream Shakespeare' (2009), a survey of 'Jacobean' films in the looser sense in which I include Giuseppe Patroni Griffi's *'Tis Pity She's a Whore* (1971), Peter Greenaway's *The Cook, the Thief, His Wife and Her Lover* (1989) and Derek Jarman's *Edward II* (1991), 'Jacobean' films define themselves against Shakespeare. They do so by adopting modes of representation that are deliberately anachronistic, disjointed, disrespectful of their source texts, and counter-cinematic. Using psychoanalyst Julia Kristeva's theory of abjection, which defines the abject as the corporeal parts of the mother an infant has to reject and repress in order to constitute her/his own identity separate from the mother, I suggest that the 'Jacobean' films position themselves as Shakespeare's abject others, as everything that mainstream Shakespeare films exclude and reject in their construction of Shakespeare as 'the epitome of good taste, order and English national identity'.[55] Embracing the position of the abject, 'Jacobean' filmmakers use the plays of Shakespeare's contemporaries as 'the platform from which to critique dominant political structures, representational modes, aesthetic values, the cultural heritage and what it means to be English'.[56]

Greenaway and Jarman have received extensive critical coverage in film studies, their films valued for their attack on Thatcherite values and an aesthetic engagement with England's past and present. By contrast, the critical response to *Noroît* and *Middleton's Changeling* is minimal. Rivette is well known in French film studies as a New Wave filmmaker, but *Noroît* has remained obscure and no criticism is, at present, available in English. The response to *Middleton's Changeling*, on the other hand, is confined to a footnote in Michael Neill's stage history, where he describes this 'bizarrely misconceived' film's anachronistic mixing of 'Jacobean costumes with sports trainers, nineteenth-century carriages with Mercedes limousines and police motorbikes, and mangled original dialogue with contemporary slang'.[57] Some more information is available on the film's website, which reproduces three press reviews.[58]

Mike Figgis's *Hotel*, with its adaptation of *The Duchess of Malfi*, is also virtually uncharted territory. Figgis himself has collected some material about the film (including a review, a monologue spoken by one of the characters, a few handwritten notes and some email exchanges) in his lushly illustrated *In the Dark* (2003). He also mentions the film at several points in his filmmaker's manual *Digital Film-Making* (2007), where he discusses some of its technical aspects. My 'Shakespearean Heritage and the Preposterous Contemporary Jacobean Film: Mike Figgis's *Hotel*' (2009) at present constitutes the only analysis of the film in print. I contend that Figgis's film cultivates a 'contemporary Jacobean' aesthetic and that it uses the Websterian text as a pre-text for an examination of the deployment and exploitation of women's bodies in mainstream cinema. The character of the Duchess of Malfi, and the resistance to patriarchal structures and power which she embodies, is refracted in the film through several female characters who enact aspects of her victimisation and claim to independence. Like the Duchess, these women ultimately fail in their assertion of individual and artistic autonomy and Figgis's denouement cannot provide a satisfactory solution to the problems his film has raised. This, I believe, is crucial to our understanding of the film: *Hotel* is too 'self-consciously implicated in the structures it is criticizing' to be able to transcend them and Figgis expresses this predicament through strategies of self-reflexivity and self-vilification. Rejecting the nostalgia of mainstream Shakespeare and heritage film, *Hotel*, I argue, embraces cultural disinheritance and presents Webster's *Duchess of Malfi* as 'a play "about" the making of *Hotel*, "about" man's control of transgressive female sexuality in the medium of film'.[59]

The corpus of critical material on Alex Cox's *The Revengers Tragedy* is slightly larger. Ben Spiller's '"Today, Vindici Returns": Alex Cox's *Revengers Tragedy*' (2003) somehow managed to be published even before the film was premiered in London and conveys a corresponding sense of roughness and urgency. Spiller comments on the film's 'alternative fictional universe whose inhabitants have rediscovered an antiquated language as a means of communication', so that the 'Jacobean dialogue [...] does not jar against the setting; and the play's excesses of violence, bloodshed and grisly gallows humour retain their early modern tang'.[60] That humour, he notes 'is brought to the fore in the film', with the 'interior shot of the limo' belonging to the Duke's sons becoming an especially memorable 'comic leitmotif as the backseat becomes more spacious as the brothers become fewer'.[61] Spiller is also the first of the film's commentators to pick up on how the death of Antonio's wife (called Imogen in the film) is represented in ways that evoke the mass hysteria at the death of Princess Diana. Jerome de Groot's brief review of the film in the same journal two months later adds to Spiller's assessment a reflection about the antecedents of the film, naming '*A Clockwork Orange* [1971], Derek Jarman's early films, *Velvet Goldmine* [1998], glam, *Bladerunner* [*sic*; 1982], cyberpunk, DIY filmmaking and the kitschy, trashy chic of *Romeo + Juliet*' as the film's main influences. For him, both the play and the film aim 'to subvert, challenge, complicate and destabilise' and succeed in doing so: *Revengers Tragedy*, he maintains, 'is an admirable example of a textual updating that stays in sympathy with the text but avoids deference'.[62]

Andrew Hartley's fuller review in 2004 picks up on 'the film's political energy' which 'stems from [the] typically British sense that class warfare is figured geographically'.[63] Vindici, whose scouse accent strongly identifies him with the film's iconic location in Liverpool, 'gives a face to the dispossessed who haunt the film's margins', his mission not merely personal but representative of an attack on 'a despised and repulsively corrupt elite'.[64] For Hartley, this concern with corrupt authority lies at the heart of *Revengers*, though he is troubled by the ending which seems to caution against revenge and the destruction of the ruling elite. Patrick J. Cook in 'Adapting *The Revengers Tragedy*', meanwhile, comments on the 'sophisticated forms of social control, modern equivalents of the Machiavellianism of Middleton's Italian court' that enable that elite to control their subjects while indulging their libidos.[65] Cook emphasises the 'extreme hybridity' of the film's style and contrasts this with the ways Shakespeare's plays have been translated into film; in his eyes, the unpredictable shifts 'between a wide range of compositions, camera angles and movements, even between color and monochrome, naturalistic cinematography and abstraction' in *Revengers* is highly effective.[66]

Finally, Gretchen E. Minton's '*The Revenger's Tragedy* in 2002: Alex Cox's Punk Apocalypse' (2009) picks up on and expands the lines of argument of her predecessors. The anachronisms that every critic of the film comments on are here described as contributing to the film's 'layered effect', which is also achieved by its blend of modern and Jacobean English and by its Liverpudlian setting: 'This setting illustrates just how broken down society has become, but it also displays a complex landscape that is itself out of joint because it includes modern architecture as well as remnants of a much older society, creating an architectural palimpsest'.[67] These disjunctions align the film both with recent Shakespeare films and with futuristic dystopias of the 1980s like *Blade Runner* and the *Mad Max* series (1979–85), while the farcical ending recalls Tarantino's 'sense of domino-effect murders'.[68] Particularly valuable, in Minton's chapter, is the way she links the film's cinematic pedigree, in which she also includes Julie Taymor's *Titus* (1999) and Michael Almereyda's *Hamlet*, to Alex Cox's previous work and the gestation of *Revengers*, drawing parallels between the director (who appears in the film) and the protagonist. Middleton's disillusion with the early years of James's reign is blended with Cox's own 'disaffection with the Blair UK', so that the film speaks urgently to the present moment.[69] For my part, I end with the hope that the present moment will speak back to these films and finally give them the extensive critical corpus they deserve.

Conclusion

The study of Jacobean drama, as this book has shown, is as varied as it is vigorous. Drawing its inspiration and methodologies from diverse disciplines, the field is leaning ever less heavily on the pillar of Shakespeare as it finds its own foundations and stability. People often ask me whether there really is something new to say about Jacobean drama. The answer is a resolute 'yes'. This is not only because resources such as *Early English Books Online (EEBO)* and *Records of Early English Drama (REED)* are making ever more documents available to researchers, with new search mechanisms that make, say, looking for references to miscarriages in Jacobean comedies and medical treatises, searching for performances by touring companies in Devon or analysing patterns of theatrical patronage easier than ever before. It is also because as new areas are explored, they inevitably reveal new lacunae in our knowledge of the drama and the period, and as our culture evolves, the questions we ask of the past change to reflect current interests and anxieties.

The research surveyed in this book is already pointing to a number of areas that need further exploration. In theatre history, we need to do more to understand performances outside London. Peter Holland has recently called for a much more thorough examination of the available sections of *REED*, records which, precisely because they are not concerned with London as the centre of theatrical culture, have 'offered the possibility of redefining what dramatic activity is in the early modern period'.[1] Shakespeare will inevitably be marginalised by such work (as is already apparent in the 2009 *Oxford Handbook of Early Modern Theatre*, which illustrates the wide variety of uses to which *REED* can be put) and by the further research that needs to be carried out to understand the Jacobean theatre companies associated with Shakespeare's lesser-known contemporaries. We need to know more about both the boys in their private theatres and the adults working in working-class venues such as the Fortune and Red Bull theatres. We also need to learn yet more about the production and circulation of texts in the period if we are to appreciate how drama was received not only in the theatre but also in the home.

Such research on the plays' production, reception and circulation will fruitfully intersect with the work of textual critics. Tiffany Stern and Simon Palfrey's groundbreaking study of actors' parts in *Shakespeare in Parts* (see p. 37), for example, has important implications for editorial practice. As Paul Whitfield White points out, 'The practice of repeated and premature cueing' which Stern and Palfrey have brought to our attention 'may now compel editors to reconsider multiple points for entering speech. The arrival of the electronic text did not occur a moment too soon, since lines of text can now join character "entrances" as having optional points of entry'.[2] Some electronic editions are in the process of being produced, but in order to bring Jacobean drama to a wider readership and to new audiences we urgently need more large-scale editorial projects along the lines of the Oxford *Middleton* and Cambridge *Jonson*, as well as smaller, cheaper single-text editions that appeal to schools and theatre companies. This work will involve new ways of looking at dramatic canons and authorship, as ever more collaborative drama is produced in print and integrated in the collected works of more than one author.

If theatre history and textual criticism are where some of the most exciting new discoveries are being made at the moment, this does not mean that the historicist and materialist criticism that has been at the heart of the discipline for the last thirty years has exhausted itself altogether. True enough, there are some signs of fatigue and repetitiveness, but in the parts of the field that are cross-fertilised by gender studies, the study of race and the body and, increasingly again, by a concern with the religious debates of post-Reformation England, historicist criticism is still producing exciting, fresh work. Important parts of the historical context, of the conceptualization of the body and of the material culture of Jacobean England are still not properly understood. As Wendy Wall's inquiry into the day-to-day workings of the early modern household has shown (see pp. 129–31), much can, for example, still be learned about the drama's representation of everyday practices and domestic politics if we pay proper attention to neglected documents such as recipe books. Countless murder pamphlets, ballads, sermons and medical texts are also waiting to be scrutinised by historically minded critics who are willing to take on board the lessons taught by New Historicists and cultural materialists. A refined grasp of the ways in which such texts are situated in their culture and are shaped by the ideologies to which they contribute will allow for a more nuanced appreciation of the political dimensions of plays that have not yet been studied from that angle.

The study of genre has not reached the end of the line, either. This is not only because of the recent attention dramatic genres have received from theatre historians and textual critics, but also because several of the smaller, more specialised genres (revenge tragedy, city comedy, tragicomedy, masque, closet drama) in particular are attracting renewed attention from feminist scholars, who are seizing on the ways in which several of these genres both represent and are embedded in the private, feminine spheres. More research is necessary to do justice to the artistic agency of female patrons and performers of courtly and domestic genres such as the masque and closet drama. I was furthermore struck, as I was writing the chapter on race, by the generic patterns that were emerging. I have not yet encountered a convincing explanation for the prominence of racial and ethnic outsiders in the court masque – this, among others, is a question that I would wish to see answered. We also do well to recall Jean Howard's call for a combination of genre study with an attention to historical context: How can we explain the evolution of generic forms and fashions? What historical pressures, we ought to ask, result in genres being modified?

One of the most interesting insights that can be gained from a study of the criticism over two centuries is that the notion of which historical pressures shape the drama changes over time. History is no longer perceived as dominated by kings, queens and their governments' policies: with the emergence of feminism, postcolonialism, Marxist criticism and cultural studies, 'history' has become more democratic and more about people than concepts, wars and debates. A lot of work is at present being done by feminist, queer and postcolonial scholars to understand how the structures of gendered, sexual and racial oppression were perpetuated, set up, and contested in the early modern period. The political agenda of present-day activists is thus shedding new light on texts which are now seen as problematic in ways that could not have been anticipated by critics of an earlier generation. *The Tempest* is no longer a play 'about' the farewell to the theatre of a Shakespeare thinly disguised as Prospero; instead, it has become a play that exposes the predicament of colonial expansion through the figures of Caliban and Ariel and that reveals the instrumentalisation and exploitation of women in marriage negotiations at the Jacobean court. The relationship between Prospero and Ariel has furthermore been subjected to scrutiny from critics and artists who have emphasised its homoerotic qualities. There is no knowing what the play will mean to future generations; all that is clear is that as the cutting edge of political activism shifts, new ways of looking at old plays will become obvious. My hunch is that ecocriticism, which has become well established in other disciplines, is about to become a much more important critical tool in this field, too, and will change our perception of the relationship between the individual and her/his environment not only in pastoral tragicomedy, but throughout Jacobean drama.

Finally, performance studies, the youngest part of the discipline, is crying out for further research. The corpus of commercially available films may be forbiddingly small, but it is growing. The archive of television productions held by the British Film Institute now also includes *Compulsion* (2009), an ITV drama that transposes the plot of *The Changeling* into twenty-first century London, setting Parminder Nagra's wealthy Asian heiress against Flowers, the middle-aged working-class chauffeur played by Ray Winstone. Further TV dramas will no doubt follow and older adaptations ought to become more widely available as demand grows. In the theatre, Roberta Barker's work on RSC productions at the Stratford-upon-Avon Shakespeare Centre Library archives has only begun to unearth the treasures located there. This work is important, but it is equally vital that we understand more about how the drama of Shakespeare's contemporaries has been staged by smaller companies, not just in Britain and the US but throughout the world. Is there a difference, I wonder, between the ways Shakespeare's contemporaries have been received in postcolonial countries as opposed to Europe? How about the opposition between Eastern and Western Europe? What does staging Jacobean drama *mean* in different locations and at different historical junctures?

It is in the nature of this book and of the vibrant fields it surveys that, as up-to-date as it is at the moment of going into print, it will begin to look out of touch within only a few years, as the avenues for research mapped out here will be pursued by new generations of scholars. When that time comes, however, this book need not be retired just yet: the criticism of the 1980s to 2010s will still provide the foundation of new research, and where the book ends, the yearly surveys of the field in *The Year's Work in English Studies* and *Studies in English Literature, 1500–1900*, together with the Shakespeare-specific round-up of criticism in *Shakespeare Survey*, will take over. These yearly surveys, which are often written by scholars at the top of their powers, will go on mapping out the scholarship of the present and the future. It is my hope that some of the readers of this book will want to be part of that future.

Notes

ACKNOWLEDGEMENTS

1. William C. Carroll, 'Recent Studies in Tudor and Stuart Drama', *SEL* 41 (2001), p. 417.

INTRODUCTION   DEFINING 'JACOBEAN DRAMA'

1. John E. Cunningham, *Elizabethan and Early Stuart Drama* (London: Evans Brothers Limited, 1965), p. 89.
2. 'Elizabethan' refers to the reign of Queen Elizabeth I, who reigned from 1558–1603; 'Jacobean' to the reign of King James I of England, who reigned from 1603–25; 'Caroline' to the reign of King Charles I, who reigned from 1625 to 1642.
3. Glynne Wickham, *Early English Stages: 1300 to 1660*, Volume 2, Part I (London: Routledge and Kegan Paul, 1963), p. xiii.
4. See Tom Rutter, 'Adult Playing Companies, 1603–1613', in Richard Dutton (ed.), *The Oxford Handbook of Early Modern Theatre* (Oxford: OUP, 2009), pp. 72–87 for an account of the major changes that took place as a result of royal patronage in 1603.
5. Gerald Eades Bentley, *The Jacobean and Caroline Stage: Dramatic Companies and Players* (Oxford: Clarendon Press, 1941), pp. 151, 186–7.
6. Rowland Wymer, 'Jacobean Tragedy', in Michael Hattaway (ed.), *A Companion to English Renaissance Literature and Culture* (Oxford: Blackwell Publishers Limited, 2000), p. 545.

1   THE CRITICAL TRAIL – EARLY VIEWS TO THE TWENTIETH CENTURY

1. Michael Cordner, 'Zeal-of-the-Land Busy Restored', in Martin Butler (ed.), *Re-Presenting Ben Jonson: Text, History, Performance* (Basingstoke: Macmillan, 1999), p. 174.
2. For the decline in Jonson's popularity, see Ejner J. Jensen, *Ben Jonson's Comedies on the Modern Stage* (Ann Arbor: UMI Research Press, 1985), pp. 7–13.
3. Theophilus Cibber, *The Lives of the Poets of Great Britain and Ireland (1753)*, Vol. 1 of 5 (Hildesheim: Georg Olms Verlagsbuchandlung, 1968), pp. 158–9. A good sense of the importance given to individual Jacobean playwrights in the mid-eighteenth century can be got from the number of pages Cibber dedicates to each: Shakespeare: 20; Jonson: 14; Beaumont and Fletcher: 10; Chapman: 5; Heywood: 3; Marston: 3; Middleton: 3; Dekker: 2; Rowley: 1. No other Jacobean playwright (except for Daniel, who did not write for the public stage) is included.
4. George Coleman, 'Critical Reflections on the Old English Dramatic Writers' in Thomas Coxeter (ed.), *The Dramatic Works of Philip Massinger*, 4 Vols (London: T. Davies, 1761).
5. Charles Lamb, *Charles Lamb's Specimens of English Dramatic Poets Who Lived about the Time of Shakespeare, Including the Extracts from the Garrick Plays*, Israel Gollancz (ed.), Vol. 1 (London: J.M. Dent and Co., 1893), p. xix.
6. Lamb (1893), p. 284.
7. With regard to Shakespeare, Lamb openly opposed the stage representation of the plays – not because he thought they were unworthy of being staged, but because contemporary actors were, he thought, not capable of representing them properly. See his remarks in Charles Lamb, 'On the Tragedies of Shakespeare, considered with reference to their fitness for stage representation' (1811), reprinted in Raymond Macdonald Alden (ed.), *Readings in English Prose of the Nineteenth Century* (Cambridge, MA: The Riverside Press, 1917), pp. 46–55.

8. Lamb (1893), p. 243.

9. Lamb (1893), p. 205.

10. Lamb (1893), p. 213.

11. A. C. Swinburne, 'Charles Lamb, 1885, 1886', in Clyde K. Hyder (ed.), *Swinburne as Critic* (London, Boston: Routledge & Kegan Paul, 1972), p. 271.

12. S. T. Coleridge, *Coleridge on the Seventeenth Century*, Roberta Florence Brinkley (ed.), (Durham, NC: Duke UP, 1955), p. 638.

13. Coleridge (1955), p. 643.

14. Coleridge (1955), p. 650.

15. Coleridge (1955), pp. 668, 678.

16. William Hazlitt, *Lectures on the Literature of the Age of Elizabeth, Chiefly Dramatic*. 1820. (London: George Bell and Sons, 1901), pp. 26, 28.

17. Hazlitt (1901), pp. 2, 1.

18. Hazlitt (1901), p. 104.

19. Hazlitt (1901), pp. 108, 109.

20. Hazlitt (1901), p. 131.

21. Hazlitt (1901), p. 105.

22. Hazlitt (1901), pp. 9–11.

23. William Archer, 'Archer Attacks', reprint of 'Webster, Lamb, and Swinburne' (1893), in Don D. Moore (ed.), *Webster: The Critical Heritage* (London: Routledge & Kegan Paul, 1981), p. 134.

24. Archer (1981), pp. 142, 141.

25. Archer (1981), p. 139.

26. Havelock Ellis (ed.), *The Mermaid Series. Thomas Middleton: The Best Plays of the Old Dramatists* (London: Vizetelly & Co., 1887).

27. John Addington Symonds, 'John Webster and Cyril Tourneur', in John Addington Symonds (ed.), *The Mermaid Series: Webster and Tourneur* (London: T. Fisher Unwin, 1888), p. x.

28. Symonds (1888), pp. xi–xii.

29. Oscar Wilde, *The Complete Works of Oscar Wilde, Volume 3: The Picture of Dorian Gray, The 1890 and 1891 Texts*, Joseph Bristow (ed.), (Oxford: Oxford University Press, 2005), p. 80.

30. E. K. Chambers, *The Elizabethan Stage*, Vol. 3 of 4 (Oxford: Clarendon Press, 1923), p. 130.

31. E. K. Chambers, *William Shakespeare: A Study of Facts and Problems*. 1930. (Oxford: Clarendon Press, 1988).

32. Chambers (1923), Vol. 1, p. 309.

33. Chambers (1923), Vol. 2, p. 3.

34. Chambers (1923), Vol. 3, p. 158.

35. See Lukas Erne, *Shakespeare as Literary Dramatist* (Cambridge: Cambridge University Press, 2003).

36. Gerald Eades Bentley, *The Jacobean and Caroline Stage*, Vol. 1 of 7 (Oxford: Clarendon Press, 1941, 1956, 1968), p. v.

37. Bentley (1941, 1956, 1968), Vol. 3, p. v.

38. Bentley (1941, 1956, 1968), Vol. 3, p. ix.

39. M. C. Bradbrook, *Themes and Conventions of Elizabethan Tragedy*. 1935. (Cambridge: Cambridge University Press, 1980), pp. 49–50.

40. Bradbrook (1980), p. vii.

41. Bradbrook (1980), p. 11.

42. Bradbrook (1980), p. 214.

43. A. C. Bradley, *Shakespearean Tragedy: Lectures on Hamlet, Othello, King Lear, Macbeth*. 1904. (London, Basingstoke: Macmillan Press, 1983).

44. A. C. Bradley (1983), p. 202.

45. A. C. Bradley (1983), p. 205.

46. A. C. Bradley (1983), p. 206.

47. T. S. Eliot, 'Seneca in Elizabethan Translation' (1927), in T. S. Eliot (ed.), *Selected Essays 1917–1932* (London: Faber and Faber Limited, 1932), p. 78.

48. Eliot (1932), p. 83.
49. Eliot (1932), p. 79.
50. Eliot (1932), p. 84.
51. Eliot (1932), p. 175.
52. Eliot (1932), p. 185.
53. Eliot (1932), p. 148.
54. Eliot (1932), p. 157.
55. Eliot (1932), pp. 153, 155.
56. Eliot (1932), pp. 161, 162, 169.
57. Eliot (1932), p. 159.
58. Una Ellis-Fermor, *The Jacobean Drama: An Interpretation*. 1937. Revised second edn (London: Methuen, 1947), pp. 1, 2, 3.
59. Ellis-Fermor (1947), pp. 10, 21.
60. Ellis-Fermor (1947), p. 43.
61. Ellis-Fermor (1947), p. 150.
62. Ellis-Fermor (1947), p. 211.
63. Ellis-Fermor (1947), p. 223.
64. L. C. Knights, *Drama and Society in the Age of Jonson*. 1937. (Harmondsworth: Penguin, 1962), p. 16.
65. Knights (1962), p. 123.
66. Knights (1962), p. 147.
67. Knights (1962), p. 148.
68. Knights (1962), p. 151.
69. Knights (1962), p. 192.
70. F. P. Wilson, 'Elizabethan and Jacobean Drama', in Ralph J. Kaufmann (ed.), *Elizabethan Drama: Modern Essays in Criticism* (New York: Oxford University Press, 1961), pp. 9, 13, 14.
71. T. B. Tomlinson, *A Study of Elizabethan and Jacobean Tragedy* (Cambridge: Cambridge University Press, 1964), pp. 215.
72. Tomlinson (1964), pp. 97, 122.
73. Tomlinson (1964), p. 133.
74. Tomlinson (1964), p. 155.
75. Tomlinson (1964), p. 208.
76. David Scott Kastan and Peter Stallybrass, 'Introduction: Staging the Renaissance', in David Scott Kastan and Peter Stallybrass (eds), *Staging the Renaissance: Reinterpretations of Elizabethan and Jacobean Drama* (New York, London: Routledge, 1991), pp. 1–2.
77. The distinction between the mainly British movement of 'cultural materialism' and its US rival 'New Historicism' is succinctly discussed in the section on 'Materialist Criticism', in Russ McDonald (ed.), *Shakespeare: An Anthology of Criticism and Theory, 1945–2000* (Oxford: Blackwell, 2004), pp. 511–64.
78. David Scott Kastan and Peter Stallybrass, 'Introduction: Staging the Renaissance', in Kastan and Stallybrass (1991), p. 2.
79. Steven Mullaney, 'Civic Rites, City Sites: The Place of the Stage', in Kastan and Stallybrass (1991), p. 21.
80. Jean E. Howard, 'Women as Spectators, Spectacles, and Paying Customers', in Kastan and Stallybrass (1991), pp. 69, 73.
81. Lisa Jardine, 'Boy Actors, Female Roles, and Elizabethan Eroticism', in Kastan and Stallybrass (1991), p. 57.
82. Jonathan Goldberg, 'Sodomy and Society: The Case of Christopher Marlowe', in Kastan and Stallybrass (1991), p. 80.
83. Stephen Orgel, 'What Is a Text?' p. 87; Random Cloud, '"The very names of the Persons": Editing and the Invention of Dramatick Character', p 90, in Kastan and Stallybrass (1991).

84. Karen Newman, 'City Talk: Women and Commodification: *Epicoene* (1609)', in Kastan and Stallybrass (1991), p. 184.
85. Ann Rosalind Jones, 'Italians and Others: *The White Devil* (1612)', in Kastan and Stallybrass (1991), p. 257.

2   THEATRE HISTORY

1. The principal revisionist is W. R. Streitberger, 'Chambers on the Revels Office and Elizabethan Theater History', *Shakespeare Quarterly*, 59:2 (Summer 2008), p. 186. See also his contribution to Richard Dutton (ed.), *The Oxford Handbook of Early Modern Theatre* (Oxford: Oxford University Press, 2009), pp. 19–38.
2. Andrew Gurr, *The Shakespearian Playing Companies* (Oxford: Clarendon Press, 1996), p. v.
3. The site was partly excavated in 1989. For an archaeologist's evaluation of the findings, see Julian M. C. Bowsher, 'The Rose and Its Stages'. *Shakespeare Survey* 60 (2007), pp. 36–48 and his and Pat Miller's *The Rose and the Globe: Playhouses of Tudor Bankside, Southwark Excavations 1988–91* (London: Museum of London Archaeology Service, 2009).
4. Andrew Gurr, *The Shakespearean Stage 1574–1642*, 3rd edn (Cambridge: Cambridge University Press, 1992), p. 104.
5. Gurr (1992), p. 102.
6. Gurr (1992), pp. 99, 114.
7. Alfred Harbage, *Shakespeare and the Rival Traditions* (New York: Macmillan, 1952) and Alfred Harbage, *Shakespeare's Audience* (New York: Columbia University Press, 1941). Ann Jennalie Cook, *The Privileged Playgoers of Shakespeare's London* (Princeton: Princeton University Press, 1981).
8. Andrew Gurr, *Playgoing in Shakespeare's London* (Cambridge: Cambridge University Press, 1987), p. 4.
9. Gurr (1987), pp. 36, 37, 38.
10. Gurr (1987), p. 22.
11. Keith Sturgess, *Jacobean Private Theatre* (London: Routledge & Kegan Paul, 1987), p. 41.
12. Sturgess (1987), p. 39.
13. John Orrell, 'The Theatres', in John D. Cox and David Scott Kastan (eds), *A New History of Early English Drama* (New York: Columbia University Press, 1997), pp. 93–112. Martin White, 'London Professional Playhouses and Performances', in Jane Milling and Peter Thomson (eds), *The Cambridge History of British Theatre: Volume I: Origins to 1660* (Cambridge: Cambridge University Press, 2004), pp. 298–338, Martin White, *The Chamber of Demonstrations Reconstructing the Jacobean Indoor Playhouse*. (Bristol: Ignition Films, 2009).
14. Gurr (1987), p. 102.
15. Scott McMillin, '*The Shakespearian Playing Companies* by Andrew Gurr', *Modern Philology*, 96:3 (February 1999), p. 382. For a critique of the 'duopoly' theory, see Roslyn L. Knutson, 'Adult Playing Companies, 1593–1603', in Richard Dutton (ed.), *The Oxford Handbook of Early Modern Theatre* (Oxford: Oxford University Press, 2009), pp. 60–8.
16. Alan C. Dessen and Leslie Thomson, *A Dictionary of Stage Directions in English Drama, 1580–1642* (Cambridge: Cambridge University Press, 1999). Updates on http://sddictionary.com/index.html.
17. Alan C. Dessen, *Elizabethan Stage Conventions and Modern Interpreters* (Cambridge: Cambridge University Press, 1984), p. 8.
18. Dessen (1984), p. 11.
19. Dessen (1984), p. 17.
20. Dessen (1984), pp. 27–8.
21. Dessen (1984), p. 107.
22. Diana E. Henderson, 'Introduction', in Diana E. Henderson (ed.), *Alternative Shakespeares 3* (London: Routledge, 2007), p. 2.
23. Stephen J. Greenblatt, 'Foreword', in Cox and Kastan (1997), p. xiii.

24. Gurr (1996), p. 372.
25. John D. Cox and David Scott Kastan, 'Introduction: Demanding History', in Cox and Kastan (1997), p. 4.
26. Cox and Kastan, 'Introduction', in Cox and Kastan (1997), p. 2.
27. Peter H. Greenfield, 'Touring', in Cox and Kastan (1997), p. 251.
28. Greenfield, in Cox and Kastan (1997), p. 252.
29. Jean MacIntyre and Garrett P.J. Epp, '"Cloathes worth all the rest": Costumes and Properties', in Cox and Kastan (1997), p. 278.
30. See also Jonathan Gil Harris and Natasha Korda's collection of essays *Staged Properties in Early Modern English Drama* (Cambridge: Cambridge University Press, 2002), in which theatre history and a reliance on Philip Henslowe's *Diary* is invigorated by the methodologies and concerns of cultural materialism.
31. Peter Thomson, 'Rogues and Rhetoricians: Acting Styles in Early English Drama', in Cox and Kastan (1997), p. 322.
32. Tiffany Stern, *Rehearsal from Shakespeare to Sheridan* (Oxford: Clarendon Press, 2000), p. 24.
33. Stern (2000), p. 11.
34. Stern (2000), p. 12.
35. Stern (2000), pp. 88–9.
36. Stern (2000), p. 3.
37. Stern (2000), p. 4.
38. Stern (2000), p. 112.
39. Stern (2000), p. 102.
40. Simon Palfrey and Tiffany Stern, *Shakespeare in Parts* (Oxford: Oxford University Press, 2007).
41. Lucy Munro, *Children of the Queen's Revels: A Jacobean Theatre Repertory* (Cambridge: Cambridge University Press, 2005), p. 27.
42. Munro (2005), p. 15.
43. Munro (2005), pp. 50, 51.
44. Munro (2005), pp. 65, 66.
45. Munro (2005), p. 71.
46. Munro (2005), p. 72.
47. Richard Dutton, 'Preface', in Richard Dutton (ed.), *The Oxford Handbook of Early Modern Theatre* (Oxford: Oxford University Press, 2009), p. vii.
48. William Ingram, 'Introduction: Early Modern Theater History: Where We Are Now, How We Got Here, Where We Go Next', in Dutton (2009), pp. 5, 7.

3 TEXTUAL TRANSMISSION

1. Andrew Murphy, *Shakespeare in Print: A History and Chronology of Shakespeare Publishing* (Cambridge: Cambridge University Press, 2003), p. 279.
2. See John Jowett's account of 'Editing Shakespeare in the Twentieth Century', *Shakespeare Survey*, 59 (2006), p. 13; see also Paul Gavin's 'A Brief History of the Edited Shakespearean Text', *Literature Compass*, 3:2 (March 2006), pp. 182–94.
3. Roland Barthes, 'The Death of the Author', in Stephen Heath (ed. and trans.), *Image – Music – Text* (London: Fontana Press, 1977), pp. 142–8.
4. Douglas A. Brooks, *From Playhouse to Printing House: Drama and Authorship in Early Modern England* (Cambridge: Cambridge University Press, 2000), p. 5.
5. Leah S. Marcus, *Unediting the Renaissance: Shakespeare, Marlowe, Milton* (London: Routledge, 1996).
6. N.W. Bawcutt, 'Renaissance Dramatists and the Texts of Their Plays', *Research Opportunities in Renaissance Drama*, XL (2001), pp. 1–24 and Lukas Erne, *Shakespeare's Modern Collaborators* (London: Continuum, 2008).

7. Erne (2008), p. 11.

8. Brooks (2000), p. 7.

9. W. W. Greg, 'The Rationale of Copy-Text*', *Studies in Bibliography*, 3 (1950–1), pp. 21, 22.

10. Greg (1950–1), p. 22.

11. Greg (1950–1), pp. 27, 30, 35.

12. Fredson Bowers, *On Editing Shakespeare and the Elizabethan Dramatists* (Richmond, VA: University of Pennsylvania Library, 1955), p. 87.

13. Bowers (1955), pp. 11, 12, 13.

14. A. W. Pollard, *Shakespeare Folios and Quartos: A Study in the Bibliography of Shakespeare's Plays* 1594–1685 (London: Methuen, 1909), pp. 64–80.

15. Bowers (1955), p. 54.

16. Bowers (1955), pp. 100, 101.

17. Paul Werstine, 'Narratives about Printed Shakespeare Texts: "Foul Papers" and "Bad" Quartos', *Shakespeare Quarterly*, 41:1 (Spring 1990), pp. 69–75.

18. Jerome J. McGann, 'The Text, the Poem, and the Problem of Historical Method' (1980–1), in Jerome J. McGann (ed.), *The Beauty of Inflections* (Oxford: Oxford University Press, 1988), pp. 117, 119.

19. Greg (1950–1), p. 36.

20. Gary Taylor, 'General Introduction', in Stanley Wells and Gary Taylor, with John Jowett and William Montgomery (eds), *William Shakespeare: A Textual Companion* (Oxford: Clarendon Press, 1987), p. 3.

21. Wells and Taylor (1987), p. 61.

22. Wells and Taylor (1987), p. 15.

23. Wells and Taylor (1987), p. 17.

24. John Lavagnino, 'Two Varieties of Digital Commentary', in Lukas Erne and Margaret Jane Kidnie (eds), *Textual Performances: The Modern Reproduction of Shakespeare's Drama* (Cambridge: Cambridge University Press, 2004), p. 195.

25. Sonia Massai, 'Scholarly Editing and the Shift from Print to Electronic Cultures', in Erne and Kidnie (2004), p. 103. For the 'Barthesian' conceptualisation of the reader as the source of meaning, see Barthes (1977).

26. Jeffrey Masten, *Textual Intercourse: Collaboration, Authorship and Sexualities in Renaissance Drama* (Cambridge: Cambridge University Press, 1997), p. 10.

27. Masten (1997), p. 9.

28. See Michel Foucault, 'What is an Author?' in Paul Rabinow (ed.), *The Foucault Reader* (New York: Pantheon Books, 1984), pp. 101–20.

29. Joseph Loewenstein, *Ben Jonson and Possessive Authorship* (Cambridge: Cambridge University Press, 2002), p. 146.

30. Loewenstein (2002), p. 1.

31. Zachary Lesser, *Renaissance Drama and the Politics of Publication: Readings in the English Book Trade* (Cambridge: Cambridge University Press, 2004), p. 21.

32. Lesser (2004), p. 17.

33. Lesser (2004), p. 117.

34. Martin Butler (ed.), *Re-Presenting Ben Jonson: Text, History, Performance* (Basingstoke: Macmillan, 1999).

35. Martin Butler, 'Introduction: From *Workes* to Texts', in Butler (1999), p. 12.

36. See the chapters by Helen Ostovich and Kevin Donovan in Butler (1999).

37. http://www.cambridge.org/features/literature/cwbj/project/default.htm, accessed 24 June 2009.

38. Butler (1999), p. 15.

39. See also the three-volume *Works of John Webster* (Cambridge University Press, 1995–2007) under the general editorship of David Gunby, David Carnegie and the late Antony Hammond, whose place was taken by MacDonald P. Jackson for the last volume. In their

combination of old-spelling text and an editorial apparatus that shows awareness of debates around 'un-editing' drama and the need to reflect the theatrical life of the play, they provide a bridge between older and newer editorial strategies.

40. Gary Taylor, 'How to Use this Book', in Gary Taylor and John Lavagnino (eds), *Thomas Middleton and Early Modern Textual Culture: A Companion to the Collected Works* (Oxford: Oxford University Press, 2007), p. 19.
41. Taylor and Lavagnino (2007), p. 58.
42. MacDonald P. Jackson, 'Early Modern Authorship: Canons and Chronologies', in Taylor and Lavagnino (2007), p. 80.
43. Taylor and Lavagnino (2007), p. 82.
44. Taylor and Lavagnino (2007), p. 82.
45. Taylor and Lavagnino (2007), p. 86.
46. John Jowett, 'Measure for Measure: A Genetic Text', in Taylor and Lavagnino (2007), p. 681. For an in-depth discussion of the problems he faced in preparing this edition, see John Jowett, 'Addressing Adaptation: *Measure for Measure and Sir Thomas More*', in Erne and Kidnie (2004), pp. 63–76.
47. Suzanne Gossett, 'Editing Collaborative Drama', *Shakespeare Survey*, 59 (October 2006), p. 214.
48. Suzanne Gossett, '*The Spanish Gypsy*: Text Edited and Annotated by Gary Taylor, Introduced by Suzanne Gossett', in Taylor and Lavagnino (2007), p. 1723.
49. Gossett (2006), p. 218.
50. Gossett (2006), p. 219.
51. Gossett in Taylor and Lavagnino (2007), p. 1723.
52. A fourth series is that produced by the Malone Society, but this only targets a specialist audience. See http://ies.sas.ac.uk/malone/index.htm for details of the series.
53. Francis Beaumont and John Fletcher, *A King and No King*, Lee Bliss (ed.) (Manchester: Manchester University Press, 2004), p. 43.

4   HISTORICAL CONTEXTS

1. E. M. W. Tillyard, *The Elizabethan World Picture*. 1943. (Harmondsworth: Penguin, 1963), p. 31.
2. Tillyard (1963), p. 37.
3. Douglas Bruster, *Quoting Shakespeare: Form and Culture in Early Modern Drama* (Lincoln: University of Nebraska Press, 2000), p. 13.
4. Jonathan Dollimore, *Radical Tragedy: Religion, Ideology and Power in the Drama of Shakespeare and His Contemporaries*. 1984. (London: Harvester Wheatsheaf, 1989), p. xiii.
5. Dollimore (1989), p. 3.
6. Dollimore (1989), p. 4.
7. Dollimore (1989), p. 107.
8. Dollimore (1989), pp. 7, 8.
9. Dollimore (1989), p. 21.
10. Dollimore (1989), p. 261.
11. Dollimore (1989), pp. 60–1.
12. Catherine Belsey, *The Subject of Tragedy: Identity and Difference in Renaissance Drama* (London: Methuen, 1985), p. 10.
13. Belsey (1985), pp. 5, 6.
14. Belsey (1985), p. 9.
15. Belsey (1985), pp. x, 2.
16. Belsey (1985), p. 23.
17. Belsey (1985), p 26.
18. Belsey (1985), pp. 36, 42, 43, 44.
19. Belsey (1985), p. 140.

20. Belsey (1985), pp. 146, 148.
21. Belsey (1985), p. 150.
22. Belsey (1985), p. 160.
23. Belsey (1985), pp. 174, 183.
24. Belsey (1985), p. 184.
25. Belsey (1985), p. 197.
26. J.R. Mulryne, 'Introduction: Theatre and Government under the Early Stuarts', in J.R. Mulryne and Margaret Shewring (eds), *Theatre and Government under the Early Stuarts* (Cambridge: Cambridge University Press, 1993), p. 4.
27. Stephen Orgel, *The Illusion of Power: Political Theater in the English Renaissance* (Berkeley: University of California Press, 1975), p. 6.
28. Orgel (1975), p. 7.
29. Orgel (1975), pp. 8, 9.
30. Orgel (1975), pp. 10, 11.
31. Orgel (1975), p. 34.
32. Orgel (1975), p. 36.
33. Orgel (1975), p. 40.
34. Orgel (1975), p. 60.
35. Stephen Greenblatt, *Renaissance Self-Fashioning: From More to Shakespeare* (Chicago: University of Chicago Press, 1980), p. 3.
36. Greenblatt (1980), p. 4.
37. Greenblatt (1980), pp. 4–5.
38. Greenblatt (1980), p. 5.
39. Greenblatt (1980), pp. 6, 8.
40. Greenblatt (1980), p. 227.
41. Greenblatt (1980), p. 253.
42. Greenblatt (1980), p. 254.
43. Jonathan Goldberg, *James I and the Politics of Literature: Jonson, Shakespeare, Donne, and their Contemporaries* (Baltimore: Johns Hopkins University Press, 1983), pp. 31, 46.
44. Goldberg (1983), p. 55.
45. Goldberg (1983), pp. 58–9.
46. Goldberg (1983), p. 114.
47. Goldberg (1983), p. 128.
48. Goldberg (1983), p. 185.
49. Stephen Mullaney, *The Place of the Stage: License, Play and Power in Renaissance England* (Chicago: University of Chicago Press, 1988), p. 14.
50. Mullaney (1988), p. 22.
51. Mullaney (1988), p. 30.
52. Mullaney (1988), p. 34.
53. Mullaney (1988), p. 92.
54. Mullaney (1988), p. 115.
55. Douglas Brooks, 'Review: *The Place of the Stage: License, Play and Power in Renaissance England*', *Sixteenth Century Journal*, 27:4 (Winter 1996), p. 1215.
56. See Mark Thornton Burnett's, 'Review: *The Place of the Stage: License, Play and Power in Renaissance England*', *Medieval & Renaissance Drama in England*, 6 (1993), pp. 240–7.
57. Douglas Bruster, *Drama and the Market in the Age of Shakespeare* (Cambridge: Cambridge University Press, 1992), p. 10.
58. Bruster (1992), p. 11.
59. Bruster (1992), pp. 10, 22.
60. Bruster (1992), p. 30.
61. Bruster (1992), p. 49.
62. Bruster (1992), p. 55.
63. Bruster (1992), p. 61.

64. Linda Woodbridge, 'Introduction', in *Money and the Age of Shakespeare: Essays in New Economic Criticism* (Houndmills: Palgrave Macmillan, 2003), p. 11.

65. Douglas Bruster, 'On a Certain Tendency in Economic Criticism of Shakespeare', in Woodbridge (2003), p. 69.

66. Bruster (2003), p. 75.

67. Jean E. Howard, *The Stage and Social Struggle in Early Modern England* (London: Routledge, 1994), pp. 72, 57.

68. Howard (1994), p. 3.

69. Howard (1994), p. 7. Howard was preceded in this by Jonathan Goldberg's *Sodometries* (1992), another key book to use a New Historicist methodology in a politically engaged way. The activist tone of this book stands in marked contrast with Goldberg's earlier *James I* (see, pp. 61–2).

70. Howard (1994), p. 17.

71. John D. Cox and David Scott Kastan, 'Introduction: Demanding History', in Cox and Kastan (1997), p. 2.

72. Diana E. Henderson, 'The Theater and Domestic Culture', in Cox and Kastan (1997), p. 174.

73. Paul Werstine, 'Plays in Manuscript', in Cox and Kastan (1997), p. 482.

74. Howard (1986), p. 19.

75. *EEBO* gathers 'about 100,000 of over 125,000 titles listed in Pollard & Redgrave's *Short-Title Catalogue (1475–1640)* and Wing's *Short-Title Catalogue (1641–1700)* and their revised editions, as well as the *Thomason Tracts (1640–1661)* collection and the *Early English Books Tract Supplement*' and is available by subscription (see http://eebo.chadwyck.com/marketing/about.htm). *REED* 'examines the historical MSS that provide external evidence of drama, secular music, and other communal entertainment and ceremony from the Middle Ages until 1642'. Twenty-five volumes, each concerned with a different geographical area, have appeared to date (see http://www.reed.utoronto.ca/index.html).

76. Peter Lake with Michael Questier, *The Antichrist's Lewd Hat: Protestants, Papists, and Players in Post-Reformation England* (New Haven and London: Yale University Press, 2002), p. xxiii.

77. Leah S. Marcus, 'Review: The Antichrist's Lewd Hat: Protestants, Papists, and Players in Post-Reformation England', *The Journal of British Studies*, 43:4 (October 2004), p. 518.

78. Lake (2002), p. xx.

79. Lake (2002), p. xxxi.

80. Lake (2002), pp. 319, 713.

81. Lake (2002), pp. xxxi, xxxiii.

82. Lake (2002), p. 205.

83. Lake (2002), p. 582.

84. Lake (2002), p. 604.

85. Lake (2002), pp. 622, 626.

86. Lake (2002), p. 392.

5   THE GENRES OF JACOBEAN DRAMA

1. Thomas Heywood, 'A Defence of Drama', in Brian Vickers (ed.), *English Renaissance Literary Criticism* (Oxford: Oxford University Press, 2003), p. 493; *Hamlet* in Stanley Wells and Gary Taylor (eds), *The Oxford Shakespeare: The Complete Works* (Oxford: Clarendon Press, 2001), 2. 2. 398–401.

2. Rosalie L. Colie, *The Resources of Kind: Genre-Theory in the Renaissance*, Barbara K. Lewalski (ed.) (Berkeley: University of California Press, 1973), p. 116.

3. Heather Dubrow, *Genre* (London: Methuen, 1982), p. 31.

4. Alastair Fowler, *Kinds of Literature: An Introduction to the Theory of Genres and Modes* (Oxford: Clarendon Press, 1982), pp. 18, 41.

5. Jean E. Howard, 'Shakespeare, Geography, and the Work of Genre on the Early Modern Stage', *Modern Language Quarterly*, 64:3 (2003), pp. 302–3.
6. M.C. Bradbrook, *Themes and Conventions of Elizabethan Tragedy*. Second edition 1980. First Edition 1935 (Cambridge: Cambridge University Press, 1980), p. 3.
7. Bradbrook (1980), p. vii.
8. Bradbrook (1980), pp. 59–60.
9. Bradbrook (1980), p. 67.
10. Robert Ornstein, *The Moral Vision of Jacobean Tragedy* (Madison and Milwaukee: University of Wisconsin Press, 1960), p. 3.
11. Ornstein (1960), p. 6.
12. Ornstein (1960), p. 24.
13. Ornstein (1960), p. 20.
14. Ornstein (1960), p. 31.
15. Ornstein (1960), p. 274.
16. Dympna Callaghan, *Woman and Gender in Renaissance Tragedy: A Study of King Lear, Othello, The Duchess of Malfi and The White Devil* (New York: Harvester Wheatsheaf, 1989), p. 1.
17. Callaghan (1989), p. 11.
18. Callaghan (1989), p. 25.
19. Callaghan (1989), p. 63.
20. Callaghan (1989), pp. 74, 90.
21. Michael Neill, *Issues of Death: Mortality and Identity in English Renaissance Tragedy* (Oxford: Clarendon Press, 1997), p. 3.
22. Neill (1997), pp. 4–5, 5.
23. Neill (1997), p. 14.
24. Neill (1997), p. 32.
25. Neill (1997), p. 34.
26. Neill (1997), p. 38.
27. Neill (1997), pp. 134, 135.
28. Neill (1997), p. 135.
29. Neill (1997), p. 169.
30. Neill (1997), p. 46.
31. Fredson Bowers, *Elizabethan Revenge Tragedy, 1587–1642* (Gloucester, MA: Peter Smith, 1959), pp. 71, 76, 109.
32. Bowers (1959), p. 134.
33. Bowers (1959), pp. 154, 155.
34. Bowers (1959), p. 187.
35. Bowers (1959), p. 283.
36. Charles A. Hallett and Elaine S. Hallett, *The Revenger's Madness: A Study of Revenge Tragedy Motifs* (Lincoln: University of Nebraska Press, 1980), p. 119.
37. Eileen Allman, *Jacobean Revenge Tragedy and the Politics of Virtue* (London: Associated University Presses, 1999), p. 32.
38. Allman (1999), pp. 20, 34.
39. Allman (1999), p. 36.
40. Allman (1999), pp. 147, 148.
41. Alison Findlay, 'Revenge Tragedy', in Alison Findlay, *A Feminist Perspective on Renaissance Drama* (Oxford: Blackwell, 1999), p. 49.
42. C.L. Barber, *Shakespeare's Festive Comedy: A Study of Dramatic Form and Its Relation to Social Custom* (Princeton, NJ: Princeton University Press, 1959), p. 4.
43. Barber (1959), p. 8.
44. Barber (1959), p. 257. Barber alludes here to the rise of Puritanism and the English Civil War.
45. Northrop Frye, *A Natural Perspective: The Development of Shakespearean Comedy and Romance* (New York: Columbia University Press, 1965), p. 6.

46. Frye (1965), p. 30.

47. Frye (1965), p. 33.

48. Frye (1965), p. 46.

49. Frye (1965), p. 49.

50. Frye (1965), p. 58.

51. Frye (1965), p. 73.

52. Frye (1965), p. 76.

53. Frye (1965), p. 79.

54. M. C. Bradbrook, *The Growth and Structure of Elizabethan Comedy* (London: Chatto & Windus, 1955), pp. 3, 7, 6–7.

55. Bradbrook (1955), pp. 119, 165.

56. Bradbrook (1955), p. 44.

57. Bradbrook (1955), p. 95.

58. Bradbrook (1955), pp. 107, 110, 108.

59. Brian Gibbons, *Jacobean City Comedy: A Study of Satiric Plays by Jonson, Marston and Middleton*. 1968. (London: Methuen, revised edn, 1980), p. 2.

60. Gibbons (1980), p. 5.

61. Gibbons (1980), p. 11.

62. Gibbons (1980), pp. 16, 38.

63. Gibbons (1980), p. 69.

64. Gibbons (1980), p. 62.

65. Gibbons (1980), pp. 117, 118.

66. Alexander Leggatt, *Citizen Comedy in the Age of Shakespeare* (Toronto: University of Toronto Press, 1973), pp. 3, 4.

67. Leggatt (1973), pp. 8, 9.

68. Leggatt (1973), p. 10.

69. Leggatt (1973), p. 12.

70. Theodore B. Leinwand, *The City Staged: Jacobean City Comedy, 1603–13* (Madison: University of Wisconsin Press, 1986). The most recent book-length study of the sub-genre is *Plotting Early Modern London: New Essays on Jacobean City Comedy*, a collection of essays edited by Dieter Mehl, Angela Stock and Anne-Julia Zwierlein, (Aldershot: Ashgate, 2004).

71. Helen Wilcox, 'Review of Subha Mukherji and Raphael Lyne (eds) *Early Modern Tragicomedy*', *The Review of English Studies*, 60:244 (April 2009), p. 308.

72. Eugene M. Waith, *The Pattern of Tragicomedy in Beaumont and Fletcher* (New Haven: Yale University Press, 1952), p. 1.

73. Waith (1952), p. 2.

74. Waith (1952), pp. 9, 10.

75. Waith (1952), p. 34.

76. Waith (1952), p. 29.

77. Waith sums these up under 8 headings (1952), pp. 36–42.

78. Waith (1952), p. 99.

79. Marvin T. Herrick, *Tragicomedy: Its Origin and Development in Italy, France, and England* (Urbana: University of Illinois Press, 1955), p. 161.

80. Herrick (1955), p. 261.

81. William Proctor Williams, '*Not* Hornpipes and Funerals: Fletcherian Tragicomedy', in Nancy Klein Maguire (ed.), *Renaissance Tragicomedy: Explorations in Genre and Politics* (New York: AMS Press, 1987), p. 144.

82. William, in Maguire (1987), p. 145.

83. James J. Yoch, 'The Renaissance Dramatization of Temperance: The Italian Revival of Tragicomedy and *The Faithful Shepherdess*', in Maguire (1987), p. 116.

84. Lois Potter, '"True Tragicomedies" of the Civil War and Commonwealth', in Maguire (1987), p. 199.

85. Gordon McMullan and Jonathan Hope (eds), *The Politics of Tragicomedy: Shakespeare and After* (London: Routledge, 1992) and Subha Mukherji and Raphael Lyne (eds), *Early Modern Tragicomedy* (Cambridge: D. S. Brewer, 2007).
86. Zachary Lesser, *Renaissance Drama and the Politics of Publication: Readings in the English Book Trade* (Cambridge: Cambridge University Press, 2004), p. 157.
87. Lesser (2004), p. 165.
88. Lucy Munro, *The Children of the Queen's Revels: A Jacobean Theatre Repertory* (Cambridge: Cambridge University Press, 2005), p. 97.
89. Munro (2005), pp. 104, 105.
90. Stephen Orgel and Roy Strong, *Inigo Jones: The Theatre of the Stuart Court Including the Complete Designs for Productions at Court for the Most Part in the Collection of the Duke of Devonshire, Together with Their Texts and Historical Documentation* (London: Sotheby Parke Bernet, 1973), p. 1.
91. Orgel and Strong (1973), p. 7.
92. Orgel and Strong (1973), pp. 8, 10.
93. Orgel and Strong (1973), p. 13.
94. Orgel and Strong (1973), p. 18.
95. Orgel and Strong (1973), p. 19.
96. Orgel and Strong (1973), p. 37.
97. Orgel and Strong (1973), p. 39.
98. Martin Butler, 'Courtly Negotiations', in David Bevington and Peter Holbrook (eds), *The Politics of the Stuart Court Masque* (Cambridge: Cambridge University Press, 1998), p. 21.
99. Butler, in Bevington and Holbrook (1998), p. 22.
100. Butler, in Bevington and Holbrook (1998), p. 26.
101. Butler, in Bevington and Holbrook (1998), p. 27.
102. Peter Holbrook, 'Jacobean Masques and the Jacobean Peace', in Bevington and Holbrook (1998), pp. 67, 69, 70, 82.
103. Hugh Craig, 'Jonson, the Antimasque and the "Rules of Flattery"', in Bevington and Holbrook (1998), p. 177.
104. Tom Bishop, 'The Gingerbread Host: Tradition and Novelty in the Jacobean Masque' in Bevington and Holbrook (1998), p. 96.
105. Bishop, in Bevington and Holbrook (1998), pp. 88, 89.
106. Clare McManus, *Women on the Renaissance Stage: Anna of Denmark and Female Masquing in the Stuart Court (1690–1619)* (Manchester: Manchester University Press, 2002), pp. 2, 3. The influence of Anna's masquing on the Caroline masque and female performance in the Restoration is powerfully traced in Sophie Thomlinson's *Women on Stage in Stuart Drama* (Cambridge: Cambridge University Press, 2005), whose first chapter revisits the territory covered by McManus using a more text-based approach.
107. McManus (2002), pp. 15–16.
108. McManus (2002), p. 113.
109. E. M. W. Tillyard, *Shakespeare's History Plays* (Harmondsworth: Penguin, 1962), p. 29.
110. Irving Ribner, *The English History Play in the Age of Shakespeare* (London: Methuen, 1965), p. 24.
111. Ribner (1965), pp. 225, 248.
112. Ribner (1965), p. 260.
113. Ribner (1965), p. 266.
114. Ribner (1965), p. 267.
115. Ribner (1965), p. 268.
116. Ribner (1965), p. 271.
117. Ribner (1965), p. 280.
118. Marsha S. Robinson, *Writing the Reformation: Actes and Monuments and the Jacobean History Play* (Aldershot: Ashgate, 2002), p. xiv.

119. Robinson (2002), p. xx.

120. Judith Doolin Spikes, 'The Jacobean History Play and the Myth of the Elect Nation', *Renaissance Drama*, New Series VIII (1977), p. 118.

121. Robinson (2002), p. 165.

122. Teresa Grant and Barbara Ravelhofer, 'Introduction', in Teresa Grant and Barbara Ravelhofer (eds), *English Historical Drama, 1500–1660: Forms Outside the Canon* (Houndmills: Palgrave Macmillan, 2008), p. 2.

123. Grant and Ravelhofer (2008), p. 5.

124. Teresa Grant, 'History in the Making: The Case of Samuel Rowley's *When You See me You Know Me* (1604/5)', in Grant and Ravelhofer (2008), p. 135.

125. Grant and Ravelhofer (2008), p. 149.

126. Barbara Ravelhofer, 'News Drama: The Tragic Subject of Charles I', in Grant and Ravelhofer (2008), p. 179.

127. Albert H. Tricomi, *Anti-Court Drama in England, 1603–1642* (Charlottesville: University Press of Virginia, 1989), p. 71.

128. Tricomi (1989), p. 67.

129. Marta Straznicky, '"Profane Stoical Paradoxes": *The Tragedie of Mariam* and Sidnean Closet Drama', *English Literary Renaissance*, 24:1 (Winter 1994), p. 119.

130. Straznicky (1994), p. 124.

131. Elaine V. Beilin, 'Elizabeth Cary (1585–1639)', in S. P. Cerasano and Marion Wynne-Davies (eds), *Readings in Renaissance Women's Drama* (London: Routledge, 1998), p. 173.

132. Margaret W. Ferguson, 'The Spectre of Resistance: *The Tragedy of Mariam* (1613)', in Cerasano and Wynne-Davies (1998), p. 185.

133. Barbara Kiefer Lewalski, 'Resisting Tyrants: Elizabeth Cary's Tragedy', in Cerasano and Wynne-Davies (1998), p. 203.

134. Margaret Anne McLaren, 'An Unknown Continent: Lady Mary Wroth's forgotten pastoral drama, "Loves Victorie"', in Cerasano and Wynne-Davies (1998), p. 231.

135. Karen Raber, *Dramatic Difference: Gender, Class, and Genre in the Early Modern Closet Drama* (Newark: University of Delaware Press, 2001), pp. 13–14.

136. Raber (2001), pp. 23–4, 24, 42.

137. Raber (2001), pp. 112, 139.

138. Raber (2001), pp. 147, 254.

6 BODY AND RACE SCHOLARSHIP

1. Sean McDowell, 'The View of the Interior: The New Body Scholarship in Renaissance/ Early Modern Studies', *Literature Compass*, 3:4 (July 2006), p. 779.

2. Peter Stallybrass and Allon White, *The Politics and Poetics of Transgression* (London: Methuen, 1986). Stallybrass and White apply the Bakhtinian notion of the carnivalesque to Jonson's *Bartholomew Fair*.

3. Mikhail Bakhtin, *Rabelais and His World*. trans. by Hélène Iswolsky. (Bloomington: Indiana University Press, 1984), p. 9.

4. Bakhtin (1984), p. 7.

5. Bakhtin (1984), pp. 11, 11–12.

6. Bakhtin (1984), p. 19.

7. Bakhtin (1984), p. 26.

8. Bakhtin (1984), p. 321.

9. Valerie Traub, *The Renaissance of Lesbianism in Early Modern England* (Cambridge: Cambridge University Press, 2002), pp. 191–2 (see also my discussion of Traub on pp. 137–9); Gianna Pomata, 'Menstruating Men: Similarity and Difference of the Sexes in Early Modern Medicine', in Valeria Finucci and Kevin Brownlee (eds), *Generation and*

Degeneration: Tropes of Reproduction in Literature and History from Antiquity through Early Modern Europe (Durham and London: Duke University Press, 2001), pp. 109–52; Maurizio Calbi, *Approximate Bodies: Gender and Power in Early Modern Drama and Anatomy* (London: Routledge, 2005), pp. xv–xvi.

10. Thomas Laqueur, *Making Sex: Body and Gender from the Greeks to Freud* (Cambridge, MA: Harvard University Press, 1990), p. 6.

11. Laqueur (1990), pp. 21–2.

12. Laqueur (1990), p. 8.

13. Laqueur (1990), p. 26.

14. Laqueur (1990), p. 52.

15. Laqueur (1990), p. 135.

16. Jonathan Sawday, *The Body Emblazoned: Dissection and the Human Body in Renaissance Culture* (London: Routledge, 1995), p. 214.

17. Sawday (1995), p. 3.

18. Sawday (1995), pp. 44.

19. Sawday (1995), p. 3.

20. Sawday (1995), p. 8.

21. Sawday (1995), p. 63.

22. Sawday (1995), p. 224.

23. Sawday (1995), p. 221.

24. Gail Kern Paster, *The Body Embarrassed: Drama and the Disciplines of Shame in Early Modern England* (Ithaca: Cornell University Press, 1993), p. 6.

25. Paster (1993), p. 9.

26. Paster (1993), p. 10.

27. Paster (1993), p. 14.

28. Paster (1993), p. 21.

29. Paster (1993), p. 24.

30. Paster (1993), p. 83.

31. Paster (1993), p. 164.

32. Ania Loomba and Jonathan Burton (eds), *Race in Early Modern England: A Documentary Companion* (New York: Palgrave Macmillan, 2007).

33. G. K. Hunter, 'Othello and Colour Prejudice', Annual Shakespeare Lecture of the British Academy 1967, *The Proceedings of the British Academy*, LIII (London: Oxford University Press, 1967), p. 139.

34. Hunter (1967), p. 159.

35. Hunter (1967), p. 161.

36. Anthony Gerard Barthelemy, *Black Face Maligned Race: The Representation of Blacks in English Drama from Shakespeare to Southerne* (Baton Rouge and London: Louisiana State University Press, 1987), pp. 1, 7.

37. Barthelemy (1987), p. 12.

38. Barthelemy (1987), p. 26.

39. Barthelemy (1987), p. 41.

40. Barthelemy (1987), p. 72.

41. Barthelemy (1987), p. 147.

42. Barthelemy (1987), p. 42.

43. Barthelemy (1987), p. 47.

44. Barthelemy (1987), p. 70.

45. Barthelemy (1987), p. 160.

46. Barthelemy (1987), p. 161.

47. Ania Loomba, *Gender, Race, Renaissance Drama* (Manchester: Manchester University Press, 1989), p. 78.

48. Loomba (1989), p. 83.

49. Loomba (1989), p. 2.

50. Loomba (1989), pp. 2, 6.

51. Loomba (1989), pp. 38–9, 48, 49.

52. Jyotsna Singh, 'Othello's Identity, Postcolonial Theory, and Contemporary African Rewritings of *Othello*', in Margo Hendricks and Patricia Parker (eds), *Women, 'Race,' and Writing in the Early Modern Period* (London: Routledge, 1994), p. 291.

53. Kim F. Hall, *Things of Darkness: Economies of Race and Gender in Early Modern England* (Ithaca and London: Cornell University Press, 1995), pp. 254–5.

54. Hall (1995), p. 2.

55. Hall (1995), pp. 6, 11.

56. Hall (1995), p. 255.

57. Hall (1995), p. 15.

58. Hall (1995), pp. 2, 19.

59. Hall (1995), p. 22.

60. Hall (1995), p. 125.

61. Hall (1995), p. 178.

62. Mary Floyd-Wilson, *English Ethnicity and Race in Early Modern Drama* (Cambridge: Cambridge University Press, 2003).

63. Floyd-Wilson (2003), p. 3.

64. Floyd-Wilson (2003), p. 4.

65. Floyd-Wilson (2003), p. 6.

66. Floyd-Wilson (2003), p. 157.

67. Floyd-Wilson (2003), p. 7.

68. Floyd-Wilson (2003), p. 15.

69. Floyd-Wilson (2003), p. 114.

70. Floyd-Wilson (2003), pp. 124, 125.

71. Daniel Vitkus, *Turning Turk: English Theater and the Multicultural Mediterranean, 1570–1630* (New York: Palgrave Macmillan, 2003), p. 3.

72. Vitkus (2003), p. 27.

73. Vitkus (2003), p. 7.

74. Vitkus (2003), pp. 8, 21.

75. Vitkus (2003), p. 22.

76. Vitkus (2003), p. 23.

77. Vitkus (2003), p. 29.

78. Vitkus (2003), p. 78.

79. Vitkus (2003), p. 99.

80. Vitkus (2003), p. 106.

81. Vitkus (2003), p. 161.

82. Vitkus (2003), p. 162.

83. Sujata Iyengar, *Shades of Difference: Mythologies of Skin Color in Early Modern England* (Philadelphia: University of Philadelphia Press, 2005), p. 7.

84. Iyengar (2005), p. 4.

85. Iyengar (2005), p. 1.

86. Iyengar (2005), p. 138.

87. Iyengar (2005), p. 180.

88. Virginia Mason Vaughan, *Performing Blackness on English Stages, 1500–1800* (Cambridge: Cambridge University Press, 2005), p. 8.

89. Vaughan (2005), pp. 5–6.

90. Vaughan (2005), p. 6.

91. Vaughan (2005), p. 75.

92. Vaughan (2005), p. 110.

93. Vaughan (2005), p. 117.

7 GENDER AND SEXUALITY

1. Sean McDowell, 'The View from the Interior: The New Body Scholarship in Renaissance/Early Modern Studies', *Literature Compass*, 3:4 (July 2006), p. 778.
2. Lisa Jardine, *Still Harping on Daughters: Women and Drama in the Age of Shakespeare* (Hemel Hempstead: Harvester Press, 1983), pp. 3, 4.
3. Jardine (1983), p. 6.
4. Jardine (1983), p. 7.
5. Jardine (1983), p. 16.
6. Jardine (1983), p. 19.
7. Jardine (1983), p. 17.
8. Jardine (1983), p. 31.
9. Jardine (1983), p. 9.
10. Jean E. Howard, 'Crossdressing, the Theatre, and Gender Struggle in Early Modern England', *Shakespeare Quarterly*, 39:4 (Winter 1988), p. 418.
11. Howard (1988), pp. 418, 421.
12. Howard (1988), p. 423.
13. Howard (1988), pp. 425, 427.
14. Howard (1988), p. 428.
15. Howard (1988), p. 429.
16. Howard (1988), p. 429.
17. Howard (1988), p. 430.
18. Howard (1988), p. 430.
19. Howard (1988), p. 436.
20. Howard (1988), p. 437.
21. Howard (1988), p. 439.
22. Stephen Orgel, 'Nobody's Perfect, or Why Did the English Stage Take Boys for Women?' *South Atlantic Quarterly*, 88 (1989), pp. 7–29.
23. Stephen Orgel, *Impersonations: The Performance of Gender in Shakespeare's England* (Cambridge: Cambridge University Press, 1996), pp. 4, 8.
24. Judith Butler, *Gender Trouble: Feminism and the Subversion of Identity* (London: Routledge, 1990).
25. Orgel (1996), p. 25.
26. Orgel (1996), p. 26.
27. Orgel (1996), p. 29.
28. Orgel (1996), p. 63.
29. Orgel (1996), p. 36.
30. Orgel (1996), p. 81.
31. Joan Kelly-Gadol, 'Did Women Have a Renaissance?' in Renate Bridenthal and Claudia Koonz (eds), *Becoming Visible: Women in European History* (Boston: Houghton Mifflin, 1977), pp. 137–64.
32. Mary Beth Rose, *The Expense of Spirit: Love and Sexuality in English Renaissance Drama* (Ithaca: Cornell University Press, 1988), pp. ix, 2.
33. Rose (1988), p. 43.
34. Jardine (1983), p. 48.
35. Rose (1988), pp. 43, 46.
36. Rose (1988), p. 58.
37. Rose (1988), p. 59.
38. Rose (1988), pp. 61, 63.
39. Rose (1988), p. 79.
40. Rose (1988), p. 83.
41. Rose (1988), pp. 80, 85.
42. Rose (1988), p. 95.

43. Rose (1988), p. 98.
44. Rose (1988), pp. 115, 131, 132.
45. The subject of heroism is treated in greater length by Rose in her next book, *Gender and Heroism in Early Modern English Literature* (Chicago: University of Chicago Press, 2002), which contains some material on Jonson and Shakespeare.
46. Rose (1988), p. 171.
47. Rose (1988), p. 175.
48. Rose (1988), p. 182.
49. Rose (1988), p. 185.
50. Rose (1988), p. 235.
51. Karen Newman, *Fashioning Femininity and English Renaissance Drama* (Chicago and London: University of Chicago Press, 1991), p. xvii.
52. Newman (1991), p. xviii.
53. Newman (1991), pp. 7, 10, 12.
54. Newman (1991), pp. 29, 30, 31.
55. Newman (1991), pp. 56, 57, 58.
56. Newman (1991), p. 68.
57. Newman (1991), p. 69.
58. Newman (1991), p. 86.
59. Newman (1991), p. 88.
60. Newman (1991), p. 137.
61. Newman (1991), p. 123.
62. Newman (1991), p. 138.
63. Barbara Hodgdon, 'Recent Studies in Tudor and Stuart Drama', *SEL*, 43:2 (Spring 2003), p. 496.
64. Wendy Wall, *Staging Domesticity: Household Work and English Identity in Early Modern Drama* (Cambridge: Cambridge University Press, 2002), p. 8.
65. Wall (2002), pp. 4–5.
66. Wall (2002), pp. 6, 10.
67. Wall (2002), p. 58.
68. Wall (2002), p. 162.
69. Wall (2002), p. 163.
70. Wall (2002), p. 166.
71. Wall (2002), pp. 177, 180, 181.
72. Wall (2002), p. 202.
73. Wall (2002), p. 203.
74. Wall (2002), pp. 225, 224.
75. Wall (2002), p. 224. I employ the term 'queer studies' as a catch-all phrase which incorporates 'gay studies', the activist form of criticism out of which 'queer studies' as we know it today evolved.
76. Heather Findlay, 'Queerying the English Renaissance', *Diacritics*, 24:2/3 (Summer- Autumn 1994), p. 227.
77. Alan Bray, *Homosexuality in Renaissance England* (London: Gay Men's Press, 1982), pp. 16, 8, 14.
78. Bray (1982), p. 25.
79. Bray (1982), p. 34.
80. Bray (1982), p. 35.
81. Bray (1982), p. 49.
82. Bray (1982), p. 51.
83. Bray (1982), pp. 54, 55.
84. Bray (1982), pp. 56, 74.
85. Jonathan Goldberg, *Sodometries: Renaissance Texts, Modern Sexualities* (Stanford: Stanford University Press, 1992), pp. xv, 18.
86. Goldberg (1992), p. 105, 115.

87. Goldberg (1992), p. 123.
88. Goldberg (1992), p. 129.
89. Goldberg (1992), pp. 164, 169.
90. Mario DiGangi, *The Homoerotics of Early Modern Drama* (Cambridge: Cambridge University Press, 1997), p. 15.
91. DiGangi (1997), pp. 12, 15.
92. DiGangi (1997), p. 29.
93. DiGangi (1997), pp. 29, 31.
94. DiGangi (1997), p. 141.
95. DiGangi (1997), p. 65.
96. DiGangi (1997), pp. 73, 74.
97. DiGangi (1997), pp. 73, 74.
98. DiGangi (1997), p. 68.
99. Michel Foucault, *History of Sexuality*, 3 volumes, translated by Robert Hurley (New York: Vintage Books, 1988–90).
100. Mary Bly, *Queer Virgins and Virgin Queans on the Early Modern Stage* (Oxford: Oxford University Press, 2000), p. 1.
101. Bly (2000), p. 10.
102. Bly (2000), p. 5.
103. Bly (2000), p. 3.
104. Bly (2000), p. 20.
105. Valerie Traub, *The Renaissance of Lesbianism in Early Modern England* (Cambridge: Cambridge University Press, 2002), p. 6.
106. Traub (2002), p. 8.
107. Traub (2002), p. 52.
108. Traub (2002), p. 8.
109. Traub (2002), pp. 15, 16.
110. Traub (2002), p. 24.
111. Traub (2002), p. 168.
112. Traub (2002), p. 37.
113. Traub (2002), p. 170.
114. Traub (2002), p. 174.

8 PERFORMANCE STUDIES

1. Sarah Werner, 'A Companion to Shakespeare and Performance', *Shakespeare Bulletin*, 25:2 (Summer 2007), p. 114.
2. See http://www.redbulltheater.com/2008/, accessed 11 November 2009.
3. J.L. Styan, *The Shakespeare Revolution: Criticism and Performance in the Twentieth Century* (Cambridge: Cambridge University Press, 1977); Jack Jorgens, *Shakespeare on Film* (Bloomington: Indiana University Press, 1977).
4. Styan (1977), p. 4.
5. Styan (1977), p. 6.
6. Styan (1977), p. 4.
7. W.B. Worthen, *Shakespeare and the Authority of Performance* (Cambridge: Cambridge University Press, 1997), p. 157.
8. Worthen (1997), p. 159.
9. Terence Hawkes, *Meaning By Shakespeare* (London: Routledge, 1992), p. 3. Original emphasis.
10. Barbara Hodgdon, *The End Crowns All: Closure and Contradiction in Shakespeare's History* (Princeton: Princeton University Press, 1991), pp. 3, 4.
11. Hodgdon (1991), p. 3.
12. Hodgdon (1991), p. 14.
13. Hodgdon (1991), p. 15.

14. Hodgdon (1991), p. 18.

15. Hodgdon (1991), pp. 18–19.

16. Hodgdon (1991), p. 21.

17. See Pascale Aebischer, *Shakespeare's Violated Bodies: Stage and Screen Performance* (Cambridge: Cambridge University Press, 2004), pp. 12–19.

18. Barbara Hodgdon, 'Photography, Theater, Mnemonics; or, Thirteen Ways of Looking at a Still', in W.B. Worthen with Peter Holland (eds), *Theorizing Practice: Redefining Theatre History* (Basingstoke: Palgrave Macmillan, 2003), pp. 88–119; Barbara Hodgdon, *The Shakespeare Trade: Performances and Appropriations* (Philadelphia: University of Pennsylvania Press, 1998).

19. Barbara Hodgdon, 'Introduction: A Kind of History', in Barbara Hodgdon and William B. Worthen (eds), *A Companion to Shakespeare and Performance* (Oxford: Blackwell, 2005), p. 7.

20. Carol Chillington Rutter, *Enter The Body: Women and Representation on Shakespeare's Stage* (London: Routledge, 2001), p. xiii.

21. Clifford Geertz, 'Thick Description: Toward an Interpretive Theory of Culture', in Clifford Geertz (ed.), *The Interpretation of Cultures* (New York: Basic Books, 1973), pp. 3–32.

22. Rutter (2001), p. xiii.

23. Rutter (2001), p. 60.

24. Rutter (2001), p. 87.

25. Rutter (2001), pp. 88–9.

26. Rutter (2001), pp. 91, 93.

27. Diana E. Henderson, 'Introduction: Through a Camera, Darkly', in Diana E. Henderson (ed.), *A Concise Companion to Shakespeare on Screen* (Oxford: Blackwell, 2006), pp. 1, 6.

28. Henderson (2006), p. 4.

29. Robert Shaughnessy, 'Stage, Screen and Nation: *Hamlet* and the Space of History', in Henderson (2006), pp. 58–9.

30. Barbara Hodgdon, 'Cinematic Performance: Spectacular Bodies: Acting + Cinema + Shakespeare', in Henderson (2006), pp. 98, 99.

31. Hodgdon, in Henderson (2006), p. 105.

32. Mark Thornton Burnett, 'Globalization: Figuring the Global/Historical in Filmic Shakespearean Tragedy', in Henderson (2006), pp. 134, 151.

33. Elsie Walker, 'Authorship: Getting Back to Shakespeare: Whose Film is it Anyway?' in Henderson (2006), p. 14.

34. Walker, in Henderson (2006), p. 18.

35. Susan Bennett, *Performing Nostalgia: Shifting Shakespeare and the Contemporary Past* (London: Routledge, 1996), p. 7.

36. Bennett (1996), p. 12.

37. Bennett (1996), p. 80.

38. Bennett (1996), p. 81.

39. Bennett (1996), p. 93.

40. Bennett (1996), p. 83.

41. Bennett (1996), p. 95.

42. Bennett (1996), pp. 110, 111.

43. Harriet Walter, 'Case Study: Harriet Walter on Playing the Duchess of Malfi', in Martin White (ed.), *Renaissance Drama in Action: An Introduction to Aspects of Theatre Practice and Performance* (London: Routledge, 1998), p. 90.

44. Martin White, *Chamber of Demonstrations* (Bristol: Ignition Films for the University of Bristol, 2009).

45. White (1998), pp. 233, 234.

46. Roberta Barker, *Early Modern Tragedy, Gender and Performance, 1984–2000: The Destined Livery* (Houndmills: Palgrave Macmillan, 2007), pp. 2, 3.

47. Ejner J. Jensen, *Ben Jonson's Comedies on the Modern Stage* (Ann Arbor: UMI Research Press, 1985), p. 3.

48. Jensen (1985), p. 52.

49. James W. Welsh, 'Shades of Ben Jonson and Stefan Zweig: "Volpone" on Film', *South Atlantic Bulletin*, 39:4 (November 1974), p. 43.

50. Welsh (1974), p. 49.

51. Karen Forsyth, 'Stefan Zweig's Adaptations of Ben Jonson', *The Modern Language Review*, 76:3 (July 1981), p. 620.

52. Forsyth (1981), p. 627.

53. Hanna Scolnicov, '*The Merchant* in *Volpone*: Narrative and Conceptual Montage in Maurice Tourneur's Film', *Ben Jonson Journal*, 8 (2001), p. 133.

54. Scolnicov (2001), p. 136.

55. Pascale Aebischer, 'Renaissance Tragedy on Film: Defying Mainstream Shakespeare', in *The Cambridge Companion to English Renaissance Tragedy* (Cambridge: Cambridge University Press, 2010), pp. 116–31.

56. Aebischer (2010), pp. 129–30.

57. Michael Neill (ed.), *The Changeling*. By Thomas Middleton. (London: A&C Black, 2006), p. xxxvii, footnote 52.

58. 'Changeling', http://www.uipl.co.uk/mc/mcsynop.htm, accessed 21 August 2009.

59. Pascale Aebischer, 'Shakespearean Heritage and the Preposterous Contemporary Jacobean Film: Mike Figgis's *Hotel*', *Shakespeare Quarterly*, 60 (2009), p. 305.

60. Ben Spiller, '"Today, Vindici Returns": Alex Cox's *Revengers Tragedy*', *Early Modern Literary Studies*, 8:3 (January 2003), paragraph 3.3.

61. Spiller (2003), paragraphs 3.5, 3.6.

62. Jerome de Groot, 'Alex Cox's *Revengers Tragedy*', *Early Modern Literary Studies*, 9:1 (May 2003), paragraphs 21.2, 21.4.

63. Andrew Hartley, 'Film Review: *Revengers Tragedy*', *Shakespeare Bulletin*, 22:4 (2004), p. 83.

64. Hartley (2004), p. 84.

65. Patrick J. Cook, 'Adapting *The Revengers Tragedy*', *Literature/Film Quarterly*, 35:2 (2007), p. 87.

66. Cook (2007), p. 88.

67. Gretchen E. Minton, '*The Revenger's Tragedy* in 2002: Alex Cox's Punk Apocalypse', in Melissa Croteau and Carolyn Jess-Cooke (eds), *Apocalyptic Shakespeare: Visions of Destruction and Revelation in Recent Film Adaptations* (Jefferson, NC: McFarland & Co., 2009), p. 136.

68. Minton (2009), p. 137.

69. Minton (2009), p. 144.

CONCLUSION

1. Peter Holland, 'Theatre without Drama: Reading *REED*', in Peter Holland and Stephen Orgel (eds), *From Script to Stage in Early Modern England* (Houndmills: Palgrave Macmillan, 2004), p. 53.

2. Paul Whitfield White, 'Recent Studies in Tudor and Stuart Drama', *Studies in English Literature, 1500–1900*, 49:2 (Spring 2009), p. 492.

Select Bibliography

GENERAL WORKS OF CRITICISM AND REFERENCE

Bentley, Gerald Eades, *The Jacobean and Caroline Stage*, 7 Vols. (Oxford: Clarendon Press, 1941, 1956, 1968).

Chambers, E. K., *The Elizabethan Stage*, 4 Vols. (Oxford: Clarendon Press, 1923).

Cunningham, John E., *Elizabethan and Early Stuart Drama* (London: Evans Brothers Limited, 1965).

Dutton, Richard (ed.), *The Oxford Handbook of Early Modern Theatre* (Oxford: Oxford University Press, 2009).

EEBO (*Early English Books Online*). http://eebo.chadwyck.com/marketing/about.htm.

English Literature: Early 17th Century. http://www.luminarium.org/sevenlit/.

Kathman, David, *Biographical Index to the Elizabethan Theater*. http://www.shakespeare-authorship.com/bd/.

Kinney, Arthur F. (ed.), *A Companion to Renaissance Drama* (Oxford: Blackwell, 2002).

McRae, Andrew, *Renaissance Drama* (London: Arnold, 2003).

REED (*Records of Early English Drama*), http://www.reed.utoronto.ca/index.html.

CHAPTER ONE: THE CRITICAL TRAIL

Archer, William, 'Archer Attacks', Reprint of 'Webster, Lamb, and Swinburne' (1893), in Don D. Moore (ed.), *Webster: The Critical Heritage* (London: Routledge & Kegan Paul, 1981), pp. 132–43.

Bentley, Gerald Eades, *The Jacobean and Caroline Stage*, 7 Vols. (Oxford: Clarendon Press, 1941, 1956, 1968).

Bradbrook, M. C., *Themes and Conventions of Elizabethan Tragedy*. 1935. Second edn (Cambridge: Cambridge University Press, 1980).

Bradley, A. C., *Shakespearean Tragedy: Lectures on Hamlet, Othello, King Lear, Macbeth*. 1904. (London, Basingstoke: Macmillan Press, 1983).

Butler, Martin (ed.), *Re-Presenting Ben Jonson: Text, History, Performance* (Basingstoke: Macmillan, 1999).

Chambers, E. K., *The Elizabethan Stage*, 4 Vols. (Oxford: Clarendon Press, 1923).

Cibber, Theophilus, *The Lives of the Poets of Great Britain and Ireland* (1753), Vol. 1 of 5 (Hildesheim: Georg Olms Verlagsbuchhandlung, 1968).

Coleridge, S. T., *Coleridge on the Seventeenth Century* (ed. Roberta Florence Brinkley) (Durham, NC: Duke University Press, 1955).

Eliot, T. S. (ed.), *Selected Essays 1917–1932* (London: Faber and Faber Limited, 1932).

Ellis-Fermor, Una, *The Jacobean Drama: An Interpretation*. 1937. Revised second edn (London: Methuen, 1947).

Hazlitt, William, *Lectures on the Literature of the Age of Elizabeth, Chiefly Dramatic*. 1820. (London: George Bell and Sons, 1901).

Kastan, David Scott and Peter Stallybrass (eds), *Staging the Renaissance: Reinterpretations of Elizabethan and Jacobean Drama* (New York, London: Routledge, 1991).

Knights, L. C., *Drama and Society in the Age of Jonson*. 1937. (Harmondsworth: Penguin, 1962).

Lamb, Charles, *Charles Lamb's Specimens of English Dramatic Poets Who Lived about the Time of Shakespeare, Including the Extracts from the Garrick Plays*, Israel Gollancz (ed.), Vol. 1 (London: J. M. Dent and Co., 1893).

McDonald, Russ (ed.), *Shakespeare: An Anthology of Criticism and Theory, 1945–2000* (Oxford: Blackwell, 2004), pp. 511–64.

Swinburne, A. C., *Swinburne as Critic*, Clyde K. Hyder (ed.) (London, Boston: Routledge & Kegan Paul, 1972).

Symonds, John Addington, 'John Webster and Cyril Tourneur', in John Addington Symonds (ed.), *The Mermaid Series: Webster and Tourneur* (London: T. Fisher Unwin, 1888), pp. vii–xxiii.

Taylor, Michael, 'The Critical Tradition', in Stanley Wells and Lena Cowen Orlin (eds), *Shakespeare: An Oxford Guide* (Oxford, NY: Oxford University Press, 2003), pp. 323–32.

Tomlinson, T. B., *A Study of Elizabethan and Jacobean Tragedy* (Cambridge: Cambridge University Press, 1964).

Vickers, Brian (ed.), *William Shakespeare: The Critical Heritage*, 6 Vols. (London, Boston: Routledge and Kegan Paul, 1974–81).

Wilson, F. P., 'Elizabethan and Jacobean Drama', in Ralph J. Kaufmann (ed.), *Elizabethan Drama: Modern Essays in Criticism* (New York: Oxford University Press, 1961), pp. 3–21.

CHAPTER TWO: THEATRE HISTORY

Astington, John, *English Court Theatre 1558–1642* (Cambridge: Cambridge University Press, 1999).

Bentley, G. E., *The Profession of Dramatist in Shakespeare's Time: 1590–1642* (Princeton: Princeton University Press, 1972).

Bowsher, Julian and Pat Miller, *The Rose and the Globe: Playhouses of Tudor Bankside, Southwark Excavations 1988–91.* (London: Museum of London Archaeology Service, 2009).

Bowsher, Julian M. C. 'The Rose and Its Stages', *Shakespeare Survey* 60 (2007), pp. 36–48.

Chambers, E. K., *The Elizabethan Stage*, 4 Vols. (Oxford: Clarendon Press, 1923).

Cook, Ann Jennalie, *The Privileged Playgoers of Shakespeare's London* (Princeton: Princeton University Press, 1981).

Cox, John D. and David Scott Kastan (eds), *A New History of Early English Drama* (New York: Columbia University Press, 1997).

Dawson, Anthony B. and Paul Yachnin, *The Culture of Playgoing in Shakespeare's England: A Collaborative Debate* (Cambridge: Cambridge University Press, 2001).

Dessen, Alan C. and Leslie Thomson, *A Dictionary of Stage Directions in English Drama, 1580–1642* (Cambridge: Cambridge University Press, 1999).

Dessen, Alan C., *Elizabethan Stage Conventions and Modern Interpreters* (Cambridge: Cambridge University Press, 1984).

Dutton, Richard (ed.), *The Oxford Handbook of Early Modern Theatre* (Oxford: Oxford University Press, 2009).

Foakes, R. A. (ed.), *Henslowe's Diary*. 2nd edn (Cambridge: Cambridge University Press, 2002).

Griffith, Eva, 'New Material for a Jacobean Playhouse: The Red Bull Theatre on the Seckford Estate', *Theatre Notebook*, 55:1 (2001), pp. 5–23.

Gurr, Andrew, *Playgoing in Shakespeare's London* (Cambridge: Cambridge University Press, 1987).

Gurr, Andrew, *The Shakespearean Stage 1574–1642*, 3rd edn (Cambridge: Cambridge University Press, 1992).

Gurr, Andrew, *The Shakespearian Playing Companies* (Oxford: Clarendon Press, 1996).

Gurr, Andrew, *The Shakespeare Company, 1594–1642* (Cambridge: Cambridge University Press, 2004).

Gurr, Andrew, *Shakespeare's Opposites: The Admiral's Company 1594–1625* (Cambridge: Cambridge University Press, 2009).

Harbage, Alfred, *Shakespeare and the Rival Traditions* (New York: Macmillan, 1952).

Harbage, Alfred, *Shakespeare's Audience* (New York: Columbia University Press, 1941).

Harris, Jonathan Gil and Natasha Korda (eds), *Staged Properties in Early Modern English Drama* (Cambridge: Cambridge University Press, 2002).

Knutson, Roslyn Lander, *Playing Companies and Commerce in Shakespeare's Time* (Cambridge: Cambridge University Press, 2001).

Knutson, Roslyn Lander, *The Repertory of Shakespeare's Company 1594–1613* (Fayetteville: University of Arkansas Press, 1991).

Leinwand, Theodore B., *Theatre, Finance and Society in Early Modern England* (Cambridge: Cambridge University Press, 1999).

Milling, Jane and Peter Thomson (eds), *The Cambridge History of British Theatre: Volume I: Origins to 1660* (Cambridge: Cambridge University Press, 2004).

Munro, Lucy, *Children of the Queen's Revels: A Jacobean Theatre Repertory* (Cambridge: Cambridge University Press, 2005).

Palfrey, Simon and Tiffany Stern, *Shakespeare in Parts* (Oxford: Oxford University Press, 2007).

Shapiro, Michael, *Children of the Revels: The Boy Companies of Shakespeare's Time and Their Plays* (New York: Columbia University Press, 1977).

Stern, Tiffany, *Rehearsal from Shakespeare to Sheridan* (Oxford: Clarendon Press, 2000).

Streitberger, W. R., 'Chambers on the Revels Office and Elizabethan Theater History', *Shakespeare Quarterly*, 59:2 (Summer 2008), pp. 185–209.

Sturgess, Keith, *Jacobean Private Theatre* (London: Routledge & Kegan Paul, 1987).

Weimann, Robert, *Shakespeare and the Popular Tradition in the Theatre* (Baltimore: Johns Hopkins University Press, 1978).

White, Martin, *The Chamber of Demonstrations Reconstructing the Jacobean Indoor Playhouse* (Bristol: Ignition Films, 2009).

Wickham, Glynne, *Early English Stages*, 2 vols. (London: Routledge & Kegan Paul, 1963–72).

Wickham, Glynne, Herbert Berry and William Ingram (eds), *English Professional Theatre, 1530–1660* (Cambridge: Cambridge University Press, 2000).

CHAPTER THREE: TEXTUAL TRANSMISSION

Bawcutt, N. W., 'Renaissance Dramatists and the Texts of Their Plays', *Research Opportunities in Renaissance Drama*, XL (2001), pp. 1–24.

Bentley, Gerald Eades, *The Profession of Dramatist in Shakespeare's Time 1590–1642* (Princeton: Princeton University Press, 1971).

Bergeron, David M., *Textual Patronage in English Drama, 1570–1640* (Aldershot: Ashgate, 2006).

Blayney, Peter W. M., 'The Publication of Playbooks', in John D. Cox and David Scott Kastan (eds), *A New History of Early English Drama* (New York: Columbia University Press, 1997), pp. 383–422.

Bowers, Fredson, *On Editing Shakespeare and the Elizabethan Dramatists* (Richmond, VA: University of Pennsylvania Library, 1955).

Brooks, Douglas A., *From Playhouse to Printing House: Drama and Authorship in Early Modern England* (Cambridge: Cambridge University Press, 2000).

Butler, Martin (ed.), *Re-Presenting Ben Jonson: Text, History, Performance* (Basingstoke: Macmillan, 1999).

Clare, Janet, *'Art made tongue-tied by authority': Elizabethan and Jacobean Dramatic Censorship.* Second edn (Manchester: Manchester University Press, 1999).

De Grazia, Margreta and Peter Stallybrass, 'The Materiality of the Shakespearean Text', *Shakespeare Quarterly*, 44:2 (Summer 1993), pp. 255–83.

Dutton, Richard, *Licensing, Censorship, and Authorship in Early Modern England: Buggeswords* (Houndmills: Palgrave Macmillan, 2000).

Dutton, Richard, *Mastering the Revels: The Regulation and Censorship of English Renaissance Drama* (London: Macmillan, 1991).

Erne, Lukas and Margaret Jane Kidnie (eds), *Textual Performances: The Modern Reproduction of Shakespeare's Drama* (Cambridge: Cambridge University Press, 2004).

Erne, Lukas, *Shakespeare's Modern Collaborators* (London: Continuum, 2008).

Gossett, Suzanne, 'Editing Collaborative Drama', *Shakespeare Survey*, 59 (October 2006), pp. 213–24.

Greg, W. W., 'The Rationale of Copy-Text*', *Studies in Bibliography*, 3 (1950–1), pp. 20–37.

Hirschfeld, Heather Anne, *Joint Enterprises: Collaborative Drama and the Institutionalization of the English Renaissance Theater* (Amherst and Boston: University of Massachusetts Press, 2004).

Holland, Peter and Stephen Orgel (eds), *From Script to Stage in Early Modern England* (Basingstoke: Palgrave Macmillan, 2004).

Jowett, John, 'Editing Shakespeare in the Twentieth Century', *Shakespeare Survey*, 59 (2006), pp. 1–19.

Lesser, Zachary, *Renaissance Drama and the Politics of Publication: Readings in the English Book Trade* (Cambridge: Cambridge University Press, 2004).

Loewenstein, Joseph, *Ben Jonson and Possessive Authorship* (Cambridge: Cambridge University Press, 2002).

Marcus, Leah S., *Unediting the Renaissance: Shakespeare, Marlowe, Milton* (London: Routledge, 1996).

Masten, Jeffrey, *Textual Intercourse: Collaboration, Authorship and Sexualities in Renaissance Drama* (Cambridge: Cambridge University Press, 1997).

McGann, Jerome J., *The Beauty of Inflections* (Oxford: Oxford University Press, 1988).

McMullan, Gordon, *The Politics of Unease in the Plays of John Fletcher* (Amherst: University of Massachusetts Press, 1994).

Murphy, Andrew, *Shakespeare in Print: A History and Chronology of Shakespeare Publishing* (Cambridge: Cambridge University Press, 2003).

Paul, Gavin, 'A Brief History of the Edited Shakespearean Text', *Literature Compass*, 3:2 (March 2006), pp. 182–94.

Pollard, A. W., *Shakespeare Folios and Quartos: A Study in the Bibliography of Shakespeare's Plays 1594–1685* (London: Methuen, 1909).

'Scholarly Editing in the Twenty-first Century', special issue, *Literature Compass*, 6 (2009). http://www.blackwell-compass.com/subject/literature/.

Stern, Tiffany, *Making Shakespeare: From Stage to Page* (London: Routledge, 2004).

Taylor, Gary and John Lavagnino (eds), *Thomas Middleton and Early Modern Textual Culture: A Companion to the Collected Works* (Oxford: Oxford University Press, 2007).

Thompson, Ann and McMullan, Gordon (eds), *In Arden: Editing Shakespeare. Essays in Honour of Richard Proudfoot* (London: Arden Shakespeare, 2003).

Wells, Stanley and Gary Taylor, with John Jowett and William Montgomery (eds), *William Shakespeare: A Textual Companion* (Oxford: Clarendon Press, 1987).

Werstine, Paul, 'Narratives about Printed Shakespeare Texts: "Foul Papers" and "Bad" Quartos', *Shakespeare Quarterly*, 41:1 (Spring 1990), pp. 65–86.

CHAPTER FOUR: HISTORICAL CONTEXTS

Barker, Francis, *The Tremulous Private Body: Essays on Subjection* (London: Methuen, 1984).

Barroll, Leeds, *Politics, Plague and Shakespeare's Theater: The Stuart Years* (Ithaca: Cornell University Press, 1991).

Belsey, Catherine, *The Subject of Tragedy: Identity and Difference in Renaissance Drama* (London: Methuen, 1985).

Bruster, Douglas, *Drama and the Market in the Age of Shakespeare* (Cambridge: Cambridge University Press, 1992).

Bushnell, Rebecca, *Tragedies of Tyrants: Political Thought and Theater in the English Renaissance* (Ithaca: Cornell University Press, 1990).

Chakravorti, Swapan, *Society and Politics in the Plays of Thomas Middleton* (Oxford: Oxford University Press, 1996).

Collinson, Patrick, 'Ben Jonson's *Bartholomew Fair*: The Theatre Constructs Puritanism', in David L. Smith, Strier, Richard and David Bevington (eds), *The Theatrical City: Culture, Theatre and Politics in London, 1576–1649* (Cambridge: Cambridge University Press, 1995), pp. 157–69.

Cox, John D. and David Scott Kastan (eds), *A New History of Early English Drama* (New York: Columbia University Press, 1997).

Diehl, Huston, *Staging Reform, Reforming the Stage* (Ithaca: Cornell University Press, 1997).

Dollimore, Jonathan, *Radical Tragedy: Religion, Ideology and Power in the Drama of Shakespeare and His Contemporaries*. 1984. Second edn (London: Harvester Wheatsheaf, 1989).

Goldberg, Jonathan, *James I and the Politics of Literature: Jonson, Shakespeare, Donne, and their Contemporaries* (Baltimore: Johns Hopkins University Press, 1983).

Grav, Peter F. *Shakespeare and the Economic Imperative: 'What's Aught but as 'Tis Valued?'* (New York: Routledge, 2008).

Greenblatt, Stephen, *Renaissance Self-Fashioning: From More to Shakespeare* (Chicago: University of Chicago Press, 1980).

Greenblatt, Stephen, *Shakespearean Negotiations: The Circulation of Social Energy in Renaissance England* (Oxford: Clarendon Press, 1988).

Haynes, Jonathan, *The Social Relations of Jonson's Theatre* (Cambridge: Cambridge University Press, 1992).

Heinemann, Margot, *Puritanism and Theatre: Thomas Middleton and Opposition Drama under the Early Stuarts* (Cambridge: Cambridge University Press, 1980).

Howard, Jean E., 'The New Historicism in Renaissance Studies', *English Literary Renaissance*, 16:1 (Winter 1986), pp. 13–43.

Howard, Jean E., *The Stage and Social Struggle in Early Modern England* (London: Routledge, 1994).

Kastan, David Scott and Peter Stallybrass (eds), *Staging the Renaissance: Reinterpretations of Elizabethan and Jacobean Drama* (New York, London: Routledge, 1991).

Lake, Peter with Michael Questier, *The Antichrist's Lewd Hat: Protestants, Papists, and Players in Post-Reformation England* (New Haven and London: Yale University Press, 2002).

Leinwand, Theodore. *Theatre, Finance and Society in Early Modern England* (Cambridge: Cambridge University Press, 1999).

Maus, Katharine Eisaman, *Inwardness and Theater in the English Renaissance* (Chicago: University of Chicago Press, 1995).

McMullan, Gordon, *The Politics of Unease in the Plays of John Fletcher* (Amherst, MA: University of Massachusetts Press, 1994).

Mullaney, Stephen, *The Place of the Stage: License, Play and Power in Renaissance England* (Chicago: University of Chicago Press, 1988).

Mulryne, J.R. and Margaret Shewring (eds), *Theatre and Government under the Early Stuarts* (Cambridge: Cambridge University Press, 1993).

Neill, Michael, *Putting History to the Question: Power, Politics, and Society in English Renaissance Drama* (New York: Columbia University Press, 2000).

Orgel, Stephen, *The Illusion of Power: Political Theater in the English Renaissance* (Berkeley: University of California Press, 1975).

Sinfield, Alan. *Shakespeare, Authority, Sexuality: Unfinished Business in Cultural Materialism* (London: Routledge, 2006).

Tennenhouse, Leonard, *Power on Display: The Politics of Shakespeare's Genres* (New York: Methuen, 1986).

Tillyard, E.M.W., *The Elizabethan World Picture*. 1943. (Harmondsworth: Penguin, 1963).

Tricomi, Albert H., *Anticourt Drama in England, 1603–1642* (Charlottesville: University Press of Virginia, 1989).

Wells, Robin Headlam, Glenn Burgess and Rowland Wymer (eds), *Neo-Historicism: Studies in English Renaissance Literature, History and Politics* (Cambridge: D. S. Brewer, 2000).

Woodbridge, Linda (ed.), *Money and the Age of Shakespeare: Essays in New Economic Criticism* (Houndmills: Palgrave Macmillan, 2003).

CHAPTER FIVE: THE GENRES OF JACOBEAN DRAMA

General

Bamber, Linda, *Comic Women, Tragic Men* (Stanford: Stanford University Press, 1982).

Colie, Rosalie L., *The Resources of Kind: Genre-Theory in the Renaissance*, Barbara K. Lewalski (ed.) (Berkeley: University of California Press, 1973).

DiGangi, Mario, *The Homoerotics of Early Modern Drama* (Cambridge: Cambridge University Press, 1997).

Dubrow, Heather, *Genre* (London: Methuen, 1982).

Fowler, Alastair, *Kinds of Literature: An Introduction to the Theory of Genres and Modes* (Oxford: Clarendon Press, 1982).

Howard, Jean E., 'Shakespeare, Geography, and the Work of Genre on the Early Modern Stage', *Modern Language Quarterly*, 64:3 (2003), pp. 299–322.

Hunter, G.K., *English Drama 1586–1642: The Age of Shakespeare* (Oxford: Clarendon Press, 1997).

Kinney, Arthur F. (ed.), *A Companion to Renaissance Drama* (Oxford: Blackwell, 2004).

Lopez, Jeremy, *Theatrical Convention and Audience Response in Early Modern Drama* (Cambridge: Cambridge University Press, 2003).

Orgel, Stephen, 'Shakespeare and the Kinds of Drama', *Critical Inquiry*, 6:1 (Autumn 1979), pp. 107–23.

Tennenhouse, Leonard, *Power on Display: The Politics of Shakespeare's Genres* (New York: Methuen, 1986).

Tragedy

Allman, Eileen, *Jacobean Revenge Tragedy and the Politics of Virtue* (London: Associated University Presses, 1999).

Belsey, Catherine, *The Subject of Tragedy: Identity and Difference in Renaissance Drama* (London: Methuen, 1985).

Bowers, Fredson, *Elizabethan Revenge Tragedy, 1587–1642* (Gloucester, MA: Peter Smith, 1959).

Bradbrook, M.C., *Themes and Conventions of Elizabethan Tragedy*. 1935. Second edn (Cambridge: Cambridge University Press, 1980).

Bradley, A.C., *Shakespearean Tragedy: Lectures on Hamlet, Othello, King Lear, Macbeth*. 1904. (London, Basingstoke: Macmillan Press, 1983).

Callaghan, Dympna, *Woman and Gender in Renaissance Tragedy: A Study of King Lear, Othello, The Duchess of Malfi and The White Devil* (New York: Harvester Wheatsheaf, 1989).

Dollimore, Jonathan, *Radical Tragedy: Religion, Ideology and Power in the Drama of Shakespeare and His Contemporaries*. 1984. (London: Harvester Wheatsheaf, 1989).

Findlay, Alison, *A Feminist Perspective on Renaissance Drama* (Oxford: Blackwell, 1999).

Hallett, Charles A. and Elaine S. Hallett, *The Revenger's Madness: A Study of Revenge Tragedy Motifs* (Lincoln: University of Nebraska Press, 1980).

Lever, J.W., *The Tragedy of State* (London: Methuen, 1971).

Liebler, Naomi Conn, *Shakespeare's Festive Tragedy: The Ritual Foundations of Genre* (London: Routledge, 1995).

Neill, Michael, *Issues of Death: Mortality and Identity in English Renaissance Tragedy* (Oxford: Clarendon Press, 1997).

Ornstein, Robert, *The Moral Vision of Jacobean Tragedy* (Madison and Milwaukee: University of Wisconsin Press, 1960).

Wymer, Rowland, 'Jacobean Tragedy', in Michael Hattaway (ed.), *A Companion to English Renaissance Literature and Culture* (Oxford: Blackwell Publishers Limited, 2000), pp. 545–55.

Comedy

Barber, C. L., *Shakespeare's Festive Comedy: A Study of Dramatic Form and Its Relation to Social Custom* (Princeton, NJ: Princeton University Press, 1959).

Bradbrook, M. C., *The Growth and Structure of Elizabethan Comedy* (London: Chatto & Windus, 1955).

Bruster, Douglas, *Drama and the Market in the Age of Shakespeare* (Cambridge: Cambridge University Press, 1992).

Frye, Northrop, *A Natural Perspective: The Development of Shakespearean Comedy and Romance* (New York: Columbia University Press, 1965).

Gibbons, Brian, *Jacobean City Comedy: A Study of Satiric Plays by Jonson, Marston and Middleton*. 1968. (London: Methuen, revised edn, 1980).

Knights, L. C., *Drama and Society in the Age of Jonson*. 1937. (Harmondsworth: Penguin, 1962).

Leggatt, Alexander, *Citizen Comedy in the Age of Shakespeare* (Toronto: University of Toronto Press, 1973).

Leggatt, Alexander, *Introduction to English Renaissance Comedy* (Manchester: Manchester University Press, 1999).

Leinwand, Theodore B., *The City Staged: Jacobean Comedy, 1603–13* (Madison: University of Wisconsin Press, 1986).

Mehl, Dieter, Angela Stock and Anne-Julia Zwierlein (eds), *Plotting Early Modern London: New Essays on Jacobean City Comedy* (Aldershot: Ashgate, 2004).

Wells, Susan, 'Jacobean City Comedy and the Ideology of the City', *ELH*, 48:1 (Spring 1981), pp. 37–60.

Tragicomedy

Bliss, Lee, 'Tragicomic Romance for the King's Men, 1609–1611: Shakespeare, Beaumont and Fletcher', in Eugene M. Waith, A. R. Braunmuller and J. C. Bulman (eds), *Comedy From Shakespeare to Sheridan: Continuity and Change in the English and European Dramatic Tradition* (Newark: University of Delaware Press, 1986), pp. 148–64.

Herrick, Marvin T., *Tragicomedy: Its Origin and Development in Italy, France, and England* (Urbana: University of Illinois Press, 1955).

Lesser, Zachary, *Renaissance Drama and the Politics of Publication: Readings in the English Book Trade* (Cambridge: Cambridge University Press, 2004).

Maguire, Nancy Klein (ed.), *Renaissance Tragicomedy: Explorations in Genre and Politics* (New York: AMS Press, 1987).

Masten, Jeffrey, *Textual Intercourse: Collaboration, Authorship and Sexualities in Renaissance Drama* (Cambridge: Cambridge University Press, 1997).

McMullan, Gordon and Jonathan Hope (eds), *The Politics of Tragicomedy: Shakespeare and After* (London: Routledge, 1992).

Mukherji, Subha and Raphael Lyne (eds), *Early Modern Tragicomedy* (Cambridge: D. S. Brewer, 2007).

Munro, Lucy, *Children of the Queen's Revels: A Jacobean Theatre Repertory* (Cambridge: Cambridge University Press, 2005).

Ristine, Frank Humphrey, *English Tragicomedy: Its Origin and History* (New York: Columbia University Press, 1910).

Waith, Eugene M., *The Pattern of Tragicomedy in Beaumont and Fletcher* (New Haven: Yale University Press, 1952).

History

Grant, Teresa and Barbara Ravelhofer (eds), *English Historical Drama, 1500–1660: Forms Outside the Canon* (Houndmills: Palgrave Macmillan, 2008).

Ribner, Irving, *The English History Play in the Age of Shakespeare* (London: Methuen, 1965).

Robinson, Marsha S., *Writing the Reformation: Actes and Monuments and the Jacobean History Play* (Aldershot: Ashgate, 2002).

Spikes, Judith Doolin, 'The Jacobean History Play and the Myth of the Elect Nation', *Renaissance Drama*, New Series VIII (1977), pp. 117–49.

Tillyard, E. M. W., *Shakespeare's History Plays* (Harmondsworth: Penguin, 1962).

Court Masque

Astington, John, *English Court Theatre 1558–1642* (Cambridge: Cambridge University Press, 1999).

Bevington, David and Peter Holbrook (eds), *The Politics of the Stuart Court Masque* (Cambridge: Cambridge University Press, 1998).

Butler, Martin, *The Stuart Court Masque and Political Culture* (Cambridge: Cambridge University Press, 2009).

Goldberg, Jonathan, *James I and the Politics of Literature: Jonson, Shakespeare, Donne, and their Contemporaries* (Baltimore: Johns Hopkins University Press, 1983).

Lindley, David (ed.), *The Court Masque* (Manchester: Manchester University Press, 1984).

Marcus, Leah S., '"Present Occasions", and the Shaping of Ben Jonson's Masques', *ELH*, 45:2 (Summer 1978), pp. 201–25.

McManus, Clare, *Women on the Renaissance Stage: Anna of Denmark and Female Masquing in the Stuart Court (1690–1619)* (Manchester: Manchester University Press, 2002).

Orgel, Stephen and Roy Strong, *Inigo Jones: The Theatre of the Stuart Court Including the Complete Designs for Productions at Court for the Most Part in the Collection of the Duke of Devonshire, Together with Their Texts and Historical Documentation* (London: Sotheby Parke Bernet, 1973).

Orgel, Stephen, *The Illusion of Power: Political Theater in the English Renaissance* (Berkeley: University of California Press, 1975).

Thomlinson, Sophie, *Women on Stage in Stuart Drama* (Cambridge: Cambridge University Press, 2005).

Closet Drama

Cerasano, S. P. and Marion Wynne-Davies (eds), *Readings in Renaissance Women's Drama* (London: Routledge, 1998).

Findlay, Alison, *Playing Spaces in Early Women's Drama* (Cambridge: Cambridge University Press, 2006).

Gutierrez, Nancy A., 'Valuing *Mariam*: Genre Study and Feminist Analysis', *Tulsa Studies in Women's Literature*, 10:2 (Fall 1991), pp. 233–51.

Raber, Karen, *Dramatic Difference: Gender, Class, and Genre in the Early Modern Closet Drama* (Newark: University of Delaware Press, 2001).

Straznicky, Marta, '"Profane Stoical Paradoxes": The Tragedie of Mariam and Sidnean Closet Drama', *English Literary Renaissance*, 24:1 (Winter 1994), pp. 104–34.

Straznicky, Marta, 'Recent Studies in Closet Drama', *English Literary Renaissance*, 28:1 (December 1998), pp. 142–60.

Tricomi, Albert H., *Anti-Court Drama in England, 1603–1642* (Charlottesville: University Press of Virginia, 1989).

CHAPTER SIX: BODIES AND RACE SCHOLARSHIP

Bodies

Bakhtin, Mikhail, *Rabelais and His World*. trans. by Hélène Iswolsky. (Bloomington: Indiana University Press, 1984).

Calbi, Maurizio, *Approximate Bodies: Gender and Power in Early Modern Drama and Anatomy* (London: Routledge, 2005).

Hillman, David and Mazzio, Carla (eds), *The Body in Parts: Fantasies of Corporeality in Early Modern Europe* (New York: Routledge, 1997).

Hillman, David, *Shakespeare's Entrails: Belief, Scepticism, and the Interior of the Body* (Basingstoke: Palgrave Macmillan, 2007).

Laqueur, Thomas, *Making Sex: Body and Gender from the Greeks to Freud* (Cambridge, MA: Harvard University Press, 1990).

McDowell, Sean, 'The View from the Interior: The New Body Scholarship in Renaissance/ Early Modern Studies', *Literature Compass*, 3:4 (July 2006), pp. 778–91.

Nunn, Hillary M., *Staging Anatomies: Dissection and Spectacle in Early Stuart Tragedy* (Aldershot: Ashgate, 2005).

Paster, Gail Kern, *Humoring the Body: Emotions and the Shakespearean Stage* (Chicago, London: University of Chicago Press, 2004).

Paster, Gail Kern, *The Body Embarrassed: Drama and the Disciplines of Shame in Early Modern England* (Ithaca: Cornell University Press, 1993).

Sawday, Jonathan, *The Body Emblazoned: Dissection and the Human Body in Renaissance Culture* (London: Routledge, 1995).

Stallybrass, Peter and Allon White, *The Politics and Poetics of Transgression* (London: Methuen, 1986).

Zimmerman, Susan, *The Early Modern Corpse and Shakespeare's Theatre* (Edinburgh: Edinburgh University Press, 2005).

Race

Barthelemy, Anthony Gerard, *Black Face Maligned Race: The Representation of Blacks in English Drama from Shakespeare to Southerne* (Baton Rouge and London: Louisiana State University Press, 1987).

D'Amico, Jack, *The Moor in English Renaissance Drama* (Tampa: University of South Florida Press, 1991).

Floyd-Wilson, Mary, 'Moors, Race, and the Study of English Renaissance Literature: A Brief Retrospective', *Literature Compass*, 3:5 (September 2006), pp. 1044–52.

Floyd-Wilson, Mary, *English Ethnicity and Race in Early Modern Drama* (Cambridge: Cambridge University Press, 2003).

Hall, Kim F., *Things of Darkness: Economies of Race and Gender in Early Modern England* (Ithaca and London: Cornell University Press, 1995).

Hendricks, Margo and Patricia Parker (eds), *Women, 'Race,' and Writing in the Early Modern Period* (London: Routledge, 1994).

Hunter, G. K., 'Othello and Colour Prejudice', Annual Shakespeare Lecture of the British Academy 1967, *The Proceedings of the British Academy*, LIII (London: Oxford University Press, 1967), pp. 139–63.

Iyengar, Sujata, *Shades of Difference: Mythologies of Skin Color in Early Modern England* (Philadelphia: University of Philadelphia Press, 2005).

Loomba, Ania and Jonathan Burton (eds), *Race in Early Modern England: A Documentary Companion* (New York: Palgrave Macmillan, 2007).

Loomba, Ania, *Gender, Race, Renaissance Drama* (Manchester: Manchester University Press, 1989).

Vaughan, Virginia Mason, *Othello: A Contextual History* (Cambridge: Cambridge University Press, 1994).

Vaughan, Virginia Mason, *Performing Blackness on English Stages, 1500–1800* (Cambridge: Cambridge University Press, 2005).

Vitkus, Daniel, *Turning Turk: English Theater and the Multicultural Mediterranean, 1570–1630* (New York: Palgrave Macmillan, 2003).

CHAPTER SEVEN: GENDER AND SEXUALITY

Cross-dressing and gender studies

Barker, Roberta, '"Not One Thing Exactly": Gender, Performance and Critical Debates over the Early Modern Boy-Actress', *Literature Compass*, 6:2 (March 2009), pp. 460–81.

Capp, Bernard, 'Playgoers, Players and Cross-Dressing in Early Modern London: The Bridewell Evidence', *The Seventeenth Century*, 18:2 (October 2003), pp. 159–71.

Daileader, Celia, *Eroticism on the Renaissance Stage* (New York: Cambridge University Press, 1998).

Dollimore, Jonathan, *Radical Tragedy: Religion, Ideology and Power in the Drama of Shakespeare and His Contemporaries*. 1984. (London: Harvester Wheatsheaf, 1989).

Greenblatt, Stephen, 'Fiction and Friction', in Thomas C. Heller, Morton Sosna and David E. Wellbery (eds), *Reconstructing Individualism* (Stanford: Stanford University Press, 1986), pp. 30–52.

Howard, Jean E., 'Crossdressing, the Theatre, and Gender Struggle in Early Modern England', *Shakespeare Quarterly*, 39:4 (Winter 1988), pp. 418–40.

Howard, Jean E., *The Stage and Social Struggle in Early Modern England* (London: Routledge, 1994).

Jardine, Lisa, *Still Harping on Daughters: Women and Drama in the Age of Shakespeare* (Hemel Hempstead: Harvester Press, 1983).

Levine, Laura, *Men in Women's Clothing: Anti-Theatricality and Effeminization, 1579–1642* (Cambridge: Cambridge University Press, 1994).

McLuskie, Kathleen, *Renaissance Dramatists* (New York: Harvester Wheatsheaf, 1989).

Newman, Karen, *Fashioning Femininity and English Renaissance Drama* (Chicago and London: University of Chicago Press, 1991).

Orgel, Stephen, *Impersonations: The Performance of Gender in Shakespeare's England* (Cambridge: Cambridge University Press, 1996).

Rackin, Phyllis, 'Androgyny, Mimesis, and the Marriage of the Boy Heroine on the English Renaissance Stage', *PMLA*, 102:1 (January 1987), pp. 29–41.

Rose, Mary Beth, *The Expense of Spirit: Love and Sexuality in English Renaissance Drama* (Ithaca: Cornell University Press, 1988).

Sinfield, Alan. *Shakespeare, Authority, Sexuality: Unfinished Business in Cultural Materialism* (London: Routledge, 2006).

Traub, Valerie, *Desire and Anxiety: Circulations of Sexuality in Shakespearean Drama* (London: Routledge, 1992).

Wall, Wendy, *Staging Domesticity: Household Work and English Identity in Early Modern Drama* (Cambridge: Cambridge University Press, 2002).

Zimmerman, Susan (ed.), *Erotic Politics: Desire on the Renaissance Stage* (New York: Routledge, 1992).

Queer Studies

Bly, Mary, *Queer Virgins and Virgin Queans on the Early Modern Stage* (Oxford: Oxford University Press, 2000).

Bray, Alan, *Homosexuality in Renaissance England* (London: Gay Men's Press, 1982).

Bredbeck, Gregory, *Sodomy and Interpretation: From Marlowe to Milton* (Ithaca: Cornell University Press, 1991).

DiGangi, Mario, *The Homoerotics of Early Modern Drama* (Cambridge: Cambridge University Press, 1997).

Dollimore, Jonathan. *Sexual Dissidence: Augustine to Wilde, Freud to Foucault* (Oxford: Oxford University Press, 1991).

Findlay, Heather, 'Queerying the English Renaissance', *Diacritics*, 24:2/3 (Summer–Autumn 1994), pp. 227–37.

Foucault, Michel, *History of Sexuality*, 3 volumes, trans. by Robert Hurley (New York: Vintage Books, 1988–90).

Goldberg, Jonathan, *Sodometries: Renaissance Texts, Modern Sexualities* (Stanford: Stanford University Press, 1992).

Howard, Jean E., 'The Early Modern and the Homoerotic Turn in Political Criticism', *Shakespeare Studies*, 26 (1998), pp. 105–20.

Jankowski, Theodora A., *Pure Resistance: Queer Virginity in Early Modern English Drama* (Philadelphia: University of Pennsylvania Press, 2000).

Smith, Bruce, *Homosexual Desire in Shakespeare's England: A Cultural Poetics* (Chicago: University of Chicago Press, 1991).

Traub, Valerie, *The Renaissance of Lesbianism in Early Modern England* (Cambridge: Cambridge University Press, 2002).

Walen, Denise A., *Constructions of Female Homoeroticism in Early Modern Drama* (New York: Palgrave Macmillan, 2005).

CHAPTER EIGHT: PERFORMANCE STUDIES

Aebischer, Pascale and Kathryn Prince (eds), *Performing Early Modern Drama Today* (Cambridge: Cambridge University Press, forthcoming 2011/12).

Aebischer, Pascale, *Shakespeare's Violated Bodies: Stage and Screen Performance* (Cambridge: Cambridge University Press, 2004).

Bennett, Susan, *Performing Nostalgia: Shifting Shakespeare and the Contemporary Past* (London: Routledge, 1996).

Butler, Martin (ed.), *Re-Presenting Ben Jonson: Text, History, Performance* (Basingstoke: Macmillan, 1999).

Esche, Edward J. (ed.), *Shakespeare and His Contemporaries in Performance* (Aldershot: Ashgate, 2000).

Figgis, Mike, *Digital Film-Making* (London: Faber and Faber, 2007).

Figgis, Mike, *In the Dark* (London: Booth-Clibborn Editions, 2003).

Henderson, Diana E. (ed.), *A Concise Companion to Shakespeare on Screen* (Oxford: Blackwell, 2006).

Hinchcliffe, Arnold P., *Volpone: Text and Performance* (Basingstoke: Humanities Press Intl, 1985).

Hodgdon, Barbara and William B. Worthen (eds), *A Companion to Shakespeare and Performance* (Oxford: Blackwell, 2005).

Hodgdon, Barbara, *The End Crowns All: Closure and Contradiction in Shakespeare's History* (Princeton: Princeton University Press, 1991).

Hodgdon, Barbara, *The Shakespeare Trade: Performances and Appropriations* (Philadelphia: University of Pennsylvania Press, 1998).

Luckyj, Christina, *A Winter's Snake: Dramatic Form in the Tragedies of John Webster* (Athens and London: University of Georgia Press, 1989).

Rutter, Carol Chillington, *Enter The Body: Women and Representation on Shakespeare's Stage* (London: Routledge, 2001).

Scott, Michael, *Renaissance Drama and a Modern Audience* (London: Macmillan, 1982).

Shaughnessy, Robert, 'Twentieth-Century Fox: Volpone's Metamorphosis', *Theatre Research International*, 27:1 (March 2002), pp. 37–48.

Styan, J.L., *The Shakespeare Revolution: Criticism and Performance in the Twentieth Century* (Cambridge: Cambridge University Press, 1977).

Werner, Sarah, 'A Companion to Shakespeare and Performance', *Shakespeare Bulletin*, 25:2 (Summer 2007), pp. 111–15.

White, Martin (ed.), *Renaissance Drama in Action: An Introduction to Aspects of Theatre Practice and Performance* (London: Routledge, 1998).

White, Martin, *Chamber of Demonstrations* (Bristol: Ignition Films for the University of Bristol, 2009).

Worthen, W. B. with Peter Holland (eds), *Theorizing Practice: Redefining Theatre History* (Basingstoke: Palgrave Macmillan, 2003).

Worthen, W. B., *Shakespeare and the Authority of Performance* (Cambridge: Cambridge University Press, 1997).

Worthen, W. B., *Shakespeare and the Force of Modern Performance* (Cambridge: Cambridge University Press, 2003).

Jacobean Drama on Film

'Changeling', http://www.uipl.co.uk/mc/mcsynop.htm, accessed 21 August 2009.

Aebischer, Pascale, 'Renaissance Tragedy on Film: Defying Mainstream Shakespeare', in *The Cambridge Companion to English Renaissance Tragedy* (Cambridge: Cambridge University Press, 2010).

Aebischer, Pascale, 'Shakespearean Heritage and the Preposterous Contemporary Jacobean Film: Mike Figgis's *Hotel*', *Shakespeare Quarterly*, 60 (2009), pp. 281–305.

Barker, Roberta and David Nicol, 'Does Beatrice Joanna Have a Subtext?: *The Changeling* on the London Stage', *Early Modern Literary Studies*, 10:1 (May 2004), paragraphs 3.1–43.

Barker, Roberta, *Early Modern Tragedy, Gender and Performance, 1984–2000: The Destined Livery* (Houndmills: Palgrave Macmillan, 2007).

Cook, Patrick J., 'Adapting *The Revengers Tragedy*', *Literature/Film Quarterly*, 35:2 (2007), pp. 85–91.

Croteau, Melissa and Carolyn Jess-Cooke (eds), *Apocalyptic Shakespeare: Visions of Destruction and Revelation in Recent Film Adaptations* (Jefferson, NC: McFarland & Co., 2009).

De Groot, Jerome, 'Alex Cox's *Revengers Tragedy*', *Early Modern Literary Studies*, 9:1 (May 2003), paragraphs 21.1–4.

Forsyth, Karen, 'Stefan Zweig's Adaptations of Ben Jonson', *The Modern Language Review*, 76:3 (July 1981), pp. 619–28.

Hartley, Andrew, 'Film Review: *Revengers Tragedy*', *Shakespeare Bulletin*, 22:4 (2004), pp. 83–89.

Jensen, Ejner J., *Ben Jonson's Comedies on the Modern Stage* (Ann Arbor: UMI Research Press, 1985).

Neill, Michael (ed.), *The Changeling*. By Thomas Middleton. (London: A&C Black, 2006).

Scolnicov, Hanna, '*The Merchant* in *Volpone*: Narrative and Conceptual Montage in Maurice Tourneur's Film', *Ben Jonson Journal*, 8 (2001), pp. 133–46.

Solga, Kim, *Violence Against Women in Early Modern Performance: Invisible Acts* (Houndmills: Palgrave Macmillan, 2009).

Spiller, Ben, '"Today, Vindici Returns": Alex Cox's *Revengers Tragedy*', *Early Modern Literary Studies*, 8:3 (January 2003), paragraph 3.1–3.14.

Welsh, James W., 'Shades of Ben Jonson and Stefan Zweig: "Volpone" on Film', *South Atlantic Bulletin*, 39:4 (November 1974), pp. 43–50.

Select Filmography

Adaptation of *The Changeling*:

Middleton's Changeling (1998). 97 minutes. Colour. UK. High Times Pictures Production.

Director: Marcus Thompson

Screenplay: Richard Coll adapting Thomas Middleton

Cast: Amanda Ray-King: Beatrice Joanna
Ian Dury: De Flores
Colm O'Maonlai: Alsemero
Guy Williams: Alonso
Richard Mayes: Vermandero

Adaptation of *The Duchess of Malfi*:

Hotel (2001). 111 minutes. Colour. UK. Moonstone Entertainment.

Director: Mike Figgis

Screenplay: Heathcote Williams adapting John Webster

Cast: Saffron Burrows: Duchess of Malfi
Salma Hayek: Charlee Boux
Lucy Liu: Kawika
David Schwimmer: Jonathan Danderfine
Rhys Ifans: Trent Stoken

Adaptation of *Edward II*:

Edward II (1991). 86 minutes. Colour. UK. British Screen.

Director: Derek Jarman

Screenplay: Derek Jarman, Stephen McBride and Ken Butler adapting Christopher Marlowe

Cast: Steven Waddington: Edward II
Andrew Tiernan: Piers Gaveston
Tilda Swinton: Isabella
John Lynch: Spencer
Kevin Collins: Lightborn

Adaptations of *The Revenger's Tragedy*:

Noroît (1976). 128 minutes. Colour. France. Mono D'Origine.

Director: Jacques Rivette

Screenplay: Eduardo de Gregorio, Jacques Rivette and Marilù Parolini

Cast: Bernadette Lafont: Giula
Geraldine Chaplin: Morag/Vindice
Babette Lamy: Régine
Kika Markham: Erika
Élisabeth Lafont: Elisa

Revengers Tragedy (2003). 106 minutes. Colour. UK. Bard Entertainments.

Director: Alex Cox

Screenplay: Frank Cottrell Boyce adapting Thomas Middleton

Cast: Christopher Eccleston: Vindice
        Eddie Izzard: Lussurioso
        Derek Jacobi: The Duke
        Diana Quick: The Duchess
        Andrew Schofield: Carlo

Adaptation of *'Tis Pity She's a Whore*:

'Tis Pity She's a Whore (1973). 91 minutes. Colour. USA. Clesi Cinematografica.

Director: Giuseppe Patroni Griffi

Screenplay: Alfio Valdarnini and Carlo Carunchio adapting John Ford

Cast: Charlotte Rampling: Annabella
        Oliver Tobias: Giovanni
        Fabio Testi: Soranzo
        Antonio Falsi: Bonaventura
        Rik Battaglia: Mercante

Adaptations of *Volpone*:

Volpone, ou l'amour de l'or (1941). 94 minutes. Black and white. France. Ile de France Film.

Director: Maurice Tourneur

Screenplay: Jules Romains adapting Stefan Zweig

Cast: Harry Baur: Volpone
        Louis Jouvet: Mosca
        Charles Dullin: Corbaccio
        Jacqueline Delubac: Colomba Corvino
        Fernand Ledoux: Corvino

Volpone (1978). 120 minutes. Colour. France. Théâtre Marigny and Panorama (au théâtre ce soir).

Director: Jean Meyer

Screenplay: Jules Romains adapting Stefan Zweig

Cast: Jean Le Poulain: Volpone
        Francis Huster: Mosca
        Jean Meyer: Corbaccio
        Claude Jade: Colomba Corvino
        Jacques Marin: Corvino

Volpone, ou le Renard (2001). 115 minutes. Colour. France. Copat.

Director: Francis Perrin

Screenplay: Jean Collette and Toni Cecchinato adapting Ben Jonson

Cast: Bernard Haller: Volpone
        Francis Perrin: Mosca
        Michel Bonnet: Corbaccio
        Eva Di Battista: Celia
        Auguste Bruneau: Corvino
        Thibaut Lorin: Lady Would-be

Volpone (2003). 90 minutes. Colour. France. GMT Productions and DD Productions.

Director: Frédéric Auburtin

Screenplay: Eric-Emmanuel Schmitt adapting Ben Jonson

Cast: Gérard Depardieu: Volpone
       Daniel Prévost: Mosca
       Gérard Jugnot: Grappione
       Inès Sastre: Colomba Bertuccio
       Jean-François Stévenin: Bertuccio

Adaptation of generic 'Jacobean' plot:

The Cook, the Thief, his Wife and her Lover (1990). 119 minutes. Colour. UK. Allarts Cook.

Director: Peter Greenaway

Screenplay: Peter Greenaway

Cast: Michael Gambon: Albert Spica
       Helen Mirren: Georgina Spica
       Richard Bohringer: Richard Borst
       Alan Howard: Michael
       Tim Roth: Mitchell

Index